The Great Restoration

'He must remain in heaven
until the time comes for God
to restore everything
as he promised long ago
through his holy prophets.'
(Acts 3:21)

The Great Restoration

The Religious Radicals of the 16th and 17th Centuries

by
Meic Pearse

paternoster
press

First published in 1998 by Paternoster Press

04   03   02   01   00   99   98   7   6   5   4   3   2   1

Paternoster Press is an imprint of Paternoster Publishing,
P.O. Box 300, Carlisle, Cumbria, CA3 0QS, U.K.
http://www.paternoster-publishing.com

British Library Cataloguing in Publication Data

A catalogue record for this book is available from the British Library.

ISBN 0 85364 800 X

This book is printed using Suffolk Book paper which is 100% acid free.

Cover design by Mainstream, Lancaster.
Typeset by WestKey Ltd, Falmouth, Cornwall
Printed in Great Britain by Clays Ltd., Bungay, Suffolk

To Ieuan, Bethan and Rhian:
this (or something worryingly like it) is the way;
walk ye in it.

Contents

Foreword

'Christendom.' For well over a thousand years, beginning in the seventh century, this is how Europeans described their civiliza-tion. It was a world in which Christianity united all citizens with a common belief, a common standard of behaviour, and a sense of mutual belonging – to be a citizen was to be a Christian. And this unity was enforced by custom and law. If you dissented from the common values of Christendom, people might well view you as someone who *chose* (the meaning of 'heretic'); and as a heretic you would be subject to the sanctions of church (excommunica-tion) and state (in extreme cases, execution). Choice was threat-ening to Christendom thinkers, who saw religious unity – even coerced religious unity – as the only alternative to chaos.

There have, however, always been Christians who have found Christendom oppressive. They have had various problems with it. Some have found its belief system to be unconvincing, a departure from the Bible as they understood it. Others have compared its standards of Christian behaviour with those of Jesus and the early church and found them strikingly – even scandalously – different. Still others have rejected the idea of a church whose membership is equivalent to that of civil society, and which one enters by infant initiation; they have sensed that a church made up of conscripts will always be flaccid.

In the sixteenth and seventeenth centuries such thinking began to spread. Christian pioneers of post-Christendom began to proliferate; and Christendom began first to quake and then slowly to disintegrate. The stories of how this happened are the substance of Meic Pearse's valuable book.

Not everyone will appreciate the author's approach. Scholars who are comfortable in Christendom have often simply ignored the people who populate his pages. These scholars may give considerable attention to the first-century origins of Christianity when Christianity itself was radical and 'sectarian'. But they tend to be uninterested in later attempts to rediscover the ethos and dynamism of early Christianity. They may simply bypass these groups in silence, concentrating in the Reformation period on the 'main players' of the Magisterial Reformation; or, if they do note the existence of the critics of Christendom, they may be dismissive. They may even imply that there is something suspect about scholars who think it worth their while to study the radicals; according to one leading historian, the Reformation radicals appeal largely to 'the young, the powerless, and the intellectually unenterprising' – the former two may apply to Meic Pearse, but hardly the latter!

But other scholars who attempt to rehabilitate the memory of Christendom's critics may be uncomfortable with Pearse as well. Those of an older generation may be disappointed in his unwillingness to trace genetic connections between the radicals who populate his pages. Confessional historians may find that he is too broad in his coverage; he deals with the unacceptable radicals as well as the radicals whom we honour. They may find that, when he treats Thomas Muentzer as well as Conrad Grebel, or the Ranters as well as the General Baptists, he muddies the waters; certainly in the search for a proper disinvention of Christendom one ought to concentrate on those people and movements who were 'right'!

But Meic Pearse's approach, I believe, is a helpful one. He takes a broad view of the early modern pioneers of post-Christendom. He is aware that when one challenges the monopolistic power of an oppressive system, all kinds of unanticipated things happen and novel expressions of Christianity suddenly emerge. These groups may agree with each other in their repudiation of Christendom, but they may disagree about virtually everything else. Some of these groups I find inspiring; others I find scarifying. But I find it helpful that Pearse wants us to see them all and to view them all with fairness and sympathy. He knows: the process of major historical change is never neat, whether in the sixteenth century or today.

I also find it useful that this book treats the Reformation radicals of both the continent and England. Generally scholars focus their attentions on one or the other. But as the author makes clear, there are parallels and interconnections which are worth studying. He doubts that the English Baptists owe as much to the continental Anabaptists as they do to the English Separa-tists and Puritans; but his treatment, which is fair-minded and rooted in a wide reading of the sources, invites readers to come to their own conclusions.

Pearse writes with authority. His reading of the original sources is most complete in his treatment of early English non-conformity, but he has also read a lot of continental materials. He thinks clearly; he writes robustly and colourfully; he tells a story with verve. Now and then he chooses an angle of vision, or a metaphor, that enables us all to see things freshly.

Why is it important to retell the story of the Reformation's radicals? Not least because, as Christendom unravels around us, it is vital that we have heroes and heroines, good examples and cautionary tales, that derive from the long struggle for a world in which Christians don't force the faith of others. We need to study, learn from and critique those who have dominated our textbooks – Luther, Calvin, the Catholic Reformation; but we need also to study, learn from and critique Hutter and Helwys, Menno and George Fox. They believed that Christendom could kill them but that it would not control the future, and subsequent centuries have shown that they were right. Meic Pearse helps us to remember them, and by remembering them to live joyfully in a world in which inducements and compulsions have disappeared and in which Jesus calls us freely to follow him.

Alan Kreider

Introduction

'What is Anabaptism?' a Jewish headmaster once asked me. As I briefly explained, I came to an awful realization.

The question had come in the middle of a job interview. I was studying for a master's degree, and my CV had made it plain that I was a church historian. The interview was for a part-time post teaching Business Studies in a Jewish school (don't laugh – this is a true story) – to help keep my family from starving while I finished my studies.

The headmaster had been admirably composed and generous upon finding a real Christian (as opposed to a 'Christian' in the usual Jewish sense of a Gentile westerner) proposing to teach in his school. Although it was nothing to do with the job I was offering to do, he had asked politely about my academic specialization, and I explained in two or three sentences what you are about to read in this book.

It was then that the most telling of analogies occurred to me. I explained that the Anabaptists were rather like the European Jewish community of the period: they stood outside the officially imposed, compulsory churches of so-called Christendom, and as a result were viciously persecuted and harassed for their faith.

Only then did the most ghastly irony strike me, and it seems to me now the most bitter that I can think of. Judaism, the headmaster's own religion, had begun as a national religious community which people entered essentially by birth; for them, it was compulsory. By the Middle Ages, however, and as it has remained into the modern world, it too had become a dissident sect. Admittedly, most Jews were simply the children of the

previous generation of Jews (though in sixteenth-century
Poland, for example, the Jewish community turned to prosely-
tizing with some considerable success) but, in the sense of being
a religious faith characterized by personal commitment to its
teachings, to its God, and to one another, Judaism was definitely sectarian. It was not a scheme for running European
society.

Christianity, on the other hand, had begun in the Roman
Empire as a dissident sectarian movement – subversive and
persecuted. As the Roman intellectual Celsus sneered, it was the
refuge of 'the foolish, dishonourable and stupid, . . . slaves,
women and little children.'[1] It did not seek to convert governments but people; it did not focus on public rituals but on the
attitude of the heart. One entered such a church by personal
regeneration. Yet by the Middle Ages – and the effects have
continued into the modern world – this church had become a
monster, claiming universal authority over human society. Its
infinitely numerous rules and regulations affected every part of
political and social life, and participation of the whole population
was compulsory. Deviations from its orthodoxy (which in any
case differed from the orthodoxy of the early church) was,
moreover, punishable ultimately by death at the stake.

Christianity and Judaism had thus traded places. The objects
of persecution (that inevitable corollary of any religion that
claims to encompass the whole of society) had changed too. The
infant church had suffered persecution from the synagogues;
medieval Christendom persecuted the Jews with a savagery that
was not abated by the Reformation, and the pogroms have
continued down to modern times.

Perhaps seeing the matter in a new light, the Jewish headmaster evidently felt he could forgive me for being a Christian. I
suspect he was sufficiently generous to have forgiven me in any
case. Either way, he passed me on to the Business Studies teacher
with the comment, 'If this man knows anything at all about
Business Studies, hire him.' So it was settled and a new part of
my education, in the mores of modern Judaism, had begun. But
that is another story.

---

[1] Origen, *Against Celsus*, iii. 44.

The much-chronicled religious upheavals of sixteenth-century Europe go by the name of the Reformation. At least, that is the title generally applied to the central eruption which led to the rise of the churches generally described as 'Protestant'. The change within the Roman Catholic church is more problematic; was it a 'Counter Reformation' – and thus a mere reaction to the emergence of Protestantism? Or was it 'the Catholic Reformation', that is the successful implementation of reforms which all sections of society had long been imploring a decadent papacy to introduce, and the delay in which had, sadly, allowed protest to become transmuted into Protestantism?

However we answer, these two dramas, Protestant and Catholic, were concerned with questions of doctrine and ceremony. Although the rival churches differed over forms of church government, they held the really basic assumption in common: they assumed, as a matter of course, that the true church should embrace the entire population and that countries were, or should be, 'Christian' in the sense that the secular authorities would uphold the true church and enforce its rulings. This was indeed what was meant by 'Christendom', and what the Protestants wanted was to reform it (hence 'Reformation') because they considered that it had become corrupted by papal domination, by the misuse of power and money, and by teachings which had misled most of the inhabitants of Europe into thinking that they could save themselves by a combination of moral effort and religious observances. The basic structure, however, they considered sound. What they wanted was to undo the accretions of the Middle Ages, and return to a church and a faith based upon Scripture, the church fathers, and the first ecumenical councils. Professor R. Tudur Jones has aptly summed up the attempt to fulfil the programme suggested by these assumptions, in the chosen title of his book – *The Great Reformation*.

It was, however, this set of assumptions which many of the radicals whose stories are told in this book were to deny. They did not wish to reform Christendom, but to abandon it. They wished to restore the model of the New Testament church, complete with its sectarian pattern of operations and its minority status as an élite fellowship of the truly converted. They saw themselves embarked upon the Great Restoration of primitive

Christianity – untrammelled by pragmatism, by political compromise with the state, or by a dual rôle as a primary means of
social control. The price of such all-out discipleship was clear to
them from the start: persecution. But then that had been the price
demanded of the early church, too. In any case, the sixteenth-
and seventeenth-century radicals were willing to pay.

By way of justification of this great enterprise, some of them
appealed to Acts 3:21, with its teaching that Christ 'must remain
in heaven until the time comes for God to restore everything, as
he promised long ago through his holy prophets'. Restoring the
New Testament church was thus given an apocalyptic significance; Christ would return when God had restored the purity of
the church. He was bound to do it, and so it was no blasphemy
to give history a nudge.

In recent times, restorationist leaders of the 'new churches'
have seen themselves involved in the same enterprise, and have
pointed to the same text by way of justification. The 'restoration'
is seen as being gradual and cumulative, with the magisterial
reformers restoring salvation by faith and biblical authority, the
religious radicals discussed in this book restoring believers'
baptism and a believers' church, the Brethren in the nineteenth
century restoring New Testament church government, and the
Pentecostals in the twentieth century restoring the gifts of the
Spirit etc. Whatever the validity of such a view of history, its
general features must surely appeal to all those who, like the
author, believe that, at the wedding of the Lamb, it will be said
'his bride has made herself ready' (Rev. 19:8).

Thus, at the end of the Middle Ages, the Roman Catholic
Church was assailed by the Protestant Reformation. This was a
protest (hence 'Protestant') against the many abuses of ecclesiastical power and unscriptural doctrines which had characterized
the medieval period. The beginning of this 'reformation' is usually dated to 1517. This was the year in which a German monk,
Martin Luther, nailed his ninety-five theses to the door of the
Schlosskirche in Wittenberg, where he was professor of Bible at
the university. Luther's theses had been occasioned by his protest
against the practice of selling indulgences, scraps of paper which
claimed to release your loved ones from purgatory, or at least to
shorten their stay there. One thing tends to lead to another, and

within three years Luther had worked out most of the framework of what would come to be regarded as Protestant theology. In the process, he had gained a sizable following, both in Germany and elsewhere.

Until fairly late on, Luther hoped that sufficient alterations could be made to the Roman Catholic church and that a final breach would be unnecessary. As late as 1541, twenty-four years after his first protest against the church of Rome, leading reformers, including Martin Bucer, John Calvin, and his own assistant Philip Melanchthon, met leading Catholic clergy at a conference in Regensburg to try to find a way of healing the rift between Protestants and Catholics. The matters they considered were certainly important: justification, faith, grace, free will and original sin were all discussed. But not the nature of the church.

Although Martin Luther and the other reformers of the six-teenth century preached justification by faith and the authority of Scripture, they did not propose to alter the social position of the medieval church in any fundamental way. To be sure, the official reformers planned to give the laity a greater say in the running of the church than they had had in the Middle Ages, but we need to ask: who, in practice, was to get that say? In general, it was those sections of the laity who ruled the country in question. Thus, at the national level, the Protestant churches of Europe were under the control of kings, princes and parliaments, and at the level of the ordinary parish, under that of the local gentry.

It was this, in part at least, that the radicals whose story we will be considering were so concerned about. Almost all of them believed that doctrinal reformation necessarily involved a funda-mental change in the church – away from an all-embracing organ of state towards a society of the committed and converted.

The radical streams described here consist mainly of the con-tinental Anabaptists of the sixteenth century, and the English radicals – separatists, Baptists, Quakers and others – of the late sixteenth and seventeenth centuries. They differed amongst themselves at least as much as modern evangelicals disagree with one another. This, however, is what one would expect from people who stressed the importance of investigating Scripture for themselves, free from legal constraints. Here you will meet, not only with orthodox biblical Christians, but with rationalists, mystics, apocalyptic visionaries and not a few downright cranks. Many were a mixture of all of these things. The wilder manifestations of these radical ideas seemed to confirm to the 'official' churches, both Catholic and Protestant, as well as to the governments who backed them, that to permit 'unofficial' churches was to invite chaos and anarchy. It was to put spiritual power into the hands of the poor and the uneducated, of servants and of women; in a word, it was to allow independence to the very same types of people whom – as Celsus had complained – the early church had attracted, and for the same reasons.

Why was this phenomenon repeated? Perhaps it is because genuine Christianity invites us all, regardless of our position in life, to a real and personal encounter with the living Christ. There is no need for priests to mediate, nor for governments to poke their noses in, telling us what we can and can't experience. When we have had that experience, moreover, when we have met with Jesus for ourselves, we will feel impelled to tell others, regardless of whether or not government permits us, or considers us fit and proper persons to be licensed to preach. We will not necessarily claim an ability to understand all the complexities of Scripture by ourselves (though those of us who are a little too sure of our total illumination by the Spirit may go so far). We will, however, insist on being allowed to differ from an interpretation that seems to us substantially at variance with our understanding of the gospel, even if that interpretation is offered to us, or imposed on us, by official clergymen. Finally, we will even be willing to differ amongst ourselves, that is from others whom we know to have the same saving experience that we do, in order that we may be faithful to what we perceive to be the truth of Christ.

And here the rubber hits the road. I am only too aware that the subject under discussion here is contentious. Modern Christians continue to disagree about the nature of the church, as well as about the doctrines that might be thought appropriate to one view of the church rather than another. Should evangelicals separate from non-evangelicals? Is baptism (the way into the church) for children, or is it for personally professed believers only? Should there be an 'established' church, and should Christians work towards a recognizably 'Christian' country?

Fortunately, perhaps, it is in that very freedom to disagree, to discuss and to debate, that no small part of our freedom in Christ consists. To assume that there is nothing left to be revealed is to quench the Spirit; we can still 'examine everything carefully, and hold fast to that which is good' (1 Thess. 5:19–21).

It should be stressed that the different groups examined in these pages do not necessarily have any continuity with one another, as if we were seeking an alternative, radical equivalent of the apostolic succession.[2] The late medieval 'heretics' considered in the first chapter are discussed, not under any delusion that they had some organic continuity with the Anabaptists who followed them (though indirect influences and consequent recep-tive predispositions towards Anabaptism in certain localities are, in fact, entirely likely), but because the Waldensians, the Lollards and the Czech Brethren bear sufficient similarities to the Anabap-tists to be deemed analogous; in them, ordinary people were making similar religious responses.

In particular, no claim is being made for there having been any organic connection between continental Anabaptism and the late sixteenth- and seventeenth-century radicals in England. These are much-disputed waters, with a number of Mennonite historians and a few Baptists who are favourably inclined to Anabaptism wishing to argue in favour of strong influence from the Dutch Anabaptists on the early English Baptists, and even upon the Elizabethan separatists. Others discountenance such claims. In all honesty, the evidence compels me, regretfully, in the direction of the latter group.

My point here, however, is that this consideration is irrelevant to my decision to tuck up both continental Anabaptists and the later English radicals in the sheets of one volume. The justifica-tion for so doing does not lie in their organic connectedness or unconnectedness but, again, in the analogous nature of the enterprise upon which both were engaged: the restoration of

---

[2]   The pioneering work by the Brethren writer E.H. Broadbent, *The Pilgrim Church*, (London: Pickering and Inglis, 1931) is sometimes unjustly accused of this. Broadbent was careful to stress, alongside the 'continuance' through the centuries of what he considered to be biblical churches, the separate, usually unconnected origins of the various groups who comprise his history.

primitive Christianity along (in the sociological sense) sectarian lines. In that respect, both constitute a common radical stream in the religious life of early modern Europe.

It is this radical stream of the sixteenth and seventeenth centuries which, though persecuted by Protestants and Catholics alike with a viciousness that has few parallels, yet succeeded in surviving and diversifying. Simply by its persistence in existing, it forced change and, though this was slow at first, the ultimate result has been the development of the pluralistic societies of today.

For this reason, the radical stream is far from being a footnote on the edges of church history, material for a minor chapter in a book on the history of the Reformation. It is central to the story of modern freedoms and – more important than that if the radicals' own insights are anywhere near the mark – of the restoration of the Christianity of the early church.

Chapter One

The Radical Background

The fire of the Reformation, as has often been observed, did not fall from a clear blue sky. The wood to build it had been lying around for some time. In late fifteenth- and early sixteenth-century Europe, laments – about the shortcomings of the church, about ignorant and immoral priests and about greedy bishops and cardinals – abounded. The studies and discoveries of the 'Christian humanist' scholars had begun to call into question some of the claims of traditionalism and the growing revival of Augustinian theology was causing some people to conclude (a number of years before Martin Luther came to a settled conviction on the point), that the righteous might, after all, be saved by their faith.

The rites and practices of the church were not noticeably more corrupt, nor the clergy more morally and spiritually bankrupt, than they had been in previous centuries, though the papacy itself possibly was. Renaissance Rome was not, except perhaps artistically, an edifying place to be. The popes were secular rulers of large parts of Italy, their capital rivalling modern Bangkok in its supply of brothels, a facility which no pope could quite bring himself to discard until Paul IV did so in the late 1550s.

Alexander VI, who reigned from 1492 until 1503, was perhaps not untypical of the Renaissance style in pontiffs. The natural arbiter of European politics, he divided the New World between Spain and Portugal, understandably awarding the vast majority to his native Spain. Immoral, a patron of the arts and a capable politician, Alexander was a man of his age. Simony – the sin of buying, or attempting to buy, spiritual authority for ready cash – was ubiquitous, and Alexander was no exception. He was

believed to have obtained the papacy itself by bribery, but perhaps some people had merely been paid to spread the rumour
that he had.

Julius II, pope from 1503–13, was lampooned by Erasmus, the
greatest scholar of the age, in a book entitled *Julius Exclusus*, in
which the pontiff's soul is depicted knocking hopelessly at the
gate of heaven, and insisting to St. Peter on his right to be
admitted. He had done more, Julius was represented as saying,
for Christ and the church than any pope before him (and in that
category Erasmus' amused readers would naturally have included Peter himself): he had annexed Bologna to the papal
territories, he had defeated the Venetians, he had driven the
French from Italy. The very fact that Erasmus thought these
activities worth pillorying is a good indication that many in
Europe now found them distasteful in one who was, supposedly,
the vicar of Christ on earth.

But the papacy was not the church, whatever its frequent
insinuations to the contrary. The details of its corruptions and
misdemeanours were not the common knowledge of every peasant across the continent: the corruptions of the local clergy were.
Drunkenness, ignorance and, as common as either, the keeping
of a concubine: these were the more local scandals of which few
could have failed to be aware. The last of these is tragic in its way,
for canon law decreed that priests must be celibate. Unable to
marry and unwilling to 'burn', many – in some areas most –
priests resorted to what, by the late Middle Ages, was a time-
honoured expedient. Erasmus himself was the son of such a
union. Several of the heroes of later chapters in our story had
similar parentage. Still, rules were rules, and if some observers
were inclined to be indulgent towards priests who kept concu-
bines, not all were so amiably disposed. The ire of many, though,
was soon to be extended, not so much to the transgressors, as to
the rule itself. Seen in the light of the concubinage problem, the
use of the term 'nepotism' to describe the corrupt assignment of
church posts to relatives was, if anything, euphemistic; 'filialism'
would frequently have been nearer the mark.

Other offences were harder to forgive. Many priests held
livings for several parishes at once, and inevitably parishes were
neglected in the process. Holders of bishoprics, moreover, were

often political appointees who saw their posts not as a spiritual ministry, but as sources of revenue, and never visited their dioceses from one year to the next.

It was not that these fallings were more widespread in, say, 1500 than they had been in 1200. Rather, increasing literacy made priestly ignorance more contemptible; heightened religious concern made clerical sins more odious. The difference is worthy of note: Erasmus was clearly pained by Julius' actions, but he could make them a matter of fun; for many, the shortcomings of the church were not so much laughable as intolerable, an offence against God. Thus, although Erasmus was one of the devoutest men of his age, his attitude looked very dated by mid-century. As the growth of towns and the spread of printing ate away at the old clerical monopoly on literacy, so the ever-increasing urgency with which men and women asked the question 'What must I do to be saved?' destroyed the traditional tolerance that had long been extended to the sometimes rather gross difference between what clergymen practised and what they preached.

There were, of course, many devout priests, many who were learned, many who were of good character; sometimes all of these qualities even coincided in one individual, as they did in Gian Matteo Giberti, who as Bishop of Verona from 1524 to 1543 even succeeded in tackling precisely these kinds of problems amongst the clergy under his charge. The very fact, however, that Giberti was the subject of a eulogizing biography merely for doing his job is itself a confession regarding the generality of bishops: such competence and zeal were the exception, not the rule.

When modern New Yorkers feel that the police are not protecting them, they tend to support groups like the Guardian Angels. Vigilantes are apt to become heroes. If we are sufficiently worried about our child's education, we try all the harder to scrape the money together for private schooling. The conspicuous failure of a service to perform its ostensible task leads inevitably to private initiatives, and the greater the perception of failure, the greater the popularity of the new alternatives. If you want a job done, do it yourself.

Western Europeans, impelled by the dearth, famine and plague of the fifteenth century, were increasingly hungry for spiritual reality. The prospect of an early death gives people pause for thought, and the Europe of the fifteenth and early sixteenth centuries was more than usually obsessed with the image of death, as countless woodprints of the period testify. The three-hundred-year plague cycle which had commenced with the Black Death in 1347–8 continued to keep population growth to a minimum, and life expectancy was low, in the cities perhaps as low as thirty years. The growing perception – for it was not universal – of the failure of the church to meet people's spiritual needs led to the growth of new forms of spirituality within the church, and of 'heresy' (or simply Christianity) outside it.

The *devotio moderna* was a fourteenth- and fifteenth-century movement whose aim was to deepen spiritual life. Apart from the Windesheim Canons, an association of Dutch monasteries, its most celebrated lay manifestation was the 'Brethren of the Common Life', a Dutch movement founded by Gerhard Groote and Florentius Radewijns in the fourteenth century.

Forbidden to preach, Groote founded a community of lay people committed to meditation and contemplative devotion to Christ. Resources were shared and the community supported itself by working, mostly copying books. This activity led naturally into the field of education, and a number of the greatest men of the age attended Brethren schools. Thomas à Kempis, author of *The Imitation of Christ*, was a pupil. So were Nicholas of Cusa, Erasmus and, for a brief time, Luther himself.

The *devotio moderna* in general, and the Brethren of the Common Life in particular, were most influential in the Low Countries and in Germany. By 1500, the movement had developed intellectual and anti-intellectual wings, but both stressed the importance of the practical following and the imitation of Christ. The historian A.G. Dickens points out that later on this distinctive spirituality made the movement very vulnerable to the blows of Luther on the one hand and of the Anabaptists on the other. (As we shall see, Anabaptism, in many varieties, was to have a great appeal in the Netherlands.) In the meantime, 'the *devotio* offered a Quakerish programme of withdrawal and rejection, not a programme of ecclesiastical revolution'.[1] The orthodoxy of the movement and its due deference to authority were never in doubt.

---

[1] A.G. Dickens, *The German Nation and Martin Luther*, pp. 19–20.

For the time being, any protest against flaws in the church was directed simply towards getting on and making a better job of it with like-minded others.

Straining the limits of Catholic tolerance a little further, but still partly contained within the church, was the apocalyptic and pro- phetic tradition. Norman Cohn has given a graphic, and some- times grisly, account of medieval apocalyptic movements in his classic book, *The Pursuit of the Millennium*. Belief in the proximity of the last judgement was not, however, confined to the spectacular cases which Cohn chronicles; it was part of the general concern with human mortality that characterized the period. Similarly, prophets were to be found in all kinds of causes. To the French, Joan of Arc had been a saint, to the English a witch; these things were a matter of perspective. At least some of the supporters of the peasants' revolt in England in 1381 had expected the dawn of a millennial kingdom in which the world's goods would be shared equally. A hundred and fifty years later, when Henry VIII sought to divorce Katherine of Aragon and marry Anne Boleyn, his way was impeded by the popularity of Elizabeth Barton, the Maid of Kent, who prophesied that Henry would be dead within six months of putting away his wife. A few years later the Pilgrims of Grace (Roman Catholic protesters against Henry's break from Rome and his assumption of the headship of the English church) sustained themselves with a prophecy concerning their leader, Robert Aske: 'Forth shal come a worm, an Aske with one eye'.[2] Local prophecies abounded, of which the historian Keith Thomas has given many English examples in his book, *Religion and the Decline of Magic*, though mostly from the Protestant period of the sixteenth and seventeenth centuries.[3] Not all such prophecies are necessarily to be despised as superstition, hysteria, or wish-fulfil- ment. In 1470, Johannes Hilten, a Franciscan in Dorpat, in mod- ern Estonia, predicted in his commentaries on Daniel and Revelation that the papacy would fall and the religious orders be brought to an end 'around 1516' by means of an irresistible monk. Not too surprisingly, once they were brought to his attention in

---

[2] K. Thomas, *Religion and the Decline of Magic*, p. 473.
[3] *Ibid.*, pp. 461–514.

1529, Luther applied these prophecies to himself. Even now, only the bravest sceptic would dare to contradict.[4]

Hilten was not entirely orthodox, from an official point of view, in any case. His prophecy came as part of the stream of anti-papal propaganda which had long characterized elements of the Franciscan order. He was imprisoned at Eisenach in 1477. Other prophets were definitely non-Catholic, or anti-papal. It is insufficiently appreciated just how unoriginal the Protestant reformers' claims to discern Antichrist in the see of Rome were; radical Franciscans, Bohemian Brethren, certain Lollards, and various local prophets had been making that very point for a long time.

The Waldensians

As modern evangelicals, anxiously surveying the pre-Reformation landscape for any sign of proto-evangelical groups, our relief at actually finding them there should make us treat them with respect. Deference demanding that precedence be given to age, we shall first consider the Waldensians. As the name suggests, these were purported to be the followers of Peter Waldo, a twelfth-century merchant of Lyons, though Professor Euan Cameron is sceptical as to whether historical continuity between Waldo (or Valdes) and the later 'Waldensians' (or 'Vaudois') of the southwestern Alps can ever be proved.[5]

Waldo had had a conversion experience which had caused him to give up his life of plenty. Admirably, he had sought to follow the injunction given by Jesus to the rich young ruler: 'If you wish to be perfect, go sell your possessions and give to the poor, and you shall have treasure in heaven; and come, follow me.' Less admirably, he had placed his two daughters in an abbey without their consent or even his wife's knowledge, and left his wife (admittedly with a large portion of his wealth) so that he could live a life of poverty, of preaching and of begging.

This was radical for a man in his position but, in itself, nothing new. Such voluntary poor included the Spiritual Franciscans, the

---

[4]   K. Deppermann, *Melchior Hoffman*, p. 79.
[5]   E. Cameron, *The Reformation of the Heretics*, p. 1.

Brethren of the Free Spirit, and the Cathars. All of these movements posed a threat to social order, acting as focal points for
social protest by the poor. The Free Spirit advocated a licentious
lifestyle – since the perfect could do no wrong. Catharism, which
gained massive support in southern France in the twelfth century,
did not really profess to be Christian at all, and was based on the
old dualism between spirit and matter, the latter being the creation
of an evil god. In this background, in which ideas were pretty fluid
between one movement and another, Waldo's protest was not
necessarily the prelude to an outburst of apostolic Christianity. In
the event, however, it became so.

By 1250, Rainier Sacchoni, a Dominican and inquisitor in
Lombardy but a former Cathar himself, could comment that
Waldensians:

> prohibit all swearing as mortal sin. They also reject secular justice on
> the ground that kings, princes and potentates ought not to punish
> evil-doers. They say that an ordinary layman may consecrate the body
> of the Lord, and I believe that they apply this to women as well for they
> have never denied it to me. . . . They say that the Roman Church is a
> church of evil, the beast and harlot which are found in the Book of
> Revelation, and that it is no sin to eat meat during Lent or on Friday
> against the precept of the Church. . . . They also say that the Church of
> Christ remained in bishops and other prelates until St. Silvester, and
> failed in him, until they themselves restored it, though they do say there
> have always been some who have feared God and been saved. They
> believe that children can be saved without baptism. [6]

There is much to comment on here. The prohibition on oaths,
which was also to be a distinctive mark of the Anabaptists, most
likely reflects straightforward biblicism; in the Sermon on the
Mount, Jesus says that any statement stronger than 'yes' or 'no'
is of evil (Mt. 5:33–7) and the Epistle of James also forbids
swearing (Jas. 5:12). For a society to profess Christianity was all
very well. The reality of political life, however, required the
taking of oaths – for all sorts of contracts, for enforcing allegiance to rulers, for submission to government commands and, by
invoking the terrors of divine judgement, for extracting the truth
in law courts. To attack oaths was to attack one of the pillars of
civil government. The biblical injunctions are so plain, though,

---

[6]   cited in R.I. Moore, *The Birth of Popular Heresy*, p. 145.

that a good deal of ingenuity, both by medieval churchmen and the Protestant reformers, was needed to evade their force. (Bucer, the sixteenth-century reformer of Strassburg, felt constrained to supply the Waldensians with a lengthy justification of oaths.)

As in so many respects, official religion required contradictory things from the people upon whom it was enforced: sufficient religiosity to take the church and its strictures seriously, but not so much zeal as to lead one into 'heresy'; enough religion to feel bound by an oath in the name of God, or taken with one's hand on the Bible, but not so much as to be worried by the indications within that very tome that one ought not to be doing this at all. For most of the Middle Ages, the ignorance of the general populace was sufficient to square this awkward circle but, with the massive growth of literacy in the early modern period encouraged by the advent of printing, this began to change. As citizens – and, indeed, peasants – of the pre-Gutenberg era, the Waldensians were merely a little ahead of their time.

The supposed rejection of secular justice to which Sacchoni refers probably reflects the conviction that fellow-Waldensians ought not to take each other to court (as indicated perhaps by 1 Cor. 6:1–8). More than three centuries later, Scipione Lentolo, a former Waldensian minister, berated his erstwhile flock for their readiness to sue one another before Catholic judges and for their failure to behave with integrity even when they did.[7] But precisely their failure in this regard draws attention to the importance of the ideal.

The Anabaptists were also to be accused of rejecting civil government because they denied the right of secular authorities to govern people's consciences by enforcing one form of religion and forbidding others. The implication behind the accusation, of course, is that the 'heretics' were really anarchists who were against all government and, although this might look like mere slander to a modern reader, one should bear in mind that to almost all people before about the late seventeenth century the idea that more than one religion in a state was consistent with social order seemed nonsensical. So for them, any attack on the

---

[7] E. Cameron, *Reformation of the Heretics*, pp. 2–3.

right of the magistracy to impose religion was an attack on civil government *per se*.

The denunciation of the church of Rome is another example of a phenomenon we have already noted. When Sacchoni reported that laymen and women 'may consecrate the body of the Lord', he was, of course, referring to communion. Waldensianism, like most medieval and early modern heresies, was an attack on clericalism and on the exclusive rights of the priesthood.

The movement had been pushed into dissent from the Church of Rome by the refusal of the Roman hierarchy to allow Waldo and his fellows to preach. Indeed, as the Waldensian movement developed preaching was not confined to fellows; it was frequently done by women as well.

Sacchoni's reference to Waldensian beliefs regarding 'St. Silvester' needs some explanation. Silvester had been bishop of Rome in the early fourth century, at the time of Constantine. Legend had it that he had been the recipient of the so-called Donation of Constantine, according to which the Bishop of Rome had been given huge wealth and sweeping ecclesiastical and temporal powers. Until 1440, when the scholar Lorenzo Valla proved the document to be an eighth-century forgery, the Donation's authenticity was accepted by orthodox and heretics alike. So, the claim that the church had fallen from grace at the time of Silvester, which was far from being exclusive to the Waldensians but was shared by some Franciscans and all kinds of 'voluntary poor', must be seen in that light. The belief that there had, nevertheless, always been those who had 'feared God and been saved' shows that sixteenth-century Protestants were not the first to face the embarrassing question – 'where was your church before Luther?' The Protestants pointed, amongst others, to the medieval Waldensians; to whom could the Waldensians point? In the absence of hard evidence, fiction had to supply the place of fact: they claimed that a companion of Silvester had rejected Constantine's 'Donation', had been excommunicated and persecuted along with his followers, and had embraced voluntary poverty in the manner of Waldo, so beginning that unbroken line of the true church which Waldo's protest had merely renewed.[8]

---

[8]   M. Lambert, *Medieval Heresy*, pp. 156–8.

Concerning Sacchoni's final statement, that the Waldensians believed 'that children can be saved without baptism', this may imply that they denigrated the rite altogether, and certainly indicates that they did not take seriously the Augustinian teach- ing (which was the orthodoxy of the Middle Ages) that children dying unbaptized would be damned. However, it is not easy to know how much credence to attach to Sacchoni's claim even for the mid-thirteenth century in which he wrote, for it is not cor- roborated elsewhere. As far as later Waldensianism is concerned, Cameron is certain that 'there is no credible trial evidence from this period to prove that the Waldenses of the western Alps entertained any heresy about baptism whatever', though he notes that inquisitors' manuals insisted the contrary.[9] Certainly, one early group of radical Waldensians in Languedoc in the late twelfth century claimed the invalidity of Catholic baptism and the validity of their own, but Waldo repudiated these over- zealous followers.

The Waldensians did not confine themselves to the Alpine valleys of France and Italy. In the centuries between their initial growth and the coming of the Reformation they expanded into Austria, many parts of Germany (even as far as Brandenburg and Pomerania), and into Poland, Hungary, Moravia and Bohe- mia. Despite persecution, therefore, by the time other, similar movements arose, the Waldensians were already well dispersed across Europe. In the early sixteenth century, Catholic oppo- nents sometimes confused them with the Bohemian Brethren, to whom our attention now turns.

The Bohemian Brethren

The Bohemian Brethren were an offshoot of the rebellion of Jan Hus, the Czech reformer of the early fifteenth century. Hus had been rector of the university of Prague, and had taught views similar to those of John Wycliffe in England, including the centrality of Scripture and the denial of the pope's power to forgive sins. He had also stressed the right of the laity to take

---

[9]   E. Cameron, *Reformation of the Heretics,* p. 85.

communion in both kinds (i.e. both bread and wine), a teaching
which was contrary to the practice of the Roman church. Invited
to the Council of Constance in 1414 with a promise of a safe
conduct, he was arrested anyway, put on trial and burned in July
1415. His supporters succeeded, by military force, in obtaining
the right to continue to give communion in both kinds, and this
church, the Utraquists, was given semi-autonomy within the
Roman Catholic church.

For a time, the more militant and radical Hussites, the
Taborites, who drew on the lower social strata for their support,
succeeded in establishing themselves under the leadership of Jan
Žižka but were defeated and destroyed by a combined Utraquist-
Catholic force at the Battle of Lipany, in 1434. The Taborites
were millenarian, expecting the imminent return of Christ;
Mount Tabor was the place to which Christ had traditionally
been expected to return. Their programme, however, was one of
violent extermination of the enemies of God.

It was as a breakaway from the more moderate Utraquists that
the Bohemian Brethren, also known as *Unitas Fratrum*, were
formed under the leadership of Petr Chelčický in the 1450s.
Whilst less adventurous in doctrine than the Taborites, they were
committed to a simple lifestyle of personal devotion. Chelčický
accepted the myth of the Donation of Constantine, and bor-
rowed the Waldensians' counter-rationale of the continuance of
a faithful remnant. His was, as one historian has described it, a
'radical reconception of Hussitism as an apostolic restitution'. [10]

In 1480, they were joined by several hundred Waldensians
fleeing from Mark Brandenburg in Germany. The movement,
though, remained predominantly Czech, despite the large numbers of German-speakers in Bohemia and Moravia. Rapidly
growing in strength despite persecution, some of its members
later united with various Protestant groups during the sixteenth
century. This fact has led various historians to claim the *Unitas
Fratrum* as Lutherans-before-Luther or Calvinists-before-
Calvin. But as another modern historian, J.K. Zeman, points
out, 'Without doing any violence to historical facts, one might

---

[10] M.L. Wagner, *Petr Chelčický*, pp. 53–4; G.H. Williams, *The Radical Reformation*,
3rd edn, p. 321.

align the Unity equally well with the Left Wing of the Reformation' – by which he means the Anabaptists. Indeed, Zeman
summarizes the work of J.M. Lochman, who found the essence
of Czech Brethrenism to consist in: 1) an emphasis on discipleship; 2) a readiness for martyrdom; 3) an origin amongst the
people rather than amongst theologians or the rich and powerful;
4) a denial that any one church body can be definitive for the
whole body of Christ on earth; and 5) amongst some elements
(e.g. the immediate followers of Chelčický), pacifism. Not unrea-
sonably, Zeman concludes: 'No one could fail to see the striking
similarities between "the essence" of Czech Brethrenism as defined by Lochman, and the basic characteristics of Anabaptism.'[11] Indeed, until the late 1520s, they practised re-baptism,
on the grounds that Catholic baptism had been administered by
unworthy priests.[12]

Despite persecution and mergers between some of the Brethren and other groupings in the sixteenth century, others maintained a distinct identity and, as the Moravians, united with
Count von Zinzendorf's fellowship at Herrnhut in 1721. The
Moravians were a decisive influence leading to the conversion of
John Wesley, and a large Moravian church exists to this day in
the U.S.

Many factors combined to make Bohemia fertile territory for
religious radicalism by the beginning of the sixteenth century: the
evident acceptance of the Hussite-derived Utraquist church, the
growth of the Bohemian Brethren, and the continued existence
of groups taking their inspiration from the wilder wing of the
Taborites and announcing the coming of some local prophet as
the ushering in of the Golden Age.

The Lollards

The Lollards were the legacy of John Wycliffe's writing and
teaching. Wycliffe had taught theology at Oxford in the 1360s

---

[11] J.K. Zeman, *The Anabaptists and the Czech Brethren in Moravia, 1526–1628*,
pp. 44–6.
[12] *Ibid.*, pp. 64–5; G.H. Williams, *Radical Reformation*, pp. 321–2, 328.

and 1370s, but had been forced from his post for, amongst other things, denying transubstantiation (the Catholic doctrine that the actual substance of the bread and wine literally becomes the body and blood of Christ at communion). Wycliffe also attacked the institution of the papacy, together with indulgences and monas- ticism. He organized too the translation of the Vulgate Latin version of the Bible into English; a later age would insist – with illuminating results – that such translations be made from the original Greek and Hebrew. Still, Wycliffe's innovation was sufficiently radical to make his success in dying in his bed at Lutterworth in 1384 (despite papal attempts to arrange a warmer demise) something of a triumph.

Wycliffe's followers were persecuted in the years that followed. Sir John Oldcastle, a Herefordshire knight, led a minor rebellion, and was executed in 1417. With its support amongst the wealthier and more educated classes destroyed, Lollardy (the name means 'mumblers' or 'mutterers') became a form of dissent amongst the lower social strata of England, with strengths in Kent, Bucking- hamshire and other rural counties as well as, later, amongst the merchants of the north-western parishes of London.

Not all confined themselves to Wycliffe's ideas. Wycliffe him- self has justly been described as the 'Morning Star of the Refor- mation'; he stressed the dominance of Scripture over Christian doctrine, of the secular government, rather than the pope, over the church, and of divine predestination over all human actions. Later Lollards tended to adhere to the first of these, to be agnostic about the second and, as often as not, inimical to the third.

Reginald Pecock, Bishop of Chichester, complained about the Lollards' biblicism in his revealingly entitled book, *The Repressor of Over Much Blaming of the Clergy*, written in 1455. They believed:

> that no governance is to be held of Christian men [to be] the service or
> the law of God, save [that] which is grounded in Holy Scripture in the
> New Testament, as some of [them] hold; or . . . in the New Testament
> or in the Old, and is not by the New Testament revoked, as some other
> of them hold.[13]

---

[13]   R. Pecock, *The Repressor of Over Much Blaming of the Clergy*, p. 5.

Either way, the Lollards' commitment to the supreme authority of Scripture, and to the primacy of the New Testament over the Old, is clear. The latter point is important for our subject; as we noticed in the Introduction, the New Testament church was sectarian in character, rather than a state-religion-in-waiting with a blueprint for running society at large like the religion of Old Testament Israel. Many of the sixteenth- and seventeenth-century radicals were to stress the New Testament at the expense of the Old for this reason.

It is safe to assume that few, if any, of the Lollards had anything as exalted as an explicit theology of the church. Such ecclesiology as they had was implicit rather than thoroughly worked out; they were *de facto* a sectarian group. The Lollards referred to themselves as 'known men'; the scriptural reference appears to have been to 1 Corinthians 14:38 ('if any one does not recognize this, he is not recognized') but the implication that the Lollards were a secret society, known only to God and to one another, is clear enough. In this the Lollards were venturing further in practice than Wycliffe had in theory for, as has been noted, he had conceived of the church continuing to embrace all, though under royal, rather than papal, authority.

Revering the Bible, especially the New Testament, the Lollards found much to criticize in the existing Catholic church. This criticism could be very damning. William Aylward, a Lollard tried in 1464, believed that 'the pope of Rome is a great beast and a devil of hell and a synagogue and that he shall lie deeper in hell nine times than Lucifer; that the Blessed Sacrament of the altar is a great devil of hell. . . .' and 'that there ought no man to be baptised until he came to old age'.[14]

By 'old age', Aylward may have meant literally that; Constantine, the first (supposedly) Christian Roman emperor in the fourth century had been baptized on his deathbed (as were many others in that age) to prevent post-baptismal sins from staining his ritually whitened soul. If, as is far more likely, he simply meant 'maturity', then this is a striking example of opposition building up to infant baptism, and all that it implies about the

---

[14] K.B. McFarlane, *The Origins of Religious Dissent in England*, p. 196.

nature of the church, even before the Reformation – let alone the sixteenth-century Anabaptist movement. (Lollard views, however, varied a great deal.)

Aylward's other protests, his denunciation of the pope as Antichrist and his rejection of the mass and transubstantiation: these were beliefs whose adherents might have been expected to jump up and embrace the Reformation of Luther, Calvin and their fellows. But dissenters who had also become used to seeing the true church as a secret society, and who doubted the validity of infant baptism: such people might be less sure that the official Reformation was indeed bringing in the New Jerusalem for which they had been waiting so long.

Pecock, in his hand-wringing over the nuisance caused by Lollards in fifteenth-century England, complained of a second trait exhibited by them:

> That whatever Christian man or woman be meek in spirit . . . shall without fail and default find the true understanding of Holy Scripture in whatever place he or she shall read and study, though it be in the Apocalypse or oughtwhere else. [15]

The Lollards were anti-intellectual, at least in the good sense of claiming that the essential points of Scripture are clear enough to all those who sincerely enquire for themselves, and that a learned élite is not required to interpose itself between God and his people. As Pecock implies with his reference to the book of Revelation, they also tended to be anti-intellectual in the bad sense, despising the value of learning and denying the value of its contribution at any point.

This anti-intellectualism was bound up with Pecock's third point about the Lollards: their unwillingness to be taught by priests was part and parcel of their anti-clericalism. Anti-clericalism has often been thought to be a phenomenon of southern Europe in the nineteenth century. But the records of radical movements in early modern Europe are full of it. The famous case of Richard Hunne, the London merchant accused of Lollardy and then murdered in prison by clerics angry because he had brought a civil case against them, brought an

---

[15]   R. Pecock, *Repressor*, p. 6.

outburst of anti-clerical protest from the merchant and political classes of London. These were outraged at the virtual immunity of clergy from obedience to the law of the land, and had long been irritated by disputes over the level of tithes, that compulsory church tax which laid such a burden upon their livelihoods. Chapuys, the ambassador in London of the Holy Roman Emperor, remarked in the 1520s that 'All the people here hate the priests'.

Elsewhere in Europe such hatred could break out with murderous results. In the 1470s, the followers of the messiah-figure Hans Böhm, the so-called Drummer of Niklashausen, had sung:

> To God in heaven we complain
> That the priests cannot be slain,

whilst their leader had denounced all clergy as the true heretics and called for them to be put to the sword. Some of the Taborites, as well as the morally dissolute practitioners of the 'Free Spirit', had done the same. Such instances are perhaps extreme examples and are more likely to reflect the hatred of the representatives of authority felt by the poor and the dispossessed than any purely religious protest against clerical shortcomings; the anti-clericalism of the Lollards was, by contrast, more middle-of-the-road, a gut-feeling compatible with easily understandable religious sensibilities, and one with which a large segment of the population could readily identify. It was a cry for the spiritual independence or autonomy of the individual, for the right to investigate the Scriptures for oneself – an assertion of the common-sense notion that all are finally equal before God.

The attack upon transubstantiation had the same effect. If bread and wine really are transformed into the body and blood of Christ every time communion is celebrated, it follows that the person who administers this miracle is very special indeed. His work of blessing the sacramental elements would then be the most vital part of ordinary Christian experience. This was pretty much the view of the priest's position in the Middle Ages.

So the denunciation of transubstantiation as so much priestly mumbo-jumbo was an attack upon the position of the clergy,

both in Christian life and the community. To state that communion was a commemorative meal, and not a miracle or a propitia-
tory sacrifice offering up Christ's body and blood afresh, was to
make the minister an ordinary mortal or, at most, the first
amongst equals. Lollardy thus not only entailed anti-clerical
protest; arguably it *was* anti-clerical protest. Not only its sacramentarianism (the technical name for the belief that communion
was commemorative only) but its biblicism, its stress upon the
ability of all devout readers to interpret Scripture, its rejection of
papal authority: all pointed towards a declaration of spiritual
independence by the individual believer.

Wycliffe's belief in predestination to salvation has been widely
hailed as his other major anticipation of the Protestant reformers
of the sixteenth century. The truth is a little more complicated. In
the first place, in thinking that God has predetermined which
individuals will be saved, Wycliffe was by no means unique
amongst late medieval churchmen. Wycliffe had been taught this
opinion by Bradwardine, who had been Archbishop of Canterbury for a few months before his death – presumably by divine
appointment – in 1349. Thomas Aquinas, the master of the schoolmen and the thirteenth-century thinker whose ideas (referred to as
Thomism) continued to dominate university departments, had
been a rigorous predestinarian, believing that every action was
finally an act of God. William of Ockham, Bradwardine's contemporary and the one who is associated with Thomism's rival school
of thought, Nominalism, was equally strong in affirming divine
predestination. In this, all were drawing on that stream of ideas in
Christian theology which had its source in Augustine (354–430),
whose thought had so dominated the Middle Ages.

Not that the medieval church had been characterized by a
general belief in predestination: far from it. Everything about
medieval religion bespoke a belief, not merely in free will, but in
the Pelagian idea that a person can put themselves right with God
by their own actions, unaided by grace, be those actions moral
good works, or sacraments, or other ritual observances such as
penance, pilgrimages, the viewing of holy relics or the purchase
of indulgences.

The views of the theologians were, in this respect, far removed
from the concrete realities of daily religious life. Even in the

mid-sixteenth century, the Council of Trent, which was designed to define Roman Catholic orthodoxy to combat Protestantism, could not bring itself to come to a hard and fast decision on the issue of predestination; the desire to uphold the teaching of Thomas Aquinas being balanced by the equal and opposite desire to condemn a central teaching of the Protestant reformers. Catholic practice, however, both before and after the outbreak of the Reformation, was to promote salvation by human effort.

The rigid predestination taught by theologians and philosophers on the one hand, and the *de facto* Pelagianism implicit in the everyday religious practice of popes, cardinals and ordinary believers alike on the other, might seem to be irreconcilable to the modern commentator. But every challenge has its hero ready to meet it and, as so often, England produced the man. Robert Holcot produced a perfect rationale for having the worst of both worlds before dying, like most of his generation in Europe, of a brief illness in the late 1340s. Salvation was, he taught, by the mercy (*potentia absoluta*) of an arbitrary God, which he nevertheless customarily channels (*potentia ordinata*) on the basis of man's works. Predestination was not, as it later came to be considered, the guarantor and undergirding of the doctrine of justification by faith. Wycliffe did not teach the latter doctrine, but implied, in a manner not very different from other commentators of his day, that the predestined elect, who could not even be certain of their own identity, would be those who brought forth good works.

It was this predestinarianism that many of Wycliffe's later followers largely rejected. The underground Lollard movement of the late fifteenth and early sixteenth centuries tended to emphasize human free will and the importance of good works as a practical expression of Christianity. This 'common-sense' approach was part of their protest against the metaphysical speculations of the schoolmen. The result was that the Epistle of James, which Luther, notoriously, was to refer to as 'an epistle of straw' (because of its emphasis upon the importance of good works as evidence of genuine faith) became one of their most treasured pieces of Scripture, as may easily be seen by the frequency with which it crops up in legal proceedings against suspected Lollards. Various portions of Scripture were copied out, circulated, read aloud at meetings, and committed to memory, especially by the illiterate. The Scriptures concerned were almost invariably from the New Testament, but the Epistle of James appears to have been used in this fashion more frequently than any other.

The truth is that, by the early sixteenth century, the Lollards were no longer 'Wycliffian' in more than the most general of senses. Groups were disparate; there was no question of any kind of national organization. For analytical purposes, reality can be distorted least by dividing them into three general tendencies.

The first may be called 'Wycliffian' in that they maintained their originator's concerns with some degree of faithfulness. These would have been the Lollards who were most willing to embrace the 'official' Reformation when Luther's ideas, and those of the other reformers, began to appear in England, often enough in books smuggled across the Channel.

The second group, and probably the largest, were those who had abandoned Wycliffe's predestinarianism, and who were most stridently anti-intellectual and anti-clerical. Many of these were more doubtful about the Protestant dawn and, though some eventually threw in their lot with it, others continued to develop their own ideas. These formed the basis for pre-Elizabethan radicalism, often influenced by continental Anabaptism, though probably never actually converted to it. Of these we shall have much more to say later.

The final tendency consisted of those individuals who had developed a miscellany of ideas, some of them far out, others simply a form of irreligion or even straight vandalism. Termed 'Lollard' by the authorities who prosecuted them, one suspects that many of their fellow victims would have been anxious enough to disown them. They continued as a nihilistic sub-current in English society, emerging, for example, in the mid-seventeenth-century movement known as the Ranters.

None of what has been said so far should be taken to mean that there was any direct continuity at all between the various movements we have described here and the continental Anabaptism of the sixteenth century. Professor Cameron's sagacious warning in respect of the Waldensians will serve us well for the Czech Brethren, for the Lollards, and for the rest of the rag-bag of radical dissenters that has been assembled here: 'One is entitled to scramble together all the references to the heresies of the sect and create a "radical" picture . . . if one wishes. However, if a heresy is not studied as it was believed, and as it may reasonably be shown to have been believed by a fair proportion of those who were accused of being its followers, then our description of it is flawed.'[16]

Fortunately, that does not answer the whole point, for what we have been looking at here (as indeed we will be doing throughout this book) is not simply continuity, but the appearance of religious phenomena which bear a similarity to one another. Modern Protestants are still trying to answer, if only for their own peace of mind, the taunt of sixteenth-century Catholics as to where their church was before Luther (or perhaps, in the case of non-pædobaptists, before Conrad Grebel, the early Anabaptist leader).

It is certainly possible to answer the jibe, but not on the basis of any kind of direct succession, apostolic or otherwise. All that can be said is that early-church doctrines, whether in respect of biblical authority, apocalyptic expectation, the priesthood of all believers, a commemorative view of the sacraments, the gift of prophecy or salvation by grace, were all recurring themes in late medieval dissent, and formed part of the climate of ideas in which some were disposed to think. There is no need to posit continuity, or even influence, between the different groups, though in some cases – notably between Wycliffe and Hus – this certainly existed.

What accounts for the recurrence of the ideas? Well, for a start, all are biblical. Vernacular Bibles were a rarity in that age but – sometimes illegally – they were becoming more common. In any case, not all laymen were ignorant of Latin, and not all clerics and theologians felt able to reconcile the contents of Scripture with official dogma. The result, amongst braver souls at least, was recurrent 'heresy'. It may be that even this is not the whole answer. The Letter to the Hebrews assures us that God spoke through the Old Testament prophets in various ways; perhaps even medieval people, living under an apostate and suffocating Christendom, were not entirely beyond his reach.

---

[16] E. Cameron, *Reformation of the Heretics*, pp. 65–6.

Chapter Two

Feathers and all: the Radical Challenge to Luther's Reformation

Andreas Bodenstein von Karlstadt

If Luther was a revolutionary, he was a pretty conservative one, and he had a tendency to become extremely irritable with those who went further – or simply faster – along the road of rebellion against Rome than he was prepared to do himself. One of these causes of irritation was Andreas Bodenstein von Karlstadt, and if Luther had to vent his spleen on anyone, then we should be thankful that his principal victim was a not entirely guiltless object of attack.

Karlstadt could be an irritating man. He was pernickety, ambitious, and awkward in his personal relations. In addition to his own earned doctorate of Divinity, he had virtually bought a doctorate in law from Siena in order to put himself in line for a lucrative official position in Wittenberg. (The plan didn't work.) Worst of all, he had the galling experience of seeing Martin Luther, his junior by about seven years, and over whose doctoral examination in 1512 he had presided as Dean of the Theology Faculty in Wittenberg, achieve undreamed-of prominence and success.

Karlstadt tried hard to be loyal. Indeed, he was persuaded by his young colleague to abandon his earlier attachment to the medieval scholastic theologians, especially Thomas Aquinas (*c.* 1225–74), and to take more of an interest in Augustine (354–430), whose writings were revolutionizing Luther's thinking.

The revival of Augustinianism, in the period before Luther's revolt of October 1517 and the beginning of the Reformation, meant an emphasis on man's inability to save himself, a belief in salvation by grace through divine predestination (not the same thing as salvation by faith) and a tendency to lay more weight upon Scripture than on the authority of medieval commentators.

As the storm was breaking in early 1518, Karlstadt began a course of lectures on Augustine's book, *On the Spirit and the Letter*, in which he stressed the difference between living under religious legalism and walking in the Spirit. Professor E.G. Rupp has pointed out that, although Karlstadt was obliged, in these lectures, to keep to the subject matter of the text he was expounding, this Law-Spirit dichotomy was, in any case, more important to him than Luther's contrast between Law and Gospel.[1]

The point is that Karlstadt was more concerned with the issues of holiness and sanctification in the inner man – attainable through the ministrations of the Holy Spirit, as opposed to outward moral and religious observances – than he was with Luther's concentration upon salvation and redemption. In stressing the inward work of the Spirit in the life of the believer, Karlstadt was anticipating an important recurring theme amongst almost all of the continental radicals.

In 1519, Karlstadt was involved in the famous Leipzig disputation between Luther and his papal opponent, John Eck, professor of theology at Ingolstadt. Indeed, as the senior academic at Wittenberg University, it was Karlstadt, not Luther, who was officially Eck's principal opponent in the debate, although it was plain that Luther was Eck's real target. For a week, Eck demolished the arguments of Karlstadt, who couldn't think on his feet like his junior colleague or, for that matter, like his opponent. Neither could Karlstadt remember quotes. Although Luther entered the lists and rescued the situation for the reformers, Karlstadt had been made to look less than brilliant. On this very public occasion, his ability had contrasted poorly with that of Luther. Forgiving our enemies is sometimes hard, but it is not as hard as forgiving our friends for rescuing us after we have made fools of ourselves, and Karlstadt proved unequal to the task.

---

[1]   E.G. Rupp, *Patterns of Reformation*, p. 59.

The situation was not helped when Luther, a few months later, made fun of Karlstadt for lecturing on the Epistle of James. Luther tended to exclude from the canon of Scripture those books teaching doctrine hard to reconcile with his own, and he described James as 'an epistle of straw'. The Wittenberg students, enthralled by the new genius, listened to Luther, and deserted Karlstadt's lectures in droves.

Karlstadt's chance was to come again just over a year later. The local prince, Frederick the Wise of Saxony, presided over a collection of several thousand holy bones, relics of the saints, and other religious clutter which would, he was sure, reduce his stay in purgatory by thousands of years. Despite this superficial adherence to religious traditionalism, he had been happy to allow 'his' academics at 'his' university to indulge in theological devia- tion of the kind that had led to the current crisis. His radicalism, however, stopped short of allowing any theoretical conclusions to be put into practical effect. Reformation must not go as far as actual reform. At least not yet. He had specifically forbidden any innovations, and Luther had been careful to oblige him.

In Luther's view, structures could be changed only after con- sciences had been changed, and that would only happen by the hearing of the Word. Preaching was enough. Even after hearts and minds had eventually been won over, moreover, alterations in services should be done so subtly 'that the common man never realizes it and no offence is caused'. As one historian has rightly commented, 'It is hard to imagine a clearer exposure of Luther's evaluation of the laity's incapacity to handle such matters'.[2]

In May 1521, however, Luther was kidnapped – by his own friends – on his way back to Wittenberg from Worms. This was no 'friendly fire' incident, but a deliberate attempt by some of the German princes to ensure their theological hero was kept out of inquisitorial clutches – long enough to write some more anti- papal diatribes at least. From his prison in the Wartburg, Luther duly obliged. Meanwhile, back in Wittenberg, Karlstadt and the other reformers kept Luther's movement going. Indeed, they speeded things up.

---

[2] *LW* 36.254 [Pelikan and Lehman eds., *Luther's Works*]; J.S. Preus, *Carlstadt's Ordinaciones and Luther's Liberty*, p. 72.

Vigils and masses for the dead were observed no more. The monasteries and convents were closed (or rather, opened, monks and nuns being allowed out as and when they pleased). Priests, monks and nuns got married. A local minor aristocrat did his bit for the Reformation and the end of clerical celibacy, by giving his fifteen-year-old daughter in marriage to Karlstadt, who encouraged others to follow suit:

> God also gave a commandment to human beings, saying, 'You are to grow and multiply.' . . . [But monks and nuns] have greater regard for anti-Christian institutions and prohibitions than for divine order. And they even think that the pope is wiser than God. Shame on them. And they dare commit abominable sins which God hates more than adultery and sodomy and yet they want to present themselves as monks and nuns and chaste persons. . . . Read the Bible and take your children out of cloisters, you lay folks – the sooner, the better – and give them in marriage. You will thus serve God, be good parents, and assist your children in gaining their salvation. [3]

In addition, at Christmas 1521, Karlstadt celebrated the first Protestant eucharist. Wearing a plain black gown rather than the usual priestly vestments, and speaking in German rather than Latin, he gave communion in both kinds to the assembled congregation. All of these actions spelled the break with priestcraft. The minister was not marked out by special, or at least not by ceremonial, dress. The implicit message was that all were (relatively) equal. The use of the vernacular meant that what was happening was supposed to be addressed to the understanding of all present; it was not just a spectacle to be adored.

Communion had generally been given in both kinds until the central Middle Ages, even by the Catholic Church, but in more recent centuries the wine had been reserved for the priest alone, hence the need for late medieval doctrines about the body and blood of Christ both being present in each of the elements separately (so that the peasant who had had only bread placed in his mouth had received the Saviour's blood as well as his body). Karlstadt's innovation broke both with this doctrine, and with the need for it. In the first place, communicants were given both bread and wine. Also the bread was given into their hands,

---

[3]　A. Karlstadt, *The Essential Carlstadt*, ed. E.J. Furcha, pp. 98–9.

not put in their mouths. One fearful member of the congregation, convinced that he really was handling the body of Christ, trembled so much that he dropped the morsel, and could not be persuaded to pick it up again. In the second place, Karlstadt refused to 'elevate the host', i.e. lift up the elements at communion for the worship of the people. By such a refusal he signalled that the communion was not a sacrifice, that the bread and wine were not the same thing as the body and blood of Christ.

Unsurprisingly, Prince Frederick was less than pleased by the activities of Karlstadt, Melanchthon and the other leaders in Wittenberg. The pattern of reform became even less sedate when Gabriel Zwilling, a monk, led an iconoclastic riot, smashing pictures, statues of Mary and the saints, crucifixes, altars and images. Again, Karlstadt had been deeply involved in creating antagonism to images.

From the perspective of four and three-quarter centuries later, this principled philistine vandalism always seems, not only unattractive, but irrational. Modern evangelicals are still not enamoured with the idea of images in church (although the odd mobile banner is gaining increasing support) but, if they are westerners, they have mostly forgotten why they do not like these things. They like seeing the Sistine Chapel as much as anyone else, even if they wouldn't want inferior but similar pictures adorning the walls of Zion Baptist Church back home. Actually destroying works of art, rather than removing them or altering attitudes towards them, seems incomprehensible. For moderns, religious images are art first and religious only after that. For sixteenth-century people, the converse was the case. In theory, an image directed illiterate parishioners to the biblical incident or character which it depicted; it was an aid to worship, not an object of worship. The reality, of course, was different. Religious images and works of art were all but universally reverenced and worshipped, especially by country people. As Karlstadt himself said, 'Who will believe us when we say that we do not love these stuffed dummies – carved or painted images, when our deeds convict us? . . . They thus destroy their worshippers.'[4] For the early Protestants, seeing around them

---

[4] *Ibid.*, p. 103.

what they felt to be the grossest idolatry (a sin that would undoubtedly lead its practitioners into hell-fire), artistic considerations merited little when placed alongside the urgent spiritual needs of the moment. It was so much the worse for the images: they were to be destroyed.

Eventually the party ended when Luther returned home in March 1522, and reversed the reforms in order to keep Frederick and other conservatives onside. Karlstadt was disgraced. Unable to remain the big fish in such a large pond as Wittenberg, he sought a smaller pond, and managed to become minister of nearby Orlamünde. There he carried through his own, more radical reforms, dressed as a peasant, did his own farming, and asked to be addressed as 'Neighbour Andreas'. As well as being extremely popular with his parishioners, he had a sizeable and growing following in the surrounding area, including at the nearby town of Jena, where he continued to publish his writings. Eventually Luther and the authorities in Wittenberg would decide to act against him.

Thomas Müntzer

In the meantime, Karlstadt was not the only radical to be causing trouble and embarrassment for Luther. If the Dean of the University gives the impression of having been awkward, cantankerous and inept, Thomas Müntzer (c. 1490–1525) has frequently had a decidedly sinister reputation.

A native Saxon, and a student of Leipzig and Frankfurt an der Oder universities, he became proof-reader for the printer Melchior Lotter. When Lotter attended the Leipzig disputation in 1519 to hear and record his heroes Luther and Karlstadt slugging it out with Eck, his proof-reader came too. Some months later, in early 1520, Luther recommended Müntzer for the job of supply preacher at the Saxon town of Zwickau.

It did not take Müntzer long to clash with the local minister. Sylvius Egranus regarded himself as a critic of the Roman hierarchy, but his was a very different programme to Luther's. He was a humanist in the Erasmian mold, more disposed than Luther to assume that, if etymological questions were resolved

and the populace educated, questions of salvation and damna-
tion might well take care of themselves. Müntzer's apocalyptic,
anti-clerical, occasionally blood-curdling sermons rather went
against the grain with Egranus, especially when he found himself
on the receiving end of some of their rhetoric. In February 1521,
he sent Müntzer a terse note, written in German rather than Latin
because, he sniffed, it was obvious that Müntzer could not abide
sound learning, or Scripture either for that matter. He added
sarcastically that 'the Spirit', about which Müntzer boasted so
frequently, must be his great educator.

There was real substance to the charge. Müntzer was beginning to emphasize spiritual illumination, rather than strict biblicism, as the key to understanding true Christian faith. His was
no introverted mysticism, however. He was starting to preach
social revolution. The lower orders of Zwickau loved it. In any
case, there was a coterie of home-grown revolutionaries in the
form of Niklaus Storch, Markus Stübner and Thomas Drechsel,
the so-called 'Zwickau prophets'.

The said 'prophets' taught the slaying of the godless – identified as the rich and anyone in authority – and the abolition of a
professional clergy and of officially imposed religion (the godly
having no need of them, since they were under the guidance of
the Spirit). They also denounced infant baptism, although
whether this was because they rejected the inclusion of the entire
population in the church, or because baptism was a mere outward work which would not be needed in this dispensation of the
Spirit, is not clear. Certainly, they did not advance to the practice
of believers' baptism.

Müntzer was mightily impressed by the Zwickau prophets
and, in terms of reciprocal influence during the years 1520–1521,
historians are divided as to which was the tail and which was the
donkey. However, when an uprising was attempted in the town
in April 1521, it failed and Müntzer, despite protestations of
having been in the bath at the time of the disturbances, was
banished. His accomplices managed to stay on until December,
when they went to Wittenberg to perplex Melanchthon and
Karlstadt during Luther's absence. Melanchthon, in particular,
got into a terrible fuss, impressed by their Bible knowledge, but
inwardly certain that their ideas were crazy. Luther sent him a

sharp letter from the Wartburg, reassuring him that the latter was the correct view.

From Zwickau, Müntzer went to Prague, where a pre-existent radical underground gave him some hope of acceptance. The disturbances caused by the revolt of Jan Hus, just over a century earlier, had left a legacy of some religious pluralism. Officially, Roman Catholics and Utraquists existed side by side. (The latter were the descendants of the most moderate Hussites, and took their name from the fact that they gave communion in both kinds, this being virtually the only concession their forefathers had succeeded in wresting from Rome.) Unofficially, Hussitism had spawned radical off-shoots, and these, together with the as yet unorganized supporters of Luther, formed a 'radical' under-world which Müntzer might hope to influence. By November 1521, however, the Utraquists and some of the native radicals had assessed Müntzer for what he was, and the major pulpits of the city were denied to him.

This setback did not prevent him from issuing his magnilo-quently titled 'Prague Manifesto' at the beginning of that month. In it, he attempted to portray himself as the great reformer of Bohemia; farcically, the document did not even get into print, and Müntzer was reduced to circulating hand-written copies. Müntzer denied having benefited from any teaching of monks or scholars. The latter had spoken of 'mere Scripture, which they have stolen from the Bible like murderers and thieves, . . . for they themselves never heard it from the mouth of God'.[5] He argued from 1 Cor. 3 that God wrote not with pen and ink, but upon the human heart, and this he did only for and in his elect.[6] Using a line of argument disconcertingly similar to that employed by modern charismatics, he maintained that God could hardly have become dumb since the canon of Scripture was completed.[7] Echoing 1 Corinthians 14:24–5, he claimed that the current exercise of prophecy would cause unbelievers to acknowledge the presence of God.[8]

---

[5]   T. Müntzer, *Collected Works*, tr. and ed. P. Matheson, p. 357.
[6]   *Ibid.*, p. 358.
[7]   *Ibid.*
[8]   *Ibid.*, p. 359.

After pledging to lay down his life for his teaching, Müntzer concluded by giving two contrasting prophecies of his own. On the one hand, God would make Bohemia a 'mirror for the whole world', the starting place of the new church. On the other hand, if the Bohemians refused to rally to 'the defence of God's word' – and one suspects that he had a military, rather than a metaphorical 'defence' in mind – then, within the year, God would cause the country to be overrun by the dreaded Turks. The former possibility was always a long shot; the latter looked a real possibility during any of the early years of the sixteenth century. [9] In the event, the real judgement of heaven expressed itself insofar as neither outcome actually occurred, either during the following year or at any other time.

Müntzer posited a 'fall' of the church from its original purity, analogous to the 'fall' of mankind in Eden. This was not, as Luther had suggested, simply the result of the corruptions of the later Middle Ages, but had occurred much sooner: 'After the death of the apostles' pupils the immaculate virginal church became a whore by the adultery of the clergy; it was the fault of the scholars, who always want to sit up top . . .' [10] That Müntzer was free from ambitions to 'sit up top' himself may be doubted. Nevertheless, the line of argument was to become a radical commonplace.

As we have seen, [11] the Waldensians believed in a 'fall' of the church around the time of Constantine. Müntzer placed it even earlier; 'after the death of the apostles' pupils' must refer to some time around the mid-second century. Perhaps he was thinking of the period after Polycarp. It was at least arguable that Irenæus, Origen and Tertullian had been the first post-apostolic 'intellectual' theologians, although Justin Martyr might have been seen in the same light. What all of the radicals were to hold in common was the view that the wrong turning had been taken by the church at a point significantly earlier than the magisterial reformers were prepared to concede. For the latter, the state of the church in the late Roman Empire had been, if not ideal, then at least fairly

---

[9] *Ibid.*, pp. 360–61.
[10] *Ibid.*, p. 360.
[11] see above, p. 17–18.

satisfactory, and its developed theology – especially as represented by the first ecumenical councils and the thought of
Augustine – provided a model with which to work. It was only
the papal accretions of the central and later Middle Ages which
needed to be sloughed off. For the radicals, on the other hand,
earlier developments were seen as constituting a 'fall'. Müntzer,
concerned to build up an anti-intellectual rationale (if that is not
a contradiction in terms), saw the development of a substantial
body of Christian apologetics and theology from the second and
third centuries onwards, together with the growth of a 'priestly'
body, as the point of 'fall'. Other radicals pinpointed the alliance
with the state under Constantine as the decisive departure from
a believers' church. Yet others felt themselves to have been
against all the world since the apostles. All were united, however,
in discerning an early date for the decisive decline of the church.

Implicit in this was the repudiation of patristic authority; for
most, especially the evangelical Anabaptists, this was to mean an
exaggerated biblicism, whilst for others it would mean the exal-
tation of 'the Spirit', whether as manifested in the lives of each
individual believer, or as with Müntzer in the person of the
supposedly anointed leader.

Müntzer's reputation was now such as to preclude the possibility of his being appointed minister by any authority aware of
his real programme. This narrowed the scope of his employment
opportunities to ill-governed hell-holes of smouldering social
tension. Happily for Müntzer, such a place existed.

The drawing of parallels between the Saxon mining town of
Allstedt and the Wild West is not fanciful. The forces of law
and order were remote, and most mayors over the previous
quarter of a century had met violent deaths. Müntzer was
appointed minister at Easter 1523, and in this atmosphere his
preaching went down well. Attempting to make the town an
alternative centre of Reformation, he drew up a German liturgy
which attracted visitors to the town from a wide area, and
swelled the local population. Some citizens went on iconoclastic
commando raids to destroy the shrines and icons of neighbouring villages.

Central authority, however, was slowly gearing itself up to
regain control of the situation. Duke John Frederick, brother of

Frederick the Wise, determined to oust the troublemaker. To ensure that no one could protest that Müntzer had been con-demned unheard though, he resolved to go through the motions of listening to him first. The prophet was therefore summoned to preach before his prince at nearby Weimar.

Müntzer can hardly have been unaware of the political reali-ties, but resolved to play the situation as it presented itself on the surface. Accordingly, his sermon appealed for the support of the princes for his brand of reformation. The second chapter of Daniel was pressed into service: only the true prophet of God, Daniel (read 'Müntzer'), could explain the vision of Nebuchad-nezzar (read 'John Frederick'). The wise men (read 'other reform-ers') who could not do this were to be killed (read 'killed'). Müntzer told his princely audience,

> The sword is necessary to wipe out the godless. . . . If, however, [the princes] do not do it, the sword will be taken from them. . . . The opposition may . . . be slain without any mercy as . . . Elijah destroyed the priests of Baal. . . . Godless rulers should be killed, especially the priests and monks who revile the gospel. . . . The godless have no right to live except as the elect wish to grant it to them, as it is written in Ex. 23:39–33.[12]

If the prince's identification of the godless differed from that of his instructor, he shared at least some of Müntzer's lethal instincts, and about a month later the pastor of Allstedt found it prudent to remove himself over the town wall one night. (This was, perhaps, one of the few genuinely Pauline actions of his entire career [Acts 9:25].) He fled south-west to meet up with the armies of peasants who were just then flaring into open revolt against their landlords.

The Peasants' War

Goaded by deteriorating social conditions and by the erosion of their traditional legal rights, the peasants of southern and central Germany and Austria spent much of the second half of 1524 and the first half of 1525 attacking aristocratic homes, clergy,

---

[12]   G.H. Williams and A.M. Mergal eds., *Spiritual and Anabaptist Writers*, p. 68–9.

monasteries and episcopal palaces. Such events were far from unprecedented; their frequency since the end of the fifteenth century amounted almost to a tradition. As uncoordinated and foredoomed to failure as most peasant revolts, they had frequently taken on a religious flavour – designating themselves 'Christian Brethren' and appealing to the natural equality of the Garden of Eden as a precedent for open access to the land in the present.

This time around, many fastened onto Luther's teachings as justification for their own actions. It soon became clear, however, that their military prospects were not the only topic about which they had been unduly sanguine. They had also been unjustifiably optimistic about the degree of support that might be expected from their peasant-turned-academic hero in Wittenberg, and in their belief that his words about the dignity and equality of all Christians should be taken at face value, rather than as representative of a merely spiritual reality.

In an attempt to refute accusations by his papal enemies that he had caused the revolt, Luther reacted by denouncing the rebels (in *Against the Murdering and Robbing Hordes of Peasants*) as 'faithless, perjured, lying, disobedient knaves'; everyone who could should 'smite, slay and stab' them, 'secretly or openly, remembering that nothing can be more poisonous, hurtful or devilish than a rebel.'[13] Luther lost out here on both counts; the smear of effectively inciting rebellion continued to cling to him, whilst his adherence to the cause of the princes, upon whose support he so much relied, lost him peasant support. The tract from which this passage comes continues to stand out even today as one of his most notoriously distasteful outbursts.

In another tract of the same year, *Against the Heavenly Prophets*, Luther turned upon the religious radicals who had plagued him, and whom he believed were the true culprits in fomenting unrest. As is the wont of conservatives attacking radicals, he lumped them all together – making all guilty of the excesses of the worst, such as Müntzer – regardless of the fact that Karlstadt had specifically rejected the offer of a 'covenantal', or ecclesiastical, alliance with Müntzer's Allstedt in July 1524. Luther

---

[13]   cited in E.G. Rupp and B. Drewery, *Martin Luther*, p. 122.

sneered that Karlstadt, who was guiltless of the violence which Müntzer had done so much to encourage, believed himself to have 'devoured the Holy Spirit, feathers and all'. [14]

Karlstadt was expelled from Saxony and turned loose into the rather frightening Germany of the Peasants' War. His pregnant wife was allowed to remain in Saxony, but was herself expelled after the birth, when she refused to allow the baby to be christened. Karlstadt had probably stopped performing in-fant baptisms before his expulsion from Orlamünde, although he had not advanced to the actual practice of believers' baptism. He had also taken a more radical stance than Luther concerning communion and now denied that the physical elements of bread and wine could assure the conscience at all; the heart alone mattered, and the elements simply played a part in the believer's mystical union with Christ. It seems that, for Karlstadt, no outward ceremonies, whether communion or baptism, mattered very much; 'spirit' was all that counted. When he had been expelled from Saxony in 1524, his brother-in-law, Dr. Gerhard Westerburg, had taken manuscripts of eight of Karlstadt's latest tracts to Basel, Switzerland, to have them printed.

Living in Orlamünde, Karlstadt had affected peasant style and dress, but the violence of the real 'common people' now unnerved him. He reached the small city of Rothenburg ob der Tauber in late 1524, where his preaching of iconoclasm and sympathy for the peasants alienated the town patricians, but where the ascendant peasant party neither understood, nor much sympathized with, the eucharistic doctrines of this intel-lectual 'man of the people', and was suspicious of his political moderation. Although he consented to be chaplain of the local peasant army, it was with the sole purpose of counselling pacific courses. One soldier amongst the many who suspected Karlstadt of treason almost succeeded in murdering him. Al-though his wife joined her husband in his faltering attempts to humour the peasants, his ordeal was ended in June when, the peasant cause in tatters, he emulated the apostle Paul at Damascus by escaping from Rothenburg in a basket let down over the wall at night.

---

[14] A. Karlstadt, *Karlstadt's Battle with Luther*, R.J. Sider, p. 97.

If Karlstadt was nervous about the peasant violence, however, involvement in the war held no fears for Müntzer. For him, the poverty of the vast mass of the population was an insuperable hindrance to their spiritual enlightenment, every minute of their time being occupied by the wretched business of staying alive. The rich and the learned he saw as parasites upon their labour. If the poor could be freed from their burden – and he was convinced that a general massacre of the rich would somehow accomplish this – then there would be achieved, as G.H. Williams expresses it, 'Restoration . . . [of the power of the early church] in the common people, the long-suffering custodians of the truth they could not articulate.'[15] And he, Thomas Müntzer, would articulate that truth for them.

Spring 1525 found Müntzer in Mühlhausen, the town having agreed to help the rebels. He wrote to Allstedt, appealing for military help from his erstwhile devotees there, and got it. The peasants of the surrounding Thuringia region were successfully stirred up, a few minor victories were won, some abbeys sacked, some nobles killed and others intimidated into joining the revolt. But the successes were illusory, and the final act of Müntzer's drama was at hand.

In May, a professional army under the Lutheran Landgrave Philip of Hesse met his peasant force of six thousand at Franken-hausen and destroyed it in minutes. Müntzer was captured after trying to flee the scene, and was tortured for information. Under torture, the bravado of his Prague Manifesto, in which he had promised his readiness to die for his beliefs, was punctured, and he gave a partial recantation. Even this, however, did not save him, for he had done too much to have any hope of securing mercy from his enemies. He was beheaded on 27th May 1525, and his body put on public display in Mühlhausen.

Karlstadt met a kinder fate. He was allowed to return anony-mously to Saxony, following a recantation. But after four years in obscurity, he re-entered the theological fray and went to Frisia in 1529 to help Melchior Hofmann, the apocalyptic Anabaptist, in his debates with the Lutheran authorities regarding the nature of the eucharist. His wanderings continued until 1534, when he

---

[15]   G.H. Williams, *The Radical Reformation*, 3rd edn, p. 126.

was offered the chair of Old Testament at the university in Protestant Basel.

The acceptance of this post, in which he ended his days, en-tailed, of course, a reversal of his long-held anti-intellectualism. Although he modified many of his other radical views, his charac-ter remained true to its old courses, and he made himself as awkward and unpopular in Basel as he had at Wittenberg, before finally succumbing to the plague in 1541.

The radical breakaways from Luther's Reformation were led by men with whom few today would care to identify. Of Thomas Müntzer, in particular, it can be said that almost no one did more to bring radical reformation into disrepute. This is an unfortunate fact, but one that needs to be faced.

There was, at the heart of Luther's theology, a passion and an irrationalism; this is not necessarily a criticism, but it is a fact. He delighted in paradox, vilified reason as 'the devil's whore', and clung to many of the folk superstitions he had learned in childhood. His brilliant theology never lost the stamp of his personal origins in the rough, credulous peasantry of central Germany. For cool, detached biblicist rationalism in the Protes-tant Reformation one must look, not to him, but to the humanist-educated reformers Zwingli and Calvin. It should come as no surprise, therefore, that the radical off-shoots of Luther's Refor-mation bore some of the characteristics of the central tree from which they sprang.

Chapter Three

The Swiss Brethren

The Slow Reformation in Zürich

If those who broke loose from Luther's Reformation bore
something of the character of their background, so too did those
who broke from the Swiss Reformation bear the imprint of
theirs. Huldrych Zwingli (1484–1531) had been parish priest of
Glarus, and then of Einsiedeln, both in Switzerland, before
being called to become Volkspriester ('people's priest') of the
Grossmünster church in Zürich in 1518. The city had some
autonomy over its own ecclesiastical affairs, and so the council
was responsible for making the appointment. A previous contact with a prostitute by the Glarus priest had, the council was
assured, been repented of, and in any case such a matter was
not considered to be particularly unusual, or even serious.

The appointment of this man had other advantages anyway:
as well as being a good preacher, Zwingli had benefited from
an excellent education in Vienna and Basel, which he had
improved upon by a degree of private study. He was a humanist
'man of letters' in the Renaissance style and, as befitted such
pretensions, maintained a considerable correspondence with
others of his ilk, the venerated Erasmus among them. Such
correspondences were more than opportunities for transmitting
information and maintaining (or gaining) friendships; they were
often written with a view to their subsequent publication, and
as such were vehicles for the full display of their authors'
erudition.

A near brush with death when he caught bubonic plague in 1519 caused the new people's priest to take his faith more seriously; this was the nearest Zwingli seems to have come to a conversion experience. Certainly he began to teach reforming doctrines after this time. The implications of the new teaching included complete local control over the church; the city council liked what it heard, and gave Zwingli its support.

Zwingli always denied preaching Lutheranism; he was simply propounding the unadulterated gospel. It was just a coincidence that his reformist preaching began shortly after the wide publicity attending 'the Luther affair', that Zwingli's doctrines bore passing resemblances to those of the Wittenberg professor, and that Zwingli possessed all of Luther's latest books. Perhaps it did not matter. Whatever Zwingli said, all reform was being labelled 'Martinist' or 'Lutheran'. In any case, his claim to independence of thought was lent some colour by the existence of a number of important differences, both in tone and in substance, between his own reforms and those of Luther.

The most obvious similarities included the dependence of both men upon powerful secular support in the territories within which they operated. Neither, moreover, wished to proceed faster than those authorities approved. For Luther, the limiting factor was the Elector of Saxony; for Zwingli, the burghers who made up the city council. The slowness of the Zürich Reformation made even the gradualism of Wittenberg seem like a whirlwind affair. Apart from Zwingli's evangelical preaching, nothing at all actually happened until 1522. That Ash Wednesday, several citizens broke the Lenten fast (when no one was supposed to eat meat) by consuming two pork sausages. Although he was a witness to this daring exploit, Zwingli was unable to summon up the courage at the time to join them, although he did defend them afterwards before the city council.

It was not until the following January that he persuaded the city fathers that religious doctrines and practices in Zürich should be decided according to Scripture. Even then, it was a full eighteen months before images and icons started to be removed, i.e. mid-1524 onwards, and the Mass was not finally abolished until April 1525. Unsurprisingly, this snail's pace soon had a group of Zwingli's disciples chafing at the bit. Conrad Grebel, the (formerly prodigal) son of a prominent council member, was the leader of this group of brilliant young scholars, who were becoming increasingly jaundiced at what they saw as their mentor's irresolute ways.

Both Luther and Zwingli identified the text of Scripture, rather than popes and councils, as the locus of religious authority. For Luther, the importance of Scripture was the fact that it pointed to the answer to man's overwhelming need. He personally had spent years of spiritual agony wrestling with the question of how an abject sinner can find a merciful God. It was Scripture, and especially the letters of Paul, which directs people to God's provision in the death of Christ, and to the need for man's response of faith. The commentaries of the medieval schoolmen had obscured the central point of Scripture, whilst the clutter of late medieval religious observances had effectively denied it. The way Luther stressed it, Scripture provided a glorious answer to a practical problem.

For Zwingli, however, the issue of scriptural authority was less desperately personal or existential. For him, it was an application of the basic *ad fontes* principle of Renaissance scholarship; to get proper perspective on any issue, it was imperative to go back to the original sources, not to later commentaries or translations. It was this which distinguished the new clarity of thought from the arid scholasticism of the Middle Ages. The original sourcebook of Christianity is the Bible, and hence its witness as to the nature of real Christianity must be decisive. This mentality is what distinguishes Zwingli's Reformation – and Calvin's too for that matter – from Luther's, even if the doctrinal differences were somewhat less than the differences in atmosphere might lead one to expect.

The most important theological difference to emerge between Luther and Zwingli was over the nature of sacraments. For Luther, a sacrament (be it communion or baptism) effected the thing it signified. Furthermore, although he rejected the Roman Catholic idea of transubstantiation, he held tenaciously to a literal reading of Matthew. 26:26, 'This is my body'. Bread and wine do indeed remain present, but so too are the body and blood of Christ. The elements do bring forgiveness when combined with faith in the promise of Christ. Similarly, baptism brings forgiveness when applied with faith. Since he could supply no convincing answer to the natural question as to why, in that case, baptism should not be restricted to those who believe, he contended first for the idea of surrogate faith (the faith of parents and sponsors coming to the aid of that of the child) and later for 'infant faith'. It could not be proved that infants do not have faith, therefore he, Luther, was free to insist that they did! Gainsayers were mere rationalists!

Zwingli, on the other hand, with his humanist's interest in etymology, pointed out that *sacramentum* originally meant an oath of allegiance of the kind that a soldier might make when entering the army. He therefore understood sacraments as signs or seals, rather than conveyors of actual spiritual benefit. He did not believe that physical acts could bring spiritual effects. The flesh of Christ, he pointed out, 'is a means of salvation to us not by being eaten, but by being slain'.[1] The New Testament language about the bread and wine being the body and blood of Christ is symbolic. Similarly, he believed that baptism was a pledge of allegiance; the water merely symbolizes the washing clean from sin that has actually been performed by the blood of Christ. The rite as a whole is a sign of God's covenant.

A Loss of Patience: Zwingli's Critics

There may be an instance in history of a yet more catastrophic shot in the foot by a theologian, but it is hard to call an example to mind. Zwingli's radical disciples, Grebel foremost among them, were already impatient that biblical warrant could apparently be followed no faster than the city council saw fit. Now they picked up on Zwingli's rationale concerning sacraments and asked why infant baptism was necessary at all. To be sure, sacraments were a response of faith commanded by God, and the person who had faith would be blessed, or reassured, by receiving them. But if baptism was essentially a sign, and did not actually 'do' anything, in the medieval-magical sense – or even in the Lutheran sense – of bringing about a spiritual transaction, then what possible 'good' could it do to a baby (who clearly had no faith) to baptize it?

---

[1] H. Zwingli, *Commentary on True and False Religion*, ed. S.M. Jackson, p. 205.

It should be said at once that, in looking at 'baptism', Zwingli did not indulge his penchant for etymology, or yet more embarrassing questions might have been asked about the dangerous effects of actually immersing a baby. His erstwhile disciples, now critics, were merely asking about the status of the person receiving baptism, not about the mode of performing it.

Zwingli could hardly claim to be unaware that pædobaptism was problematic; he had recently confessed himself that

> Although I know, as the Fathers indicate, that children were baptized from early times, I also know that the practice was not as common as it is in our day and age. Rather, together, they were instructed publicly when they reached full understanding. . . . And when they had faith firmly established in their hearts and were able to affirm it with their lips, they were baptized.

Although he added that 'This manner of instruction I should like to see adopted again in our own day', he immediately qualified it by the concession that 'inasmuch as children are baptized so early, we undertake to instruct them' when they become old enough to understand.[2]

A number of people in Zürich and in the outlying villages under the city's rule began to withhold their children from being christened. Grebel's own daughter, Rachel, born on 6th January 1525, was amongst these. Officialdom began to panic. If it became a matter of personal choice as to who was, or was not, part of the official church, then the chief moral, social and political 'handle' on ordinary people's lives – or, in sociologese, 'means of social control' – would have gone, and with it any possibility of stable social order. Political pressure from the neighbouring Catholic Swiss cantons was already severe, on account of the religious reforms that had already been made in Zürich, and religious dissent within the city was thus a luxury that was even less affordable than under normal circumstances.

The rather cautious oligarchs of Zürich had only slowly been persuaded of the merits and advantages of Zwingli's programme. The radical demands of Grebel and his group represented the first flickerings of exactly the kind of religious anarchy which the more conservative among them had feared all along might

---

[2]   H. Zwingli, *Writings*, tr. E.J. Furcha, i., pp. 100–101.

accompany such departures from tradition, and which their Catholic critics and neighbours were even now insisting was its logical outcome. No one likes to be reminded that 'I told you so'; the best way of avoiding such reminders was to suppress the radicals.

Accordingly, a disputation was called for 17th January 1525 to discuss the merits of Zwingli's case, on the one hand, and that of the radicals, on the other. The official notice announcing the forthcoming debate was not entirely impartial: 'Whereas some have expressed erroneous opinions that young children should not be baptized', the mayor and council ordered all who held such opinions to appear before them, 'after which our lords will take whatever further action is appropriate.'[3] Although it was plain to the nascent Anabaptist group that this was intended to be a visit to the straighteners, rather than a genuine opportunity to vindicate their cause, there seemed to be no option but to attend, and they duly did so.

The verdict of the council as to who had won the debate was not altogether a surprise. The day after the disputation a council mandate decreed that 'All those who have hitherto left their children unbaptized shall have them baptized within the next eight days. And anyone who refuses to do this shall, with wife and child and possessions, leave our lords' city, jurisdiction, and domain, and never return, or await what happens to him.'[4]

The dissidents were thus left with a choice, and they did not hesitate. On the evening of 21st January 1525, the decisive event in the birth of Anabaptism took place: the first believers' bap-tisms of modern times. A group of about fifteen met in a house in the Neugasse, close to the Grossmünster. The house was owned by the mother of a member of the group. Felix Mantz, her son by a Catholic priest, was about twenty-seven years old, and no mean scholar, being proficient in Latin, Greek and Hebrew. Also present was Georg Cajakob, or Blaurock, a priest of Chur, in Rhaetia.

There are several accounts of what took place at the meeting, and although there is no sharp contradiction between the

---

[3] L. Harder ed., *The Sources of Swiss Anabaptism*, p. 333.
[4] *Ibid.*, p. 336.

versions, the Klettgau/Cologne letter is perhaps to be preferred to the more usually quoted Hutterian Chronicle:

> After fear lay greatly upon them, they called upon God in heaven, that he should show mercy to them. Then Jörg arose and asked Conrad for God's sake to baptize him; and this he did. After that, he baptized the others also.[5]

The baptisms were by affusion, not immersion; bathtubs were a rarity, and no special baptistery had been dug in Mantz's mother's floor. Baptism by immersion was to take place the following month, when Grebel baptized Wolfgang Ulimann, an ex-monk, stark naked in the River Rhine – an action which required a higher degree of discipleship in February than it might have done at another time of year.

Crossing the Jordan, crossing the Rubicon, burning one's boats: all of the metaphors for describing the watery event in the Neugasse seem to be similarly aqueous. The city council had the same instinct: they threatened to drown the 're-baptizers' with a third, and terminal, baptism and, although they did not rush to impose this ultimate penalty, they did not shrink from inflicting it after other measures had failed to prevent the spread of the movement.

Chaos in St. Gall

That spread was both dramatic and turbulent in the opening months. The Neugasse group was no isolated circle of dissident intellectuals, but merely the most active amongst a large number of people in Zürich and its environs who had been preaching against pædobaptism for about a year. Wilhelm Reublin, priest at the nearby village of Wytikon, had been one of the first to preach against the practice, and had been imprisoned for doing so the previous August. Johannes Brötli, a former priest now married and living as a farm labourer, had taught the same in Zollikon. Andreas Castelberger, a lame bookseller, had been spreading the same views. As a result, a number of people had withheld their children from baptism.

---

[5]   *Ibid.*, p. 342. For the reasons for my choice of documents, see *ibid.*, p. 338–40.

Antipædobaptism is not, however, the same thing as actual Anabaptism, since the former might simply dissipate itself in the belief that the rite is not necessary at all. The two ministers of nearby Schaffhausen, in particular, could not be heaved over the hump from the former view to the latter, and Grebel found himself unable to persuade the hitherto sympathetic Dr. Sebastian Meyer and Dr. Sebastian Hofmeister to join the new movement.

The reverend doctors were overshadowed, however, by the large numbers who did respond, including many in their own town of Schaffhausen. 'Wildfire' is no overstatement of the speed – and, as it was to prove, the lack of control – in the early spread of Anabaptism. That spring saw the movement appear in Basel, Bern, Constance, St. Gall, Schaffhausen, Chur and the German region of Swabia.

Perhaps the most unfortunate outbreak was that in St. Gall, 40 miles to the east of Zürich. The mayor of the town was the scholar Vadian, Grebel's brother-in-law, who briefly viewed the movement with favour before reverting to support for Zwingli. Wolfgang Ulimann, fresh from his icy ordeal in the Rhine, took over the leadership of a group of unruly evangelicals there. Grebel visited the town for a fortnight in April 1525, and it was then and immediately afterwards that very large numbers of the local inhabitants were drawn into Anabaptism. Grebel baptized many in the river there. He still hoped that the local council would adopt his ideas; despite his proclamation of believers' baptism he had not yet arrived at a clear view of a believers' church separated from the world. This fact is demonstrated by the form of the baptisms themselves, which were rather indis- criminate, and were conferred upon all who requested it. No attempt was made to organize the newly baptized into gathered churches.

It was from amongst this disorganized mass that the excesses broke out, although even then it was only the activities of a minority which brought disrepute upon the movement as a whole. Some people burned copies of the New Testament because 'the letter kills'; others took to acting and speaking like little children in order to be fit for the kingdom. There was sexual immorality, presumably on the usual rationale (such things had happened before and have happened since!) that acts of the flesh do not matter, since the disposition of the spirit alone counts with God. One woman declared she was predestined to give birth to Antichrist. Children lay in comas for several hours – 'dying with Christ to the world'. One man was even (at his own request) beheaded by his brother, it apparently having been revealed to him that this was the will of God. Embarrassingly, perhaps, for modern charismatics, there were also outbreaks of speaking in tongues! G.H. Williams, the master-historian of this period, sums up the motivation and significance of these phenomena well: 'In this degeneration of the movement one seems to see beneath the lifted weight of centuries of ecclesiastical domination a squirming, spawning, nihilistic populace on its own, confused by the new theological terms . . . and by the new biblical texts seized upon with an almost maniacal glare.'[6] Williams adds that these outbursts in St. Gall had almost nothing in common with the sober evangelicalism of the Anabaptist leaders.

His analogy with lifting a heavy stone in a flowerbed, and observing the hundreds of ugly creepy-crawlies suddenly exposed to the light, strikes exactly the right note. The population of western Europe had been under the rocklike religious tutelage of the papacy for centuries, and now various brands of biblicism were making an appeal for their loyalty. It is small wonder that, amidst the confusion, some people responded in ways that, to an outsider, seem less than rational. We have observed the same phenomenon in eastern Europe in our own day. Released from long servitude, mature judgement is exhibited, not by the many, but by the few; larger numbers turn to Stalinism, the Cossacks, Quixotic Tsarism, the drug culture, fascism, organized crime, racism, the White Brotherhood and to name-it-and-claim-it evangelists. The wonder is, not that the free enquiring spirit promoted by sixteenth-century Anabaptism facilitated so many outbursts of bizarre behaviour, but that, relatively, it prompted so few.

---

[6] G.H. Williams, *The Radical Reformation,* 3rd edn, p. 228.

Persecution

The bizarre behaviour in St. Gall served simply to prove what the spokesmen for official Protestantism had been saying all along. To permit religious freedom, or to promote religious change at a pace faster than the secular authorities approved, was to court anarchy. And anarchy could not be permitted. It was inevitable that the machinery of official repression would be brought to bear, and this happened sooner rather than later.

Some 35 converts had been made in the village of Zollikon, just outside Zürich, during the week following the first baptisms in the city in January 1525. At the end of it, Georg Blaurock challenged the right of the local priest to preach in his own pulpit, interrupting him (with the encouragement of many in the con- gregation) to the point where Blaurock was threatened with arrest by the magistrate.

On Monday 30th January, he, Felix Mantz and some 25 Zollikon Anabaptists were arrested and imprisoned for their activities. Mantz and Blaurock were separated from their disci- ples, and Zwingli, with Leo Jud and Caspar Megander (the other leading reformers of Zürich) and several council members, came to visit the remainder to dissuade them from their Anabaptism.

Zwingli opened with the assertion that no rebaptism is to be found in Scripture. This argument, of course, failed to interact with the central contention of the radicals, namely that infant baptism was no baptism at all, and that, therefore, the believers' baptism which they practised was not rebaptism. Even so, the peasants to whom Zwingli appealed either did not have much theological sophistication, or else simply decided that a prag- matic argument was as good as any other: they pointed to Acts 19:1–7, where Paul is reported to have baptized some Ephesians who had previously been baptized by John the Baptist. Zwingli was reduced to arguing that, contrary to all appearances, 'baptism' there meant 'instruction'.

No one was convinced by Zwingli's instruction (or 'baptism'!) on this point, but upon their promise to assemble in groups of not more than four, and not to preach or baptize, they were released on 8th February. This promise was not kept and, after Blaurock was released ten days later, they were all rearrested in

March for their continuing evangelism. After two weeks, most of the Anabaptists yielded to the authorities, paid fines and were released. Blaurock was banished and went to the Grisons, where Mantz joined him after escaping. Mantz was arrested yet again in July, handed over to the Zürich authorities and kept in prison until October.

In the meantime, the Anabaptist movement had suffered its first two martyrs. Bolt Eberli was a peasant farmer who had helped lead the rapid growth in St. Gall. Rather unwisely returning to his native town of Lachen, in the still Catholic canton of Schwyz, he and his companion, an unnamed priest, were arrested and burned as heretics on 29th May 1525. They were to be the first of many.

Felix Mantz was drowned by the Zürich authorities at three o'clock on the Saturday afternoon of 5th January 1527, following the decree of the previous March that the death penalty be imposed for rebaptizing. He had been arrested only a few weeks after his release in October 1525, this time in Grüningen, where he had been apprehended along with Grebel and Blaurock. They had been transferred to Zürich, from whence they again escaped; the lax security is a cause for wonderment! He rejoined Grebel in preaching in the towns and villages of eastern Switzerland, but Grebel died of the plague during yet another evangelistic tour in August 1526. Mantz's final arrest was in Graubünden the following December and, once again, Blaurock was captured with him. Transferred to Zürich, Mantz was drowned in the River Limmat the same day that sentence was passed, his mother calling encouragement to him from the riverbank.

Blaurock, as a foreigner from the Grisons, was merely badly beaten and then expelled; in the following two months he was thrown out of Bern and Biel as well. The old saw has it that, 'Home is the place where, when you have to go there, they have to take you in', and he returned to his native turf in the Grisons. [7] But the dictum is wrong and, in April, he was banished from home. Venturing into the Austrian Tyrol, he gained many

---

[7] The American poet Robert Frost is, as far as I can trace, the originator of this particular goody.

converts over a two-year period before being arrested and tortured, along with a fellow-leader, Hans Langenegger, in August 1529. The following month they were both burned at the stake.

With the martyrdom of Blaurock, all three of the earliest ringleaders were dead. But others had been put to death for their Anabaptist faith in the meantime. Jakob Falk and Heini Reimann, two farmers from Gossau, a town some 15 miles south-east of Zürich, became Anabaptists in the summer of 1525 after listening to Grebel, and themselves baptized several new converts. Arrested in May 1526, they were kept in prison whilst they wrangled with the courts but refused to recant. They were sentenced and drowned on 5th September 1528. Others imprisoned with them recanted and were released, but two of these, Heine Karpfis and Hans Herzog, were later arrested as having returned to Anabaptism and were drowned in March 1532.

Michael Sattler

By that time, several more important leaders had both arisen and been martyred. Of these, arguably the most important was the former prior, Michael Sattler. So glowing are all the accounts that we have of Sattler – even from his Protestant opponents – and so appalling the cruelty of his execution, that it seems safe to conclude that, in him, we are dealing with one of the very greatest of the early Anabaptist leaders.

He was born in south-west Germany about 1490, and became a Benedictine monk at a monastery near Freiburg. Convinced of the essential truth of the Protestant reformers' ideas, he left the cloister and got married to a former Beguine, a heinous sin in the eyes of the Roman Catholic authorities, and one which would be raised at his trial as amongst the most serious of the charges against him.

Converted to Anabaptism during 1525, he went to Zürich but was expelled as an undesirable alien. From thence he went to Strassburg, where a number of other radicals were already beginning to gather.

It is at least arguable that the Strassburg of the 1520s and 1530s is amongst the most interesting places, politically and religiously

speaking, in the whole fascinating European scene of those decades. The city itself had a degree of autonomy within the Holy
Roman Empire. It was then, as it was to remain for several
centuries more, a centre of German culture and economic life
before the various disasters of late nineteenth- and twentieth-
century history made the region a part of the French state. For
a variety of reasons, including its internal political instability,
Strassburg was then perhaps the most religiously tolerant city in
Europe – a title fairly easily won.[8] That fact virtually guaranteed
an increase in the city's religious pluralism, as refugees of various
shades and hues sought sanctuary within its walls, where they
jostled or merged with, or else simply anathematized, the various
homegrown radicals.

The official situation was that Strassburg's leading clergymen,
Martin Bucer and Wolfgang Capito, were slowly moving the city
in the direction of Reformed, rather than Lutheran, Protestantism. Apart from the insecurity of their position, and the unwillingness of much of the population to accept the social discipline
which such a religious departure might demand, Capito in particular was temperamentally disinclined to persecute dissenters,
whilst both he and the less leniently minded Bucer were extremely
impressed by the Anabaptist former prior who now confronted
them.

The debate with Bucer and Capito helped Sattler himself to
see the issues in a clearer light. Believers' baptism could not
possibly coexist with a state-supported church; it demanded a
congregation restricted to committed believers only. He began
preaching this message in the Black Forest area around the town
of Horb, where he was successful in planting an Anabaptist
church.

Sattler was a leading figure in calling together and organizing
the Schleitheim Conference of Anabaptist leaders on 24th
February 1527, and was the probable author of the resultant
Schleitheim Confession, which was to be definitive of evangelical

---

[8] See the essay by L.J. Abray, 'Confession, conscience and honour: the limits of
magisterial tolerance in sixteenth-century Strassburg' in O.P. Grell and R. Scribner
eds., *Tolerance and Intolerance in the European Reformation*, pp. 94–107 for a balanced
appraisal.

Anabaptist distinctives. It was while he was at the conference, however, that his church was detected by the authorities, and upon his return to Horb he found himself, his wife and a number of friends under arrest. He was taken to the nearby village of Binsdorf because of the protests of the Horb population at these arrests. From thence he wrote a letter to the remnants of his congregation: clearly anticipating his own death, he warned his flock not to flee 'the surefooted and living way of Christ, namely through cross, misery, imprisonment, self-denial and finally through death.'[9] It is not, one fears, an emphasis that would hold much appeal today, but it was certainly necessary in the circumstances.

Although the local authorities were not anxious to commence a case that was certain to end in the death sentence, the imperial government based in Vienna had no such qualms. Indeed, it was eager to get proceedings underway, presumably to serve as a deterrent to further radical activity. The trial, therefore, exhibits something of that ubiquitous political dimension of sixteenth-century Germanic Europe, the struggle between local jurisdiction and autonomy and the powers of central – especially imperial – government. Because of political jostling, the trial did not begin until 17th May.

Sattler found himself facing a number of charges. The first stated that he had broken the imperial mandate outlawing Lutheranism. Sattler denied the charge, pointing out that the mandate attacking Lutheranism had ordered people to follow only 'the gospel and the Word of God' which, he added with a nice sense of humour, was precisely what he and his fellows were doing. The second charged him with sacramentarianism, which Sattler admitted; the body of Christ was at the right hand of the Father and so could not be in the bread of communion. The third charge was that he did not believe infant baptism to be necessary to salvation; again, Sattler admitted the charge, pointing out that faith was what saved a person. Accused in the fourth charge of denying the efficacy of the 'sacrament of unction' with oil, Sattler was disposed to haggle: oil was good stuff since it, too, had been made by God, but no amount of clerical or papal jiggery-pokery could improve upon it, 'for the pope has never made anything

---

[9]   M. Sattler, *The Legacy of Michael Sattler*, ed. J.H. Yoder, p. 58.

good'. The fifth charge claimed that he despised 'the mother of God and the saints'. Sattler disagreed: Mary was a marvellous woman, but that didn't mean she was a mediatrix between God and mankind; even she 'must like us await judgement', whilst 'we who live and believe are the saints'. One can almost hear the Catholic officials wince as they had to listen to this defence, trampling as it did on the core sensitivities of popular Catholic piety.

Accused of denying that Christians should take oaths, he pleaded guilty, pointing to the scriptural justification for his position. Charged with forsaking his order of monks and getting married, he pointed to the fornication in which, he said, most monks lived. Were his accusers the men whom the apostle Paul had prophesied would, in the last days, forbid marriage?

The last accusation picked up on what was perhaps Sattler's most provocative remark of all. In a hyperbolic expression of Anabaptist pacifism, he had apparently suggested that, 'If the Turk were to come into the land, one should not resist him, and, if it were right to go to war, he would rather go to war against the Christians than against the Turks'. Already guaranteed a rather unpleasant execution at some time in the very near future, the ex-prior decided there was no point in wasting the rhetorical possibilities presented by the requirement to answer this charge. It was wrong, he insisted, to resist evil with evil, for 'thou shalt not kill'.

> As to me saying that if waging war were proper I would rather take the field against the so-called Christians who persecute, take captive, and kill true Christians, than against the Turks, this was for the following reason: the Turk is a genuine Turk and knows nothing of the Christian faith. He is a Turk according to the flesh. But you claim to be Christians, boast of Christ, and still persecute the faithful witnesses of Christ. Thus you are Turks according to the Spirit. [10]

It was not a speech calculated to tickle the ears of his audience.

He was sentenced to have his tongue cut out, to be chained to a wagon, to have his body torn seven times with red-hot tongs, and finally to be burned at the stake. Two days later, on 20th May, the sentence was carried out. We must assume that only a

---

[10] *Ibid.*, pp. 70–73.

piece of his tongue was, in fact, cut out, since all of the subsequent accounts mention him exhorting the onlookers and praying audibly. Four others were beheaded shortly after the execution. His wife, after the failure of attempts by the Countess of Zollern to persuade her to recant, was drowned eight days later in the River Neckar.

The manner of Sattler's death, and his dignity and defiance in suffering it, made a profound impression, not only upon those who witnessed it, but upon those who read or heard about it – and the local Anabaptists made sure that the news spread widely and quickly. Several printed accounts of the trial and martyrdom were in circulation almost immediately.

Wolfgang Capito, the Strassburg reformer, wrote two letters: one to the Horb council on 31st May protesting at the treatment of Sattler and the remaining prisoners; the other to the prisoners themselves, criticizing the points upon which he, Capito, disagreed with them, but otherwise exhorting them to remain steadfast. Some did, but others recanted and had various punishments and penances imposed upon them. Capito's liberal-mindedness was very unusual amongst the magisterial, or state-church, Protestant reformers, to the point of inconsistency with his overall position. Practical experience of the actual exercise of power would come to harden Protestant attitudes in the years ahead, and make the liberality of Capito seem naïve.

The Schleitheim Confession

In passing, it has been necessary to gloss over, somewhat, the all-important *Schleitheim Confession*. To that document we must now return. The conference, and the confession of faith which resulted from it, had been necessary for two main reasons. In the first place, the early Zürich leaders had been dying off – with strong encouragement from the secular and ecclesiastical authorities – at a quite alarming rate, and it was now clear that none of the magisterial Protestant leaders would, or could, consider taking on board Anabaptist ideals. That being so, the new movement needed to define itself, and quickly, before it petered out into merely so much disparate, inchoate protest. Secondly – and this will be dealt with in the following chapter – a number of radicals had imbibed a little too deeply from the wells tapped by Thomas Müntzer and were preaching, not so much the need for separation from the world, as its imminent destruction, sometimes with the thinly concealed implication that the godly themselves might someday do the destroying. A number of others had (as we have seen) already fallen into antinomianism and libertinism, characterized by immoral behaviour. A check was needed on this too, and the covering letter referred to such teachers as 'false brothers and sisters'. The *Schleitheim Confession*, then, seems to have been aimed at establishing a platform *vis-à-vis* both external forces – i.e. the state churches – and unwelcome internal forces.

The *Confession*, or 'Brotherly Union' as it called itself, made seven affirmations. They were not concerned with the issues of Christology and the resurrection that had preoccupied the theologians at Nicæa and Chalcedon over a millennium before. Neither did they labour the primacy of Scripture (as opposed to tradition or papal authority) as Luther, Zwingli and the other magisterial Protestants were doing. Rather, the *Schleitheim Confession* tends to presuppose all of these things, concentrating only on the areas in which the Anabaptists differed from others.

A position was taken on the nature of communion, which was becoming such a bone of contention between Lutherans and Zwinglians, but the subject was treated in a passing phrase and the clause dealing with it concentrated instead on who was to be allowed to participate. For the *Schleitheim Confession* was not concerned with doctrine (in the traditional sense) at all, but rather with practical matters related to the life of a true Christian church. If one text sums up the burden of Anabaptist Christianity, it is the exhortation of James to be 'doers of the word, and not hearers only'. The *Schleitheim Confession* told its readers, not so much what to believe, as what to do; the beliefs were implicit in the practice.

Firstly, baptism was to be given only to those who had repented, had faith in Christ for the forgiveness of their sins, and desired to live a life of discipleship. Secondly, based on Matthew 18:15–18, the ban was to be employed against wayward members of the church, who were to be shunned by the others to maintain the purity of the fellowship. Thirdly, Anabaptist breaking of bread was to be confined to the committed; members might not also take communion in their parish churches.

The fourth section dealt with separation from 'the world'. Christians should have nothing to do with 'popish and repopish works and idolatry', a reference to Catholic and Protestant ('repopish') religious ceremonies. Nor should they have anything to do with 'church attendance, winehouses, guarantees and com - mitments of unbelief'; the juxtaposition of ideas in this phrase gives almost as much pleasure four and three quarter centuries later as it must have done to its first composers. A 'guarantee of unbelief' was a nicely polemical reference to an oath. Anabaptists refused to swear, and so it was particularly easy for the governing authorities, when they were inclined, to detect them. To swear that one supported the official church, or that one was not an Anabaptist, was to give a guarantee that one was not a true believer.

The fifth article laid down the functions of a shepherd, or pastor in the church, and the qualifications for being one. He should be supported by his own congregation and arrangements were to be made for his immediate replacement should he be arrested or martyred, a feature seldom found in evangelical churches today. Sixthly, pacifism was Christ's will for Christians, and for this reason they should not serve as magistrates, even if the opportunity arose. Finally, because of the clear biblical commands not to do so, they should not swear oaths. [11]

In the *Schleitheim Confession*, the self-identification of the evangelical Anabaptists as a body of believers separated from the world comes to full tide. Separatism is the *Confession's* constant motif, and every article deals in some way with such separation. Baptism and communion are for committed, converted believers only; those lapsing into unrepented sin are to be excluded; believ - ers are to have no truck with the world and its religious ceremon - ies; churches are to support their own pastors without outside help; Christians are to have nothing to do with civil government or with its ultimate means of sustaining itself, the sword; they should not take oaths, even though these were a requirement of civil society.

---

[11]   *Ibid.*, pp 34–43.

Pre-modern western society, like Muslim societies today, viewed religious dissent as, in a very real and tangible sense, a betrayal, a rejection by the dissenter of his or her community, which justified the community in retaliating by excluding them, either by expulsion from the actual territory where the dissident lived, or – as in the cases of Felix Mantz, Michael Sattler and others – by exclusion from the world itself. If the wider world experienced religious dissent as a form of treason, then the sentiments expressed in the *Schleitheim Confession* might be seen as a compounding of the felony.

The Swiss Brethren had come to birth as the result of impatience with the slowness of official reform in Zürich. In the process, however, the movement had abandoned the attempt to re-form Christendom, the medieval *corpus christianum*, and had instead explicitly adopted the separation from the world that had always been implicit in their programme. The Anabaptists were henceforth seeking to restore primitive Christianity as they understood it. Indeed, one of their number, Wolfgang Brand-huber, who paid for his opinions with his life in 1529, identified the restoration of a true baptism and a true eucharist as key elements in the restoration of a true and pure church in prepara-tion for Christ's second coming.[12] The insistence upon conver-sion and discipleship, and a willingness to accept persecution and a life as sheep amongst wolves, were resonant, not of 'Christen-dom', but of the pages of the New Testament. Though there were many deviations from the path by those whom we must nonethe-less designate 'Anabaptist', this was to be the definitive pro-gramme of the evangelical Anabaptists in the years that lay ahead.

---

[12] W. Klaassen, *Living at the End of the Ages*, p. 69.

Chapter Four

All Things Common

Marxism, Anabaptism and the Peasants' War

However pacifist and world-denying the signatories to the *Schleitheim Confession* may have been, the birth of Anabaptism took place against the background of widespread and terrifying peasant rebellions. Moreover, the programme of those peasant insurgents – or rather, of Müntzer on their behalf – did include an element of economic levelling. For example, the demands made in 1525, just prior to their comprehensive annihilation on the battlefield of Frankenhausen, included:

1. Free and unadulterated preaching of the Gospel;
2. Free usufruct of forest, water, pasture, and rights of chase;
3. Destruction of excessive nobles' castles, and distribution of their provisions amongst the [peasants'] army;
4. Abandonment of noble titles in favour of God's honour alone. Thereafter restitution of nobles' property . . ., save for provisions, again to be shared amongst the common man. [1]

Given the approximation of the Peasants' War to a form of class struggle on the one hand, and the geographic and temporal prox - imity of that struggle to the birth of Anabaptism on the other, it is not surprising that, by and large, Marxist historians have chosen to regard the whole Anabaptist movement as a continuation of the Peasants' War by other means. What is meant by this is that

---

[1] from T. Scott, *Thomas Müntzer: Theology and Revolution in the German Reformation*, p. 162.

Anabaptism provided social protest with a religious face. Alternatively, once it had failed on the battlefield it provided a 'sublimation' of that protest in a religious form – a sort of religious consolation for failure, by embodying in spiritualized fashion the *real* (and, for Marxists, 'real' consistently means material, or politico-economic) aspirations of the participants.

It must be conceded at once that there is something in this explanation. There is no doubt that Anabaptism, especially when it is broadly defined, attracted very many people who had been drawn to the peasant cause in the fighting of 1524–25. In that sense, civil tumult acted as a recruiting ground for religious radicalism. Modern Christians, however, have nothing to fear from making such a concession, any more than they would by conceding to a chemist that people are, after all, mostly water. Marxism explains everything about religion except, of course, the religious part. To say that various forms of religious expression can embody political or social causes, or that religion can console people who have been denied the fulfilment of their worldly aspirations does not, *ipso facto*, 'explain' the religious phenomenon itself.

Many Anabaptists were to go to their deaths for their faith, whilst most were to undergo danger, hardship and suffering; their 'real', or this-worldly, aspirations were thereby willingly forgone, not promoted, as a result of their religious activity. And the consolation in the hereafter for having been martyred in the here-and-now is one of which the Marxist can know nothing. It is precisely the *religious* element in people's motivation for which Marxist analysis of religion cannot account. The reductionism that seeks to explain away religious movements as merely the sublimation of material, economic forces makes no more sense than an attempt to 'explain' Mother Teresa by reference to the chemical elements that made up her body; the result is not so much an explanation as an abstraction.

That said, it is important not to downplay the interconnection between the early Anabaptist movement and the social ferment of the mid-1520s. This, some historians of Anabaptism – perhaps in an attempt to sanitize the movement, and to emphasize the pedigree of the Swiss Brethren as solid, twentieth-century-style evangelicals – have been wont to do, minimizing the interconnections between 'nasty' Müntzer and 'nice' Grebel, Mantz, Blaurock and co. There is no doubt that Grebel and his peers were not preaching with half an eye, as it were, on social revolution, but the unpalat-able fact of their correspondence with Müntzer (the Marxists' prophet of modern class-warfare) must be faced, if only to bring out the contrast between their approach and his.[2]

Grebel wrote two letters to Müntzer in September 1524, before the first believers' baptisms in Zürich, but after (although Grebel was unaware of the fact) Müntzer had left Allstedt for Mühlhausen. The second letter is a lengthy postscript to the first, and both were sent by the same messenger. Given that Müntzer was not where the senders expected him to be, it is to be doubted whether either missive ever arrived. The contents are, nevertheless, enlightening.

Grebel and his fellows describe themselves as 'seven new young Müntzers', and Müntzer himself as 'someone who is of a common Christian mind with us'. 'You and Karlstadt,' they inform him, 'are regarded among us as the purest proclaimers and preachers of the purest Word of God', whose books 'have almost immeasurably instructed and strengthened us'.

In context, however, much of this is seen to be mere flattery, and the fellow-feeling expressed simply reflects their common radicalism and their common experience of repudiation by the 'official' reformers, Luther and Zwingli, who were compromising with the secular authorities. Müntzer was in danger from Luther, who 'wants to deliver you to the axe and hand you over to the prince, to whom he has bound his gospel'. The Zürich circle, on the other hand, complained that 'Around here there are not even twenty who believe the Word of God'. They were unaware of the precise differences between the various radicals, and inquired whether Müntzer and Karlstadt were of one mind on all matters: 'We hope and believe you are'.[3]

---

[2] The East German state made a hero of Müntzer, raising statues to him and naming streets after him. Marxist historians have described his movement as the *Volksrefor-mation*, or 'people's Reformation', to distinguish it from the Protestantism of Martin Luther, which represented bourgeois interests. See E.G. Rupp, *Patterns of Reformation*, pp. 157–8; H-J. Goertz, *Thomas Müntzer: Apocalyptic Mystic and Revolutionary*, pp. xvi, xviii–xix, 15–18.
[3] L. Harder, *The Sources of Swiss Anabaptism*, pp. 284–94.

When it came down to brass tacks though, the Zürich dissidents were uneasy about a number of aspects of Müntzer's programme, and were not afraid to say so. They advised him to 'preach only God's Word unflinchingly', and to 'defend only divine practices, . . . and to reject, hate, and curse all the schemes, words, practices, and opinions of all men, even your own'. The Zürichers had heard of Müntzer's new German liturgy and German chanting, and let him know that 'this cannot be good' – not, of course, because they preferred Latin, but because they disapproved of liturgy and chanting altogether. He had also set up tablets in his church, setting forth the ten commandments; his correspondents reported that 'we learned with sorrow' of this, and hoped that 'you will again destroy the tablets.' Most of all, they feared his advocacy of violence and were quite confrontational on the subject. 'The gospel and its adherents are not to be protected by the sword, nor [should] they [protect] themselves, which as we have heard through our brother is what you believe and maintain.'

Despite their pacifism, a trait which the majority of evangelical Anabaptists were to maintain throughout their history, the radical background of a number of them was forged in the Peasants' War. It was a fact which was to have divisive and, in the 1530s, catastrophic consequences for later developments.

Hans Hut is a good example of an Anabaptist leader whose background included involvement in these social upheavals. He was a bookseller who had been entrusted with the printing of some of Müntzer's tracts, and in whose house the prophet had stayed one night on his flight from Mühlhausen. Hut had been with Müntzer at the Battle of Frankenhausen and, despite capture by the Landgrave's forces afterwards, had been released as a noncombatant. But a fortnight later he was preaching in the town of Bibra that 'The subjects should murder all the authorities, for the opportune time has arrived: the power is in their hands'.[4] He had already rejected infant baptism and had refused to allow his own child to be christened. When forced to flee to Augsburg, he was baptized at the hands of Hans Denck, in May 1526.

---

[4]   G.H. Williams, *The Radical Reformation*, 3rd edn, pp. 167–8.

Hut, like his mentor Müntzer, saw himself as living in the end times, and there was a sharply apocalyptic tone to his preaching which did not abate after his formal adoption of Anabaptism. He had a keen interest in prophecies and dreams. For him, the advance of the Ottoman Turks into Christendom, reaching ever closer to Vienna, was a judgement of God and a sign of the end – a concept which struck a chord with the jittery population of central Europe. Those who repented would face persecution and suffering, but true Christians would eventually slay the godless and rule the earth with Christ. In the interim, no violence was to be used, but believers' baptism was the sign without which destruction at the hands of the saints would be certain.

Such preaching, in which a present outbreak of violence was scarcely smothered beneath promises of future retribution, helped to create an atmosphere of extreme emotional tension and ambivalence. Present suffering and mistreatment were 'contextualized', and so made easier to bear, by being juxtaposed with future, perhaps imminent, revenge.

Balthasar Hubmaier

Balthasar Hubmaier (1481–1528) is another example (although a more orthodox one) of an Anabaptist leader whose radicalism emerged in the context of the Peasants' War. A native of Friedberg in Bavaria, he had studied at Freiburg from 1503 to 1506 under John Eck, the Catholic apologist who later was to make such a mess of Karlstadt's self-respect at the Leipzig disputation with Luther. Hubmaier followed his mentor to the University of Ingolstadt in 1512, where he received his doctorate shortly afterwards, and was soon (1515) made prorector of the university. Shortly after this, Hubmaier was appointed chaplain to Regensburg Cathedral, where his abilities in preaching could be used more fully.

Unfortunately, his oratorical skills were given full play in rather a bad cause. Regensburg was going through one of its periodic bouts of anti-Semitism; the city had a sizeable, walled-off Jewish quarter, to the inhabitants of which both the civic authorities and ordinary tradespeople were in debt. In many places, Jews had been debarred from most professions except for that of money-lender, which was fortunate, given that princes and merchants alike needed credit, and the medieval religious conscience had forbidden Christians from the practice of 'usury' – the lending of money at interest. Medieval hypocrisy, however, then blamed the Jews for performing an economically necessary function which had, effectively, been forced upon them.

Generally speaking, the princes and the higher clergy tended to protect Jews – if only because they were more aware of the long-term implications of eradicating or expelling them. Ordin- ary traders, by contrast, saw only the fact of their own present indebtedness, and were the more easily persuaded by the junior clergy that this was due to incorrigible wickedness on the part of their creditors. If town councils sided with the merchants and local clergy, as they did at Regensburg, then anti-Semitism be- came one more element in the battle between central government and local privileges.

In this context, Hubmaier's anti-Semitic preaching appeared to make him a champion of the people. He denounced the Jews as 'idle, lecherous, and greedy', and in February 1519 he per- suaded the council that the Jews were defaming the Virgin Mary.[5] It seems that the council was, in no small part, swayed by Hubmaier and the frenzy which he had helped to stir up when it expelled the Jewish population of the city, demolished the syna- gogue and caused a new Catholic church, *zur Schönen Maria*, to be erected in its place. (When heaven apparently showed its approval in the form of miraculous cures performed on the site, the church instantly became a place of pilgrimage.)

It would be pleasant to surmise that Hubmaier's anti-Jewish venom was merely a part of his Catholic period, and as such discarded when he was converted to evangelical Anabaptism. Unhappily this is not exactly the case. Although the later Hub- maier did not continue the anti-Semitic theme, neither did he repudiate his earlier activities in this regard. Indeed, when ques- tioned about them in Zürich in 1526, he recalled that 'When I was a preacher in Regensburg, I saw the great oppression that the population suffered from the Jews. . . . Then I said to the

[5] H.A. Oberman, *The Roots of Anti-Semitism*, pp. 77, 84.

people from the pulpit, that they ought not to suffer in this wise for the future'.[6] There is really nothing to be said in Hubmaier's defence on this subject, except perhaps to remind ourselves of the date; if Hubmaier's conversion was to convince him of the wrong-headedness of so many of the assumptions of his society, it is a pity that it does not appear to have convinced him of the wrong-headedness of this too.

It is not known why Hubmaier chose, at the height of his popularity in bustling Regensburg, to accept the position of priest in the small town of Waldshut, near the Swiss border. G.H. Williams speculates that, even at this stage, he was repelled by the excesses of the Mariolatry attendant upon the developments in Regensburg.[7] In any event, Hubmaier did not begin to move decisively in an evangelical direction until 1522 and 1523, when he read Luther, visited Zwingli in Zürich, got married, and began to preach upon the Pauline epistles in his new parish. As popular there as in Regensburg, he began a rapid reformation of the town. The imperial authorities grew concerned and demanded Hubmaier's arrest; this call was supported by the traditionalist elements within the town but opposed by the generality of the citizenry.

If Hubmaier had anticipated the social upheaval of the Peasants' War of 1524–25, he could hardly have selected a more strategic site than Waldshut from which to influence events. The rebellion began in Stühlingen, only 14 miles away, but the peasants there sent a force of armed men to Waldshut, in July and August 1524, to make an alliance against Ferdinand I of Austria. Thomas Müntzer spent part of that winter in the area, but although his ideas impressed the pastor of Waldshut, he does not seem to have met Hubmaier in person. It was in this context – as the military crisis of the Peasants' War was reaching fever pitch, and with Hubmaier and his Waldshut parishioners in the middle of it – that Wilhelm Reublin arrived from Zürich, preaching believers' baptism.

In truth, Reublin did not bring his doctrine to a place unprepared. Hubmaier had maintained his contacts with Zürich and

[6] H.C. Vedder, *Balthasar Hubmaier: the Leader of the Anabaptists*, pp. 43–4.
[7] G.H. Williams, *The Radical Reformation*, 3rd edn, p. 149.

so was well aware of the debates that had been raging there; he had concluded some months previously that infant baptism was a delusion, and had preached as much to his people. In April, Reublin came and baptized Hubmaier and sixty others; Hubmaier continued the work, with the assistance of a milk bucket and the water from the fountain in the town square, and baptized another three hundred.

Hubmaier had created, in effect, an evangelical state employing – almost enforcing – believers' baptism, and allied with the local peasant rebels. For him, radical reformation suited his rôle as champion of the people; as with his anti-Semitic campaign in Regensburg, it had become a part of the struggle for a more egalitarian society. Priestcraft, clericalism and ritual were to be brought to an emphatic end and, in baptism, each was to have the opportunity to declare for themselves their faith in the promises of God.

Uniquely amongst the leaders of the Swiss Brethren, he was to continue to maintain that a believers' church could be supported by the state. Grebel and his circle had, for a short time, vaguely thought something of the kind; it had quickly become clear to them though that state support *meant* an all-embracing church (as a way of running society), and that conversely to call for a believers' church was to demand the destruction of precisely that monolith. The idea that a pure church could somehow coexist with state-supported Christianity was a confusion with which Hubmaier continued to live, and of which, although they have not inherited it from him, many twentieth-century English-speaking Christians have yet to be disabused.

With such beliefs, he considered it no waste of time to make one more effort to convince Zwingli of the truth of believers' baptism. In truth, he had little else to do that December, since Waldshut had fallen to Catholic troops three weeks before Christmas, enforcing the mass recantation of the populace and Hubmaier's flight to Zürich, and he was arrested within four days of his arrival in that city. The attempt failed: browbeaten by his captors, he agreed to recant. However, he used the opportunity of what was intended to be his recantatory sermon in the Fraumünster church to recant his recantation and to expound his views of believers' baptism. For this extraordinary foray into melodrama, he was thrown back into prison. Although Zwingli was familiar with Hubmaier's tract of autumn 1524, a plea for religious toleration entitled *On Heretics and Those Who Burn Them*, the Swiss reformer had a firmer grasp of the realities of power than the refugee pastor from Waldshut, and now decided to employ the rack as an instrument of further persuasion. Hubmaier was unable to bear this and wrote out the recantation required of him, which he then read out in three churches in and around the city.

In April 1526, his credibility in tatters with local Anabaptists and non-Anabaptists alike, he was released and allowed to leave the city secretly, so that he might not be apprehended by agents of the Austrian authorities, to whom recantations given to a Protestant government meant nothing. Via Augsburg, he made his way to Moravia.

Nikolsburg, like the rest of Moravia, was a city with a fair amount of autonomy from the imperial authorities. So when its German-speaking congregation turned evangelical under the influence of its pastor, Oswald Glaidt, the local rulers, Lord Leonhard and Lord Hans von Liechtenstein, did not fear immediate retribution from the Habsburgs. The lords already governed over Catholics and several varieties of Hussite. In July 1526, Balthasar Hubmaier arrived in town and swiftly converted both pastor and lords to Anabaptism. As in Waldshut, the generality of the population followed suit. One wonders how far this was really a believers' church.

Anabaptist refugees, notably from Catholic Austria, flocked to the safe haven of Nikolsburg. Amongst the new arrivals was Hans Hut, who now believed that the peasant uprisings had been wrong because their participants had sought their own glory rather than that of God and had, in any case, acted too early in the apocalyptic scheme of things. The main features of this scheme he felt able to discern. The Turks were being used as an instrument of God's judgement upon an apostate Christendom, and the saints would eventually rise to take the Kingdom by force. In the meantime, the godly should be pacifist. This G.H. Williams describes as 'apocalyptically oriented pacifism (or suspended bellicosity)'.[8]

---

[8]   *Ibid.*, p. 269.

Arriving in Nikolsburg in the spring of 1527, he quickly exacerbated a division which was already in the making there. Jakob Wiedemann headed a group that held Christian discipleship to be best expressed by community of goods and by complete separation from the state. Hubmaier, meanwhile, thought a Christian magistracy, such as was actually instituted in Nikolsburg, to be not only possible, but praiseworthy and that, for the restraint of evil-doers, it was permissible that the sword be wielded by Christians. Unsurprisingly, the Lords von Liechtenstein saw things Hubmaier's way, and when Hut came along offering to speak up for Wiedemann he was arrested as a subversive character.

But the imperial forces were already trying to catch up with Hubmaier. If Frederick of Austria was unwilling to provoke the princely supporters of magisterial Protestantism, whose support he needed against the Turks, he was at least determined to crush the frightening spectre of Anabaptism. Already Hubmaier's proliferating writings were being printed in Moravia and spread from thence throughout the adjacent German-speaking lands. Indeed, so dangerously influential were Hubmaier's writings that they were eventually to be placed on the notorious papal *Index* of prohibited books, alongside the works of Luther and Zwingli themselves.

One of these writings, penned during his imprisonment in Zürich, but only published in the safety of Nikolsburg, concluded with a prayer which shows his acute awareness of his own human frailty, and which proved to be sadly prophetic:

> This is my faith. . . . I pray thee faithfully, wilt thou preserve me therein graciously until my end. And if through human fear and weakness, through human tyranny, torture, sword, fire, or water I should even be driven away from it, even so I herewith appeal to thee, O my merciful Father, restore me again with the grace of thy Holy Spirit and let me not depart in death without this faith. [9]

In July 1527, the Lords von Liechtenstein were required by Ferdinand to give up their pastor to the Austrian authorities and, perhaps frightened for their own safeties if they refused,

---

[9]   B. Hubmaier, *Balthasar Hubmaier: Theologian of Anabaptism*, eds. Pipkin and Yoder, p. 240.

they complied. Hubmaier and his wife were taken to Vienna. The authorities were at least as keen to bring him to book for his seditious support of the rebels in Waldshut as for his continuing heresies, and took some months to prepare the case against him. The Roman Catholic authorities succeeded in wresting a partial recantation from him, but on the issues of baptism and communion he refused to back down.

Early in March 1528, he was tortured on the rack in an attempt to gain a full recantation, but found new courage to resist the demands pressed upon him. On 10th March, he was burned at the stake whilst his wife, who was to be executed by drowning in the Danube three days later, cried out to him to have courage. The most highly trained theologian of Anabaptism's first generation had joined the fast-growing list of martyrs.

No Needy Person Among Them: The Hutterite Experiment

The group with which Hubmaier had debated in Nikolsburg continued to develop under the leadership of Jakob Wiedemann and Hans Hut. It is true that the undertones of Hut's brand of pacifism looked rather more lethal than Hubmaier's traditional insistence that a Christian could serve as a magistrate or, in a just war, as a soldier. Still, whatever its peculiarities, Hut's and Wiedemann's group was at least pacifist, and so in the main-stream of evangelical Anabaptism to a greater degree than was Hubmaier.

Where the group differed from most Anabaptists was in its insistence on communism. This too, however, was an attempt to restore the Christianity of the New Testament, and in particular that of the Jerusalem church as described in Acts 4:32. But unlike the proto-socialism of Müntzer's peasants (so beloved by the twentieth-century East German government), the sharing of goods was to be restricted to the microcosm of the voluntary community of committed believers, not imposed on all and sundry by all-wise social visionaries.

Hut's apocalypticism was gradually left by the wayside; he had prophesied the Second Coming for three and a half years after the Peasants' War, or after the death of the 'two witnesses' of

Revelation 11:3–7 – identified by him as Thomas Müntzer and the Mühlhausen agitator executed with him, Henry Pfeiffer. In any case, Hut escaped Lord von Liechtenstein's prison in Nikolsburg, and left for Vienna, where he established a church of about fifty people. September 1527 found him in Augsburg, where he was detected and arrested. Following torture, he died in an apparently accidental fire in his prison cell; the glowing future which his captors clearly had in mind for him was thus pre-empted.

Wiedemann's group was expelled from the protection of Nikolsburg, and formed a colony in Austerlitz in 1529. Similar colonies developed nearby as Anabaptist refugees poured in from Austria and Germany. Jakob Hutter (c. 1502–36) had become the chief leader of the Tyrolean Anabaptists, following the burning of Georg Blaurock in September 1529 and now, while he himself continued to work in the Tyrol, he organized the removal of some of his flock to Moravia to escape the ever fiercer persecutions being visited on them by the Catholic authorities.

Wiedemann's group split over various issues, including its leader's authoritarian ways, and his belief (imbibed from Hut's ironic twist upon Augustine) that since baptism was necessary to salvation, children dying before coming to an age where they could legitimately be baptized would be damned. That way, whether either side saw it or not, would in the long run have led to a return to infant baptism.

Although Hutter eventually assumed the leadership of the largest anti-Wiedemann faction from 1533, it was not without an exercise of judgement beginning well and truly with the household of faith, with all manner of unseemly sins, divisions and recriminations amongst leaders and others being brought to light. Neither were Hutter's apostolic pretensions notably less than Wiedemann's had been.

Many of the would-be communists could not refrain from secretly hanging on to some money for themselves by way of provision against future disasters; exposure led to discipline, which in turn led to anger either from the supporters of the one punished, or from those who felt that the person concerned had not been punished harshly enough. Even communism in microcosm, it seems, runs up against human nature, regenerate or otherwise.

Hutter and his wife were captured in the Italian Tyrol in November 1535. Aware that they had a key leader in their hands, the Catholic authorities nevertheless failed to extract either in-formation or a recantation from him. This was despite the liberal use of torture, including putting him tied and gagged into icy water, pulling him out, then beating him and pouring flaming brandy into his wounds.[10] In February 1536, he was burned at Innsbruck. Although his wife escaped prison, she was recaptured two years later and likewise put to death. It is from Hutter that the movement he led, and which continues to exist, mainly in the United States and Canada, takes its name.

John Amon took over as leader after Hutter's martyrdom until his own death in 1542, when the mantle passed to Leonard Lanzenstiel. But perhaps the leader whose influence was most abiding, after that of Hutter himself, was Peter Riedemann (1506–56).

In 1540–41 Riedemann had produced, whilst ensconced in the fairly benign prison conditions provided for him by that most unwilling of persecutors, Count Philip of Hesse, a *Confession of Faith* which was to become a standard point of doctrinal refer-ence for the Hutterites. His purpose in writing the work was quite clearly to vindicate the movement from accusations of heresy:

> In order that no man, including the authorities – who, perhaps at the instigation of others, have already stretched out and laid their hand upon the Lord's people of peace – may bring further guilt upon them-selves by violating the apple of the Lord's eyes, we desire to give an account of our faith, doctrine and life as much in sequence as is possible, through which we believe every man should see and recognize suffi-ciently that we are not heretics and seducers, as we are blasphemously called . . .[11]

Lanzenstiel felt badly in need of Riedemann's help in leading the flock, but only after an exhortatory letter, in 1542, was he finally persuaded to escape from custody (a laughably simple feat in his circumstances) and return to Moravia.

In the early 1540s the Hutterite communities prospered. Hard work, thrift, and the pooling of expenses led inevitably, in the

---

[10]   *The Chronicle of the Hutterite Brethren*, i., p. 145.
[11]   Peter Riedemann, *Confession of Faith*, p. 9.

long run, to wealth, and the Moravian lords were glad to have
people who farmed hitherto intractable wilderness and produced
high-quality goods. The local economy was boosted by their
presence. Local non-Anabaptist craftsmen, however, were re-
sentful of their competition; communal living reduced overheads
and allowed lower prices, whilst the specialization and the division of labour resulting from relatively large enterprises enabled
high-quality goods to be produced. Here we see some of the very
same features at work which had created popular anti-Semitism,
together with the same protective response on the part of those
– the hierarchy – who were in a position both to take a larger
view of the economic effects of the minority's presence and to
benefit from it.

Although compelled by Ferdinand to expel them (they went
to Hungary) in the years after 1547, the nobles encouraged them
to return as soon as the trouble had died down. Thus the
Hutterites prospered, both numerically and materially, for most
of the rest of the sixteenth century. Numbers have been very
variously estimated, but twenty thousand may not be too far wide
of the mark for this period. Many of their landlords mistreated
them, but usually not too much, for they valued the Hutterites
as good workers.

The *Hutterite Chronicle* – a sort of collective diary – may be
seen variously as an invaluable historical record, as a heroic
testament of faith through endurance, or as a lovingly nursed
catalogue of wrongs perpetrated against the community. But the
very extent of the depredations and thefts visited with such
incredible persistence upon the various Hutterite settlements is
itself a testimony, both to their resilience and to their productiv-
ity. When the emperor tried, in 1596, to extract a large loan with
menaces, the Hutterite leaders had to work hard to persuade
local officials that it was 'wrong to think that we possessed such
wealth'.[12] Had the poverty been as self-evident as all that, the
issue would never have arisen. 'Everybody knows', the elders
argued, that the Hutterites have nothing to do with trade or usury
and earn their bread with hard manual labour, and 'it is impossible to accumulate great wealth like that.' The conclusion pal-

---

[12] *Chronicle of the Hutterite Brethren*, i., p. 531.

pably did not follow from the premise. In addition to the economic advantages of communal living, the Hutterites' pacifist
and anti-clerical consciences did not allow them to pay either
taxes for war – the chief purpose of most state taxation in the
pre-modern period – or tithes.[13] In 1604, the emperor again
looked to the Hutterite communities for a loan of twenty thousand guilders. Though they complained that 'we did not have
enough to feed ourselves', rumours still persisted that 'we had
large reserves of money. It troubled us deeply that no one
believed we were in need.'[14]

The scale of the repeated losses sustained by the Hutterites
over many years, including capital goods and money, does tend
to lend credence to the outsiders' suspicions, however unjustifi-
able the mistreatment of these Anabaptists may have been. Certainly the mutual sharing of resources, between settlements as
well as within them, increased their resilience to blows that would
have destroyed any other community.

In the seventeenth century the Hutterites' troubles began again,
and during the Thirty Years War (1618–48) many of them were
unspeakably treated.[15] The war against the Turks which followed
brought further suffering. Massacres, persecution and defection
reduced them, by 1665, to a rump: a contemporary estimated just
one thousand. The remaining Hutterites moved into Hungary and
Transylvania, but communal living broke up under the pressure.

Following further persecution, they moved on in the years
after 1770 to the Ukraine and to Russia, before removing to the
U.S. in the 1870s, on the assurance that their pacifism would be
respected, and finally to Canada in 1918 after the violation of
that assurance during the First World War. In both Russia and
North America, communal living was eventually, after many
failures and much difficulty, resumed, and this is now the general
model for modern Hutterites, who have in the twentieth century
established communities in many different countries. Thus has
their perspective on the restoration of the New Testament church
itself been restored.

---

[13] *Ibid.*, i., pp. 549, 551.
[14] *Ibid.*, i., pp. 567–8.
[15] *Ibid.*, i., pp. 647–68 gives the gruesome details.

Chapter Five

Visions of Vengeance

The Rise and Fall of an End-time Prophet: Melchior Hofmann

Thomas Müntzer and Henry Pfeiffer were not the only appellants to the rôle of the two prophets of Revelation 11; the furrier-turned-preacher Melchior Hofmann[1] was identified by friends in Strassburg in 1530, and thenceforward by himself, as the returned Elijah. The city of Strassburg, moreover, was to be the New Jerusalem. Disconcertingly, Hofmann does not fit the picture of the insane ranter that these two claims, taken in isolation, might suggest. His biography, however, is somewhat bizarre, or interesting, according to point of view.

Hofmann was born in Swabia, in south-west Germany, some-time around 1493–95. By 1522, he was combining his original trade as a furrier with the work of an itinerant Lutheran evangelist in the fur country of the Knights of the Teutonic Order, where the modern Baltic republics of Estonia and Latvia are now situated and where, at that time and for long after, the nobility and town merchants were German-speaking – the rural peasants and urban plebeians being Estonians and Letts. Hofmann was the kind of person who found it hard to stay in the same place for long. It was not so much an itch to travel; he just kept getting kicked out of one city after another.

---

[1] Hofmann's name is variously spelled: 'Hoffmann', 'Hoffman', but I have chosen 'Hofmann' here in deference to majority usage, and because it accords more with standard modern German.

If he had confined himself to spreading orthodox Lutheran ideas in the normal pedestrian Lutheran manner, i.e. by arrange- ment with the secular authorities, he might, perhaps, have had an easier life. But as a lay preacher working on the fringes of the Protestant-influenced areas, it was always possible for him to take his own line, and this he did with enthusiasm.

At Wolmar (Valmira), Livonia, in 1523, he was imprisoned and then expelled for preaching, alongside justification by faith, that God was about to bring a swift judgement upon those who failed to accept his message, that nuns were 'brides of the devil' and that images of the saints were 'painted dummies'. [2]

In Dorpat (Tartu), to which he had fled by the autumn of 1524, he quickly built up a sizeable following amongst the younger German merchants and the Estonian lower classes. There his preaching was directed against images and against confessions to the priest. Pastors, he claimed, should be elected by their parish- ioners who, if they were godly, should also be allowed to share from the Word of God or to prophesy. Such egalitarian senti- ments were unlikely to recommend themselves to the city authori- ties and so, in January 1525, a mob of Hofmann's enthusiastic followers made a tour of the city churches and convents destroy- ing the images within them and, in three cases, razing the churches themselves for good measure. The cathedral became something of a battleground in the process and there were several people dead at the end of it all. In the circumstances, the city council's treatment of him, merely expelling him to Riga, was extraordinarily lenient.

Hofmann obtained a letter of endorsement for his ministry from a clearly ill-informed Martin Luther. After creating friction in Reval (Tallinn) he was once again expelled in 1526, and this time he left Livonia altogether for Sweden. The Germans had been the majority in Stockholm up until a few years before, but now they found themselves on the defensive against the policies of the new Swedish king. As Germans, they were inclined towards Lutheranism, and as newly disadvantaged, they were open to radical ideas of the sort which Hofmann, who now obtained a position as preacher at the German Lutheran Church there, was

[2] K. Deppermann, *Melchior Hoffman*, p. 36.

only too happy to supply. Here he wrote tracts, including an exposition of the apocalyptic twelfth chapter of Daniel, got married, and had a baby son.

It was inevitable that the Swedish government would look upon Hofmann as a troublemaker, and he was obliged to move on again. This time he went to Lübeck, and from thence to Kiel, at that time in Danish territory. Surprisingly, the Danish king gave Hofmann his backing at first. In 1529, however, he was expelled for his views on the eucharist.

Hofmann's opinions on this subject were, to put the matter at its kindest, of a very idiosyncratic type. They amounted, however, to a species of sacramentarianism, a mystical variation on Zwingli's view that the bread and wine in no sense contain the body and blood of Christ. Such ideas, of course, put him definitively outside of the Lutheran fold.

Hofmann was required to defend himself at the Flensburg Disputation in April 1529. Such debates were, as we have seen in Zürich, a form of theological show-trial, the ostensible purpose of which was to establish the truth or otherwise of certain doctrines, but which were actually a public ritual to justify the condemnation of a particular viewpoint and those who held it. Karlstadt made an attempt to attend in order to speak up for Hofmann, but was refused a safe-conduct and had to resort to meeting him secretly to provide moral support.

Following the inevitable outcome, Hofmann made the decisive move of his career. He went to Strassburg, *via* East Frisia. During his stopover in the Lowlands, he tried to encourage the local sacramentarians and made many vital contacts. Sacramentarianism in Frisia and the Netherlands was not dependent upon Zwingli, but had developed quite independently under the native leadership of Cornélis Hoen and Hinne Rode. It was very extensive and there were secret conventicles across the Netherlands, some of which had already faced persecution. Perhaps the most notable of the sacramentarian martyrs was Wendelmoet Claesdochter, a widow of Monnikendam, who had been executed two years earlier in 1527. Her interrogation and final defiance at her martyrdom are recorded in the *Martyrs Mirror*, an immense collection of accounts of persecuted – mostly Dutch – Anabaptists and radicals:

Then the monk exclaimed: 'Mother Weynken, will you gladly die as a
Christian?'
Ans. 'Yes, I will.'
Ques. 'Do you renounce all heresy?'
Ans. 'I do.'
Ques. 'This is well. Are you also sorry that you have erred?'
Ans. 'I formerly did err indeed, and for that I am sorry; this however is
no error, but the true way, and I adhere to God.'
When she had said this, the executioner began to strangle her, which
when she felt it, she cast down her eyes and closed them, as though she
had fallen into a sleep, and gave up the ghost. [3]

In eastern Frisia, the area visited by Hofmann, the peasants
had for long enjoyed an unusual degree of personal freedom,
having only minimal labour obligations to their lords, and often
being able to help choose their local priests, who were expected
to live with a concubine in order to keep everybody else's wives
safe!

As the religious situation there began to drift towards a free-
for-all in the late 1520s, the local Count, Enno II, found himself
under threat of attack from the Catholic Emperor Charles V. As
it became clear that the neighbouring German Lutheran states
would not help defend him because of the radicalism currently
permitted within the county, Enno began to call for moderation
and for orthodox Lutheranism, thus coming into conflict with
the more radically inclined amongst his own subjects. Hofmann
sought to galvanise the latter, and gained support from some
nobles. In June, however, he was encouraged to leave for Strassburg, perhaps – although this was not how things were to turn
out – to enlist the moral support of the reformers there.

In Strassburg, Hofmann quickly and inevitably fell into the
company of one of the several rival Anabaptist congregations.
The city remained very tolerant, although Bucer was anxious to
expel Anabaptists, whether natives or refugees. The latest arrival
joined a group which included the prophets Lienhard and Ursula
Jost and Barbara Rebstock. Hofmann now adopted belief in
human free will and the universality of divine grace, and allowed
himself to be baptized as a believer in April 1530. More ominously, he accepted the prophecies of his companions to the effect

---

[3]   Thieleman van Braght, *Martyrs Mirror*, p. 424.

that he was the returned Elijah, one of the two end-time prophets who was to announce the imminent judgement. In line with his unique insights into the impending apocalypse, he published his exposition of the Book of Revelation and two books of the Josts' prophecies.

Hofmann also adopted a peculiar Christology, which was to be a distinguishing mark both of his followers and of groups derived from his movement for long afterwards. His view has generally been described as Monophysite (i.e. recognizing only one nature in Christ), although that is a little harsh; his idea was certainly seriously unorthodox though not, perhaps (except to a stern judgement), heretical in the sense that, say, Arianism or Docetism are heretical.

Simply put, Hofmann taught that Christ did not take his human flesh from Mary, but brought it with him from heaven. In defence of this, he argued from John's dictum that 'the Word became flesh', and appealed to the teaching of Paul that 'the first man [Adam] was of the dust of the earth, the second man [Christ] from heaven' (1 Cor. 15:47). Hofmann's central argument, however, was that, had Christ really taken flesh of Mary, 'then it would have been the cursed flesh of Adam in which he had redeemed us'.[4] As Hofmann's recent biographer, Klaus Deppermann, explains, 'the devil would have been deceived if Christ took flesh from Mary, a sinful daughter of Adam', for then 'it would logically follow that sinners were redeemed by sin . . . that filthy people were cleansed and purified by filth'.[5]

In May 1530, the month following his baptism, Hofmann went on a preaching mission to the Netherlands, the astonishing and instantaneous success of which was so great that the historian is absolutely required to make some gesture in the direction of explanation. What can be said? Well, in the first place, it must be remembered that the sacramentarian movement in the Netherlands was very large, and that Hofmann had already won credibility within it. Zwingli's sacramentarianism in Zürich had led some of that reformer's more radical followers to the irresistible conclusion that, if communion was indeed a human act, rather

---

[4]   M. Bucer, *Handlung inn dem offentlichen gesprech . . . gegen Melchior Hoffman*, Biv.
[5]   K. Deppermann, *Melchior Hoffman*, p. 225.

than a divine one, then baptism must be too. Communion was an act of worship and a calling to mind by the participants of Christ's sacrifice for sin, not an infusion of grace; for only faith in Christ's sacrifice could call forth grace. In the same way, baptism was a plea before God for a good conscience on the part of the one being baptized, and a pledge of obedience, marking that person off as dead to self and alive to Christ. Like communion, it was not a *means* of grace but rather a sign that, through faith in Christ's death, grace had already been received.

By its nature, believers' baptism was implicit. Only if the ceremony somehow does some 'good' *in itself* can infant baptism be defended. So, those who accepted sacramentarianism in respect of communion were strongly predisposed to accept believers' baptism. This Hofmann now preached to the Dutch sacramentarians who already possessed a network of conventicles through which the new practice could rapidly be spread, and which could quickly take on the life of Anabaptist churches.

In the second place, the Netherlands was currently experiencing a series of both natural and man-made disasters: flood, plague and, from 1528–36, famine caused by war in the Baltic region (from which the Low Countries received much of their grain supply). Amidst such calamities, divine irruption into history of the kind offered by Hofmann seemed to present a likelier hope for the immediate future than any human palliatives; indeed, the various woes might be viewed as portents of just such an intervention. In such circumstances, heightened eschatological expectations were only to be expected, and most of the pamphlets published in the Netherlands were on such subjects. Hofmann's preaching, of course, had always borne precisely such an aspect, and it certainly added to his appeal now.

In speaking of Dutch Anabaptism, then, we are discussing a phenomenon that came to almost instant fruition by means of the rapid transformation of the pre-existent sacramentarianism. Because Hofmann was the instigator of the transformation, it was also strongly apocalyptic, contained within itself a call for social revolution, and held to his deviant Christology. In particular, the combination of apocalyptic expectation and social protest made early Dutch Anabaptism internally unstable and a destabilizing force within Dutch society.

Hofmann's first port of call was Emden, where he converted the large sacramentarian group and baptized three hundred. In November, he baptized Sicke Freerks (also known as Snijder), who then went to his home town of Leeuwarden and converted the sacramentarian conventicle there to Anabaptism. Freerks became the first Dutch Anabaptist martyr a few months later, when he was beheaded before a sympathetic crowd on 21st March 1531. Freerks had a local reputation for godliness and piety, and his martyrdom shocked many around Leeuwarden, including Obbe and Dirk Philips, sons of a local priest. The Philips brothers, already sacramentarian sympathizers, now turned Anabaptist. Anxious about the bloodthirsty rhetoric of many of their fellows, they counselled pacifism and an evangelical theology, although they accepted Hofmann's Christology (which had, in any case, pre-Reformation precedent in Dutch popular heresy).

Another of Hofmann's converts was Jan Volkerts (also known as Trijpmaker). Soon claiming to be 'the new Enoch', the second prophet of the Apocalypse, he went to Amsterdam and founded an Anabaptist congregation there. Arrested in the autumn of 1531, he recanted and, perhaps under torture, gave the names of fifty of his converts to the Court of Holland. Seven were, like him, beheaded on 5th December and their heads put on public display in Amsterdam, an action which left the more leniently minded local council at loggerheads with the Court.

It was not fear of persecution, however, which caused Hofmann to leave the Netherlands early in 1533 and return to Strassburg. He went back with the express purpose of delivering himself to the authorities there, convinced by the prophecy of one of his East Frisian supporters that he must be imprisoned for six months and that then the Lord would appear to deliver his people.

From his prison cell, he called for the temporary suspension of believers' baptism, citing by way of justification the book of Ezra. The enemies of the children of Israel had wanted to stop them 'restoring the walls and repairing the foundations' (4:12) of Jerusalem, an enterprise analogous to the restoration of the church in which the Melchiorites were now engaged. And so (4:24) 'the work on the house of God in Jerusalem came to a standstill until the second year of the reign of Darius King of Persia'; believers' baptism, Hofmann decreed, should be suspended for two years.

Although his commands from prison in Strassburg were at first obeyed by his devotees in the Netherlands, the self-styled prophet of the end times was about to lose control of the movement he had created. The Lord did not appear to usher in the Kingdom, or even to achieve the more mundane task of releasing his prophet from incarceration. Hofmann was to remain in prison until his death in 1543. At least as damaging as the disproof of his prophecies was the appalling blow that was to strike at the public image of his movement, and of Anabaptism as a whole, as a result of the events at Münster and elsewhere. A catastrophe was about to unfold.

The Sword Unsheathed: Münster

The most sinister of Hofmann's converts was undoubtedly Jan Matthijs, a baker from Haarlem. He now challenged Hofmann's authority on the question of the suspension of believers' baptism. If this was reasonable in itself, however, he soon followed up the challenge by ordaining twelve 'apostles', a move ominously redo - lent of personal messianic claims. He also began to preach the imminent destruction of all tyrants, by which he meant the ecclesiastical and secular authorities.

Obbe Philips, recollecting events from the vantage-point of about 1560, described Matthijs and his manner of asserting his ministry:

> There arose a baker of Haarlem named John Matthijs, who had an elderly wife whom he deserted, and he took with him a brewer's daughter who was a very pretty young slip of a girl and had great knowledge of the gospel. . . . He carried her secretly with him to Amsterdam. . . . Now when he came there, he professed to have been greatly driven by the Spirit and [told] how God had revealed great things to him which he could tell to no one, that he was the other witness, Enoch.
>
> Now when the friends or brethren heard of this, they became appre - hensive and knew not what they should best do. . . . They had also heard that Cornelius Polterman was Enoch.
>
> When John Matthijs learned of this, he carried on with much emotion and terrifying alarm, and with great and desperate curses cast all into

hell and to the devils to eternity who would not hear his voice and who would not recognize and accept him as the true Enoch. Because of this, some went into a room without food and drink, in fasting and prayer, and were almost all as disconsolate over such threats as if they lay in hell. For we were at that time all unsuspecting and no one knew that such false prophets could arise in the midst of the brethren. [6]

With the Melchiorite leaders in mental turmoil, Matthijs abruptly changed the emotional temperature by sending into the room a young child proclaiming peace and offering the hand of friendship. The baker's combination of psychological warfare and superspiritual bullying was of the type by which charlatans have ever been wont to compel the submission of sensitive, self-doubting believers. It worked then, as it has worked many times since. Matthijs' cause, however, was more dangerous than most.

Some of Matthijs' apostles now went to Münster, a city of some fifteen thousand souls in the north German Rhineland, which was undergoing a particularly volatile period of politico-religious turmoil. Traditionally ruled by a Catholic prince-bishop whose spiritual prestige was rock-bottom, Lutheranism had recently been making some headway in the city, with the encouragement of a prominent pastor, Bernhard Rothmann, and the support of the city council, and in the teeth of opposition from the bishop. In the late spring and summer of 1533, Rothmann began to teach a sacramentarian view of communion and, as a logical corollary, to denounce infant baptism. This split the reforming party. Rothmann and his supporters were ordered to leave the city, the Lutherans having made common cause with the Catholics. However, when several prominent Catholics tried to expel the Lutherans too, the Lutherans changed sides once more and allowed Rothmann to stay, on the condition that he ceased preaching.

It was in this somewhat delicately poised situation that Rothmann received the emissaries of the new Enoch in January 1534. He submitted to baptism, along with a fellow-pastor of the city, Henry Rol, and a key patrician supporter, Bernhard Knipperdolling. Within a week, over a thousand citizens had been similarly

---

[6] G.H. Williams and A.M. Mergals eds., *Spiritual and Anabaptist Writers*, pp. 213–14.

baptized in their own homes. Rothmann's support was large and prepared to use force, and the council felt unable either to arrest or to expel him without serious disturbance. The vacillation was to prove fatal.

In February, the emissaries' mentor arrived, along with many Anabaptist refugees fleeing vicious persecution and coming to what they were now promised would be the real New Jerusalem, the site of the Second Coming of Christ. Talk of Hofmann and Strassburg as the focus of the messianic hope was now forgotten, and believers' baptism had become, not a symbol of dying to self and rising again in Christ, but the badge of obedience to the Münsterite cause and the apocalyptic kingdom. Matthijs declared that the time to destroy the godless was at hand.

After a series of political intrigues, Matthijs succeeded in taking control of the city and appointing a new council, with Knipperdolling as mayor. There was an influx of economic refugees from the surrounding area, who were sufficiently des- perate to give credence to Matthijs' vision of an egalitarian utopia about to be ushered in by the hand of God. In late February and early March, all citizens who refused to submit to rebaptism were expelled, leaving their possessions behind them. Unchivalrously, many of these left their wives amongst their other belongings, thereby enabling the new régime to introduce polygamy in May. The 'surplus' women were required to repu- diate their erstwhile husbands, and to become second (or third, or fourth) wives to the remaining men. The extent of polygamy increased as men were lost in the coming siege.

In March, Matthijs ordered all books except the Bible to be destroyed, and a huge fire was made in the cathedral square for this purpose. As the historian Norman Cohn has rightly com- mented, 'This act symbolized a complete break with the past, a total rejection above all of the intellectual legacy of earlier gen- erations'.[7] It was also copying a feature (albeit in a vastly exag- gerated form) of the Roman Catholic Church, which assiduously encouraged the burning of books it deemed heretical. As the Khmer Rouge would seek to do in the Cambodia of the 1970s, the purpose in Münster was the destruction of everything –

---

[7] N. Cohn, *The Pursuit of the Millennium*, p. 267.

including people – which might evoke previous conditions, and to invent the world anew. There was to be no going back.

Although Rothmann busily produced writings during the period of the kingdom of Münster, he was also a vital part of the leadership of the city. Access to thoughts other than those of the new leadership was severed. In Rothmann's exposition of the restoration alluded to in Acts 3:21, the day of grace was already past, and retribution alone now remained for the impenitent. 'What was begun by Erasmus, Luther and Zwingli, has now been gloriously established in the truth' – by the Münsterites.[8]

Any semblance of adherence to evangelical Anabaptism now disappeared. It became a capital offence to be unbaptized, a nice irony considering that this was precisely the situation in Catholic and Protestant states, in respect of infant baptism. The Old Testament, moreover, was now brought into service to justify the new programme – another development which stood Anabaptism on its head. If the entire population of a given piece of territory is to be governed as a 'Christian society', recourse must perforce be made to the Old Testament by way of justification; the New Testament knows nothing of a 'Christian country'. The Old Testament history of Israel gives a picture of laws, military arrangements and patterns of social organization which can be appealed to by way of precedent for a godly commonwealth. It was to the Old Testament that Catholic and magisterial Protestant teachers had, without exception, appealed when seeking to justify the apparatus of a 'Christian state' and to denounce evangelical Anabaptism. The New Testament, they taught, provided an account of the beginnings of Christianity, but the precepts of the Sermon on the Mount were 'counsels of perfection' which ordinary believers could not, and should not, hope to follow literally; the lifestyle described in the Book of Acts was only for the transitional period of the establishing of the Church.

Evangelical Anabaptism, by way of contrast, had tended to reverse this type of hermeneutic: it had emphasized the typological significance of the Old Testament, whilst stressing the need for literal adherence to the precepts and the pattern provided by the New Testament church. But the aberrant Anabaptists of

---

[8]   W. Klaassen, *Living at the End of the Ages*, pp. 30–31, 77.

Münster had taken over a city in order to run it as a godly utopia embracing the whole population; it was inevitable that they would have to resort to force to do this, and equally inevitable that they would have to revert to the Old Testament in an attempt to find scriptural warrant for their actions.

One important New Testament precedent was maintained, however: Rothmann taught that communism, as implied in Acts 4:32–35, was the model for a true Christian community. (This was perhaps necessary to give the new government control over all of the city's resources, since Münster was now besieged by the mercenary army of the bishop.) Private ownership of houses, and even of food, was forbidden. Money was abolished, which perhaps didn't matter too much as the siege meant that there was soon very little to buy with it. People caught harbouring money, food, or anything else, were liable to execution. There was a text to justify this, of course: 'All the sinners among my people will die by the sword' (Amos 9:10).

Perhaps the real meaning of that text extended to leaders too, for Matthijs was literally cut to pieces in a skirmish with the besiegers outside the city walls on 4th April. He seems to have believed that he would defeat the enemies of God almost single-handed, a belief in which he seems to have been encouraged by his lieutenant, Jan Beuckels van Leiden.

Beuckels' undoubted military ability and political judgement had dictated that he content himself with remaining in the city during the aforesaid skirmish. His prescience was rewarded when he immediately became Matthijs' successor. He abolished the city council and replaced it with twelve elders, or 'Judges of the Tribes of Israel'. Following his introduction of polygamy the following month, he set a good example by taking Matthijs' widow – such 'a pretty young slip of a girl' – and 14 others, later personally beheading one who was sufficiently unwise as to criticize him.

On 29th July, there was an insurrection in the city over the issue of polygamy. Jan Beuckels was captured briefly, but when he refused to reverse his order on polygamy the rebels hesitated, and a group of loyalists arrived and captured the insurgents. About fifty of them were executed.

Beuckels organized the defences of Münster well. A successful sortie was made into the enemy camp. Propaganda was sent to the ill-paid besieging soldiers, inviting them to join the defenders, and in June two hundred did so. Others simply deserted. On 25th May, and again on 31st August, the besiegers were repelled after sustaining terrible losses. After the latter victory Beuckels had himself crowned king over the messianic city and caused coins to be struck – the ban on money notwithstanding – showing his likeness.

Persecuted beyond endurance and encouraged by the appeals from Münster, Dutch Anabaptists made their way to the heavenly city. As a recent historian has commented, they 'thought they were escaping not only the severe persecution of tyrants but also the great judgement day of God'.[9] In March 1534, perhaps as many as twelve thousand started to make their way towards Münster from all across the Netherlands. Whilst some of them succeeded in reaching their destination, most were apprehended. Eleven ships were prevented from crossing the Zuiderzee, but 30 others, containing some three thousand men, women and children, reached the far side, where they were found to be in possession of some fifteen hundred weapons of various kinds. The weapons, however, had been brought merely because they had been told to do so by the messengers from Münster; no thought had been given to using them, and a handful of soldiers was sufficient to arrest their holders, no resistance being given. A few leaders were executed there and then by the representatives of the Court of Holland, but the rest had their possessions confiscated and were sent home, where about another hundred were put to death. The Court limited its blood-lust to this, not from any natural clemency, but from a desire not to damage the economy by depopulating the countryside.

Melchiorite activity in the Netherlands was not, however, restricted to attempts to reach Münster. On 22nd March 1534, several of its adherents ran through the streets of Amsterdam with cries of 'repent' and 'woe to the godless'. The runners carried swords, and declared that the new part of the city had been given to the children of God. Amongst them were those who had baptized and commissioned Obbe Philips, who was becoming increasingly horrified by the direction which events were taking.

---

[9] C. Krahn, *Dutch Anabaptism*, p. 146.

A wanted man in his native Leeuwarden, he had fled to the relative anonymity of Amsterdam, where he was now attempting to dissuade the Melchiorites from participation in the growing madness. His evangelical followers were to become known as Obbenites. When the swordsmen were arrested and executed, curiosity drove Obbe to view the bodies, in order

> to know which in the heap those three were who had baptized us and had proclaimed such calling and promise to us. But we could not identify them, so frightfully were they changed by the fire and smoke, and those on the wheels we could not recognize either, nor tell one from the other.[10]

Philips' curiosity was more than mere ghoulishness; a doubt had been sown in his mind which would later cause him to repudiate the validity of his own baptism and ordination at the hands of these false prophets. In the meantime, he got on with the business of rescuing as many Anabaptists as he could from the Münsterite fanaticism.

Almost a year later, with the Münster siege becoming desperate, Amsterdam Melchiorites again offered symbolic help. On the night of 10th February 1535, twelve men and women proclaimed the 'naked truth' of the new Eden and the impending apocalypse by running through the streets of the city, similarly unattired. One of the women was later found to be a Catholic, who had simply been caught up in the (rather chilly) excitement of the moment. Sixteenth-century governments stood no nonsense from streakers, and so they were beheaded.

Stadholder Hoogstraten, however, was already in possession of even more disconcerting information about the Amsterdam Melchiorites. According to the interrogation evidence of one prisoner, Jannetgen Thys, there were sixty secret adherents in the city militia, plus two magistrates and a senior city councillor. The only thing that had prevented an insurrection already happening, she said, was division amongst the leadership; the influence of the Philips brothers was clearly beginning to have its effect.

On 30th March, a group of about three hundred men and women under the leadership of Jan van Geelen, an emissary from Münster, captured the Oude Kloster at Bolsward. They

---

[10]   G.H. Williams and A.M. Mergal eds., *Spiritual and Anabaptist Writers*, p. 219.

were immediately besieged by the forces of Stadholder van Toutenburg. Repeated assaults and bombardment by heavy artillery killed 130 of the defenders. Van Geelen escaped but, of those captured when the monastery was overwhelmed on 7th April, 37 were beheaded, and the remaining 132 taken to nearby Leeuwarden, where 55 were put to death.

On 10th May, violence broke out in Amsterdam. A group led by the ubiquitous Jan van Geelen planned to capture the town hall on an evening when the councillors were present. Clearly, every attempt had been made to involve all the local Melchiorites in the attack, but the Obbenites had refused to have anything to do with violence, whilst Jacob van Campen, another local leader, had taken the mediating position that force should not be used unless God gave a clear sign to that effect, and he could discern none. So it was a depleted force of about forty that turned out for this particular meeting.

Three or four people, including a burgomaster, were killed. The insurgents dug in for the night, but the morning brought the inevitable attack by the outraged authorities. The outcome was predictable: all of the defenders were killed. During the fighting, Van Geelen dodged bullets to climb to the top of the tower; his fatal jump was the work of a moment and, as well as being a suitably theatrical exit, meant he escaped the certain torture that would have resulted from his having been captured. Van Campen was captured though and, despite having refused to help the revolutionaries, suffered the cutting off of both his tongue and his right arm before the more merciful removal of his head.

Meanwhile, back in Münster, things were going from bad to worse. Starvation had set in. Very unwillingly, Beuckels allowed some old men, women and children to leave (others had for some time been fleeing as opportunity presented itself), but almost all of the men were killed by the besiegers through whose lines they had to pass. In May, the remaining population was estimated at nine and a half thousand, consisting of just nine hundred men, five and a half thousand women and the rest children, almost all of whom were now in a piteous condition. The besieging army numbered about three thousand and, in one of the few concessions to ecumenism that would be made for many years yet, included both Protestant and Catholic forces.

On the night of 24th June, two men betrayed a weak point in the defences to the bishop's army. These now burst into the city and, on the morning of the 25th, it fell amidst scenes of appalling carnage. The killing continued until the 27th, by which time virtually all of the men were dead, including all but two dozen of a group of three hundred who had surrendered on the under-standing that their lives would be spared. Between fifteen hun-dred and two thousand of the women had also died, many in summary executions. Attics and basements were assiduously searched for any signs of life. The Bishop came to see the carnage but could not bear the stench.

Bernhard Rothmann seems to have been fortunate, in the sense that he probably died in the fighting.[11] The messianic King John, plus Bernhard Knipperdolling and one other leader, were less fortunate. After interrogations in which Beuckels made a partial recantation, the three were tortured to death with red-hot irons on a public platform, in January 1536. Their bodies were hung in cages from the tower of one of the churches.

Melchior Hofmann: an Appraisal

The disaster at Münster was complete. For at least two centuries to come, 'Anabaptism' would be dismissed out of hand as amounting (whatever its advocates might say to the contrary) to a desire to reattempt the Münster experiment: to destroy ordered society and to seek a communist utopia, to bring in the millennial kingdom at the point of a sword and to slaughter all who resisted.

Goaded by vicious persecution and misled by manipulators, thousands of Melchiorites had indeed sought many of these goals. Disturbances had broken out in many parts of the Neth-erlands in support of the heavenly city of Münster. These Dutch Anabaptists had thus turned the vision of their Swiss and South-German originators on its head.

---

[11]   Information later given to the authorities by Jan van Batenburg may indicate that Rothmann did, in fact, survive and continue his career as an Anabaptist leader. See C. Krahn, *Dutch Anabaptism*, p. 168.

But how far was Hofmann responsible for it all? He remains the most enigmatic of all of the early Anabaptist leaders. Is he to be dismissed as a wild visionary and unstable preacher of social revolution? Or was he a badly flawed evangelical who bears no real responsibility either for the activities of the megalomaniacs Jan Matthijs and Jan Beuckels at Münster, or for those whom they duped or terrorized into obedience?

Certainly, those who today look upon the Anabaptist movement with favour, or who trace their own spiritual lineage from continental Anabaptism, are inclined to view Hofmann with considerable caution. Whilst the writings of most of the significant evangelical Anabaptist leaders are available in modern English editions, those of Hofmann are not. Given that Hofmann is the vital link between the original Swiss and South-German Anabaptism and the later Dutch/North-German Mennonites, this is a strange omission. Over four and a half centuries later, however, Hofmann's at least partial responsibility for the catastrophic events of 1534–35 makes him a continuing embarrassment. Bearing in mind his activities in the Baltic area in the mid-1520s as a renegade promoter of the Lutheran reformation, his affinity with the spiritual direction that characterized Thomas Müntzer's career, and the social instabilities that made it possible, are undeniable.

But perhaps a more charitable assessment is possible. Hofmann denounced the activities of his Dutch disciples unambiguously; it was, after all, his authority which Matthijs had overturned. He was not in close touch with developments in Münster; interviewed in prison in Strassburg in November 1534, he appeared to believe that Matthijs was still in control, whereas he had in fact been dead since the preceding April. If Hofmann's preaching had aroused passions which later got out of control, the raw material – both in terms of religious dissent and social grievance – had been lying around before ever he arrived in the Netherlands. He had not taught his disciples to use the sword, and never approved their doing so. He consistently favoured religious toleration. His central doctrines were, firstly, an expectation of an imminent apocalypse – which proved unduly optimistic as to timing but which was, in itself, hardly inconsistent with the New Testament hope; secondly, a Christology which most orthodox Christians today would reject, but not in anything like the same harsh terms with which they would reject the Christology of, say, the Jehovah's Witnesses; and thirdly, a call for believers' baptism and for churches of the committed, which would be accepted by many millions more today than Hofmann could ever have had the means to reach.

Chapter Six

A Little Reconstruction

The Aftermath of Münster

A worse blow to the Anabaptists' reputation than the Münster débâcle would be hard to envisage. It certainly gave the rulers of Europe ample reason to redouble their persecution of radicals of all descriptions. Many Anabaptists fled to England, though when Henry VIII, not known for the quality of his mercy in other spheres, began burning them, a number returned to the Nether-lands. It was in these circumstances of crisis that about twenty representatives of the various streams of Dutch Melchiorites agreed to meet to discuss their future (if any). The convention, paid for by an Englishman named Henry, took place at Bocholt, in August 1536.

In the absence of several key figures, David Joris was the most important leader actually present. Before ever becoming a Melchiorite, he had been bored through the tongue as a sacra-mentarian in 1527, a distinction he shared with the Münsterite leader Jan Matthijs. At Bocholt, he held the middle ground between the mainline Melchiorites and evangelical Obbenites on the one hand, and the shattered remnants of the Münsterites and the Batenburgers on the other. This last group were the followers of yet another 'new Elijah', Jan van Batenburg, who rather surprisingly considered the Münsterites to be altogether too moderate.

Batenburg's people continued to practise communism amongst themselves, as well as polygamy. They also plundered churches and committed other acts of terrorism. Their basic rationale was that all outside of their group should be killed; indeed, their leader cheerfully threatened to kill Joris with his own hands.

The remaining Münsterites (there was still a fair number in the towns and villages of Westphalia) considered massacring the godless to be a pointless exercise, for the moment at least. Münster had been a nasty mistake. But God would soon set up his kingdom – a number continued to believe that Münster would be the location – and then would be the time to unsheathe the sword again. The mainline Melchiorites also felt that the kingdom was imminent, but did not accept that the sword was a legitimate way of expressing it. The Obbenites went further and denied that the kingdom was about to be established; indeed, they rejected the emphasis upon prophecy that had encouraged the belief that it was.

Joris was able to cobble together a meaningless agreement between the disparate factions. They agreed on baptism, although the Batenburgers no longer practised it, since the day of grace had passed and only vengeance now remained. (In any case, like attending Catholic churches, not baptizing helped them to avoid detection.) Concerning violence, the various representatives concluded that it was, as the historian G.H. Williams expresses it, 'justifiable but inexpedient, since the millennium was clearly not yet at hand'.[1] They also agreed on Hofmann's Christology and the doctrine of free will. Nevertheless, C. Krahn is hardly unjust when he describes the conference's significance as 'probably more important in assessing existing differences than in achieving unity.'[2]

Joris was much admired by his own followers, and the Bocholt conference enhanced his reputation. One disciple was so overcome by the qualities of her leader that she sent him a letter declaring him to be – perhaps not surprisingly – one of the two prophets of the apocalypse. Thus did Joris join company with Müntzer, Pfeiffer, Melchior Hofmann, Jan Volkerts Trijpmaker, Cornelius Polderman, Jan Matthijs and Jan van Batenburg.

---

[1] G.H. Williams, *The Radical Reformation*, 3rd edn, p. 583.
[2] C. Krahn, *Dutch Anabaptism*, p. 167.

The sender of the letter, Anneken Jansdochter, had to flee to England shortly afterwards with her husband. Fleeing back again in January 1539, she was overheard singing a hymn on board the ship – apparently a sure sign of not being a pious Catholic – and was arrested and drowned in Rotterdam. She made adoption arrangements for her infant son with a woman in the crowd on the way to her execution, and with him left a letter, of exceptional beauty and pathos, to be given him when he had grown up – so that he might understand what his parents had done.

She clearly had a talent for impressive correspondence; her earlier missive to Joris had caused him, he later claimed, to be in a trance for a week after receiving it. He now saw himself as 'the third David'; Moses had given the law, Christ the gospel in the flesh, he the revelation of the Spirit. Sadly, he was able to persuade a number of Dutch Melchiorites of the truth of his claims. After Batenburg's apprehension and execution in 1538, a number of that prophet's followers transferred their allegiance to Joris also.

Many historians believe that the reason for the Batenburgers' adherence was Joris' subtle espousal of sexual libertinism. At Bocholt he had pushed the issue of polygamy to one side, but now he began to claim that his followers should make confession of their sexual sins and temptations to one another in order to overcome sexual shame, which many have taken to be evidence of his libertine tendencies. His recent biographer, Gary Waite, is sure, however, that Joris' support for polygamy at this stage cannot be proved.[3] Even the author of 'The Anonymous Biography of David Joris' (possibly Joris himself, but certainly someone close to him) admitted that he 'bore the reputation . . . of a woman chaser'.[4] Publicly, the prophet took the view that sexual relations, even within a monogamous marriage, were sinful unless specifically for the purpose of procreation.[5] But much later, in 1553, Joris is on record as saying that 'it is all the same whether you have one, two, or four [wives] so long as you obey God and the truth'; polygamy

---

[3] D. Joris, *The Anabaptist Writings of David Joris, 1535–1543*, ed. G.K. Waite, p. 156.
[4] *Ibid.*, p. 66.
[5] *Ibid.*, pp. 132, 172–3.

was, after all, permissible.[6] On this subject a strange ambivalence seems to surround, not only Joris' reputation, but also his own feelings and inclinations.[7]

Joris argued that neither attending the services of the Catholic or Protestant state churches nor having one's infants baptized did any harm; indeed, it helped one to evade detection and persecution. In this he was as good – or as bad – as his principles, and from 1543 lived under an assumed name as a member of the Reformed church in Basel, whilst covertly continuing to exercise his 'real' rôle as a messiah (albeit an entirely secret one) to his own disciples. For those inclined to Platonic dualism and spiritualist interpretations of Scripture, what harm could there be in participation in the state churches? After all, what counted was the inner life of the spirit, and this remained untouched by mere outward ordinances, be they Catholic or Protestant.

The Revival of the Evangelicals: Dirk Philips and Menno Simons

The Münsterites and Batenburgers could hardly survive, except as lingering terrorist movements, and then only until they were tracked down by the authorities or until their adherents became disillusioned with waiting for the moment of action – after that moment had clearly come and gone. The Davidjorists, mystical and esoteric, had perhaps a better future, but one which was closely bound up with the fortunes of their messianic leader. After his lifetime, his movement, too, would dissipate although, as we shall see in chapter 7, it might be said to have continued (in a somewhat mutated form) *via* the Family of Love.

Of the remaining Melchiorite forces, this left those who attempted to remain faithful to Hofmann's ideals, and the pacifist evangelicals under Obbe and Dirk Philips. With the former in disarray and their prophet still an enforced guest of municipal hospitality in Strassburg, the future clearly belonged to the

---

[6] *Ibid.*, p. 308.
[7] Joris' reputation for personal promiscuity seems to have originated only with the doubtful testimony of his secretary after Joris' death. See G.H. Williams, *The Radical Reformation* (3rd edn), p. 730.

evangelicals. In addition to their organization, these last had the advantage of being able to claim to have been vindicated by the disaster at Münster. Had they not always warned against those very actions which had precipitated the catastrophe that had now unfolded all around them?

Nevertheless, it was Joris who, for a while at least, appeared to be the most prominent amongst the surviving Melchiorite leaders. When Jan van Batenburg was arrested in 1538, he gave every appearance of co-operating with the authorities by providing them with the names of leading Anabaptists (though omitting to mention that these were also his enemies; he gave no information about his own circle): David Joris was at the head of his list.

The strength of those Anabaptists who wished to gather the remnants into an evangelical movement was not helped by the defection, in 1541, of one of the Philips brothers, who had done so much to secure just such an outcome. Obbe had slowly become disillusioned with Anabaptism over several years; his was a delayed reaction to the Münster fiasco. By the time of Obbe's defection from the movement that bore his name, however, another leader was emerging within the ranks whose status would outstrip even his, and whose leadership would be decisive in rebuilding the shattered remnants of Dutch Anabaptism along evangelical lines.

Menno Simons had been born in the village of Witmarsum, Frisia, in 1496, and had entered the Franciscan monastery at nearby Bolsward as a boy. In 1524 he became assistant priest in the parish of Pingjum, just up the road from his home village. It was not until two years later, however, that he began to read the Bible for himself. When he did so, it was to clear up doubts that had been raised in his mind concerning the Catholic doctrine of transubstantiation, doubts almost certainly placed there by the spread of sacramentarian influence.

He had barely been priested a year before 'it occurred to me, as often as I handled the bread and wine in the Mass, that they were not the flesh and blood of the Lord'. (That the same thought was occurring to literally thousands of others in the Netherlands during those years, he neglects to mention.) The issue was resolved for him, but not in the way that his superiors would have wished, and only by raising all manner of other questions in his mind, questions which a more punctilious dedication to professional advancement might have left undis-turbed. His readings in the New Testament convinced him of the falsity of transubstantiation, whilst his perusal of Luther persuaded him of the authority of Scripture over that of human institutions.

During the years 1528–31, Simons began to gain a reputation locally as an 'evangelical' preacher, though he was later to deny strenuously that this reputation was in any way deserved, for although he had taught scriptural doctrine, he had not had the courage of his convictions. As the sacramentarian movement was transformed into Anabaptism from the summer of 1530 onwards under the influence of Melchior Hofmann's visits, Simons could not but be aware of ongoing developments. When Sicke Freerks (Snijder) was beheaded at nearby Leeuwarden in March 1531 for having been rebaptized, the assistant priest of Pingjum consulted his senior pastor, who was forced to admit that infant baptism had no basis in Scripture. In view of this biblical silence, Simons turned to his other source of theological ideas – the writings of the magisterial Reformers – for light on the subject. Luther 'taught me that children were to be baptized on account of their own faith', but 'I perceived that this also was not in accordance with the Word of God'. Bucer fared no better in Menno's esti-mation: 'He taught that infants are to be baptized so that they might be the more carefully nurtured in the way of the Lord', but this idea was also 'without foundation'. Finally, Bullinger 'pointed to the covenant and to circumcision', but this idea too he found 'to be incapable of scriptural proof'. From this, his conclusion was obvious: in view of the deafening silence of Scripture and the equally insupportable claims of the magisterial Reformers, who could not even agree amongst themselves, 'I realized that we were deceived in regard to infant baptism'.[8]

The discrepancy between Menno's private opinions and the requirements of his public office was now fairly considerable. His problem was hardly alleviated by the fact that many of the Anabaptists known to him – some of whom he had been respon-sible for converting to believer's baptism – began to espouse the

---

[8] M. Simons, *Complete Writings*, pp. 668–9.

revolutionary views of the Münsterites which repelled and appalled him. His biblical learning was now such that 'I could silence these persons beautifully', but he found that, when he did so, the godless applauded and were confirmed in their impenitence, whilst the Anabaptists remained unimpressed 'because I myself still did that which I knew was not right' by retaining his position in the Catholic church. Indeed, he had recently been promoted to take charge of his home parish of Witmarsum. The terrible fighting at the Oude Kloster in Bolsward was a mere stone's throw from his parish, and Menno's brother is thought to have been among the Münsterites who perished in the ensuing carnage.

It seems to have been this latest disaster, so close to home, which finally prompted his decisive step out of the Catholic church into evangelical Anabaptism. His own account of his conversion is so moving and powerful that it deserves quoting at some length:

> After this had transpired the blood of these people, although misled, fell so hot on my heart that I could not stand it, nor find rest in my soul. . . . I saw that these zealous children, although in error, willingly gave their lives and their estates for their doctrine and faith. And I was one of those who had disclosed to some of them the abominations of the papal system. But I myself was continuing in my comfortable life and acknowledged abominations simply in order that I might enjoy physical comfort and escape the cross of Christ.
>
> Pondering these things my conscience tormented me so that I could no longer endure it. I thought to myself . . . if I through bodily fear do not lay bare the foundations of the truth, nor use all my powers to direct the wandering flock . . . – oh, how shall their shed blood, shed in the midst of transgression, rise against me at the judgement of the Almighty and pronounce sentence against my poor, miserable soul!
>
> My heart trembled within me. I prayed to God with sighs and tears that He would give to me, a sorrowing sinner, the gift of His grace, create within me a clean heart. . . . I began in the name of the Lord to preach publicly from the pulpit the word of true repentance, to point the people to the narrow path, . . . also the true baptism and the Lord's Supper. . . . After about nine months or so, the gracious Lord granted me His fatherly Spirit, help, and hand. Then I, without constraint, of a sudden, renounced all my worldly reputation, name and fame, my unchristian abominations, my masses, my infant baptism, and my easy life, and I willingly submitted to distress and poverty under the heavy cross of Christ. [9]

---

[9]   *Ibid.*, pp. 670–1.

Menno's conversion, in January 1536, was to lead him into a lifetime of hardship as a fugitive from the authorities. It was also to lead to what was arguably the most fruitful ministry of all the Anabaptist leaders of the sixteenth century.

For the first year, he travelled about, but took little active part in leadership, preferring to devote his energies to private study of the Scriptures. Harold Bender's biography reflects well the ominous nature of his new existence: 'Traces of his movements during this time have been preserved in the records of martyrs who were punished several years later for sheltering him.'[10] He was ordained as a leader in 1537, about a year after his decision to join the Anabaptists, probably by Obbe Philips at Groningen. He got married at about the same time, to a woman named Gertrude.

From the time of his ordination onwards, his pre-eminence amongst the evangelical Anabaptists was increasingly assured. That he should have received his office at the hands of Obbe is ironic, for it was this man, after whom the evangelical Melchiorites had hitherto been named, who now began to lose heart – a delayed reaction to the disasters of the mid-1530s. Obbe reflected on all that had been done, on how he and the brethren had been deceived, and how they still remained so certain of their own dissident beliefs and, above all, on how his own ordination had been at the hands of Willem Kuyper and Bartholomeus Boekbinder, two of Jan Matthijs' supposed apostles.[11] How could such an ordination possibly be of God? Surely his own ministry was no ministry at all?

These were fair questions, but not ones which either his brother Dirk or Menno Simons, both of whom had been ordained in their turn by Obbe, allowed to trouble them unduly. For Obbe, however, they were overwhelming. In 1541 he turned his back on the movement he had led, and had done so much to form out of the ruins of the Melchiorite enterprise, and retreated to a kind of evangelical spiritualism: there was no one true church, even if the Anabaptists did give closest expression to the truth; Scripture was not necessarily to be understood literally; if

---

[10] *Ibid.*, p. 14.

[11] G.H. Williams and A.M. Mergal eds., *Spiritual and Anabaptist Writers*, p. 216.

the old church of Rome was corrupt, attempts to start again from scratch led only to deception; each person should follow Christ in his own heart and not be too harsh on his neighbours who might think, or act, differently. He lamented the 'ban [i.e. shunning, or excommunication], condemnations, blasphemy, backbiting, judging' practised by any Christians who 'could suffer neither the love nor benefit of another who was not of their belief, sect, opinion, and who did not say yes and amen to all their enterprises and onslaughts'.[12]

His sympathies clearly lay with the Anabaptists, but he could no longer give his assent to their categorical assertion of the exclusive rightness of their own positions and the falseness of all others. If they were, then why had God allowed so many of the godly to be so terribly misled? 'All prophecies', he bewailed years later, 'were false and lying, for the tables were always turned the other way. Those who denounced others as godless were such themselves.'[13] More than two decades later, he declared himself to be 'miserable at heart' that he had ordained others to leadership within the movement, since his own ordination had been at the hands of 'false brethren' and, as such, surely invalid.

His latter years were spent pretending to be a state-church Protestant in Rostock. Lest any be tempted to draw parallels between his Nicodemism (or, for that matter, his spiritualism) and the case of David Joris, it should be remembered that Obbe's case is entirely devoid of anything resembling Joris' pretensions to messiahdom. Obbe's was a quietism born of self-doubt and of despair at ever attaining to religious certainty; Joris' dualism is esoteric, and – like all gnosticisms – sanguine in its expectation that secret knowledge will indeed be revealed to the chosen few.

Menno and Dirk, meanwhile, continued their labour of reconstruction undeterred by Obbe's defection. In the early years, they worked mainly in the northern Netherlands. Menno was so successful that, as early as 1541, the Friesland authorities formulated a plan whereby captured Anabaptists might be pardoned if they betrayed him. The following year the Emperor, Charles V, put a price on his head and offered pardon to anyone who

12 *Ibid.*, pp. 224–5.
13 *Ibid.*, p. 222.

delivered him into the hands of officialdom. By that time, Menno was operating further south, in the vicinity of Amsterdam, but in 1543 he removed to East Frisia, and for the next three years he operated both there and in the diocese of Cologne, where persecution was relatively light, and where the edicts of the emperor in Vienna had little effect.

There was, in particular, a large Anabaptist congregation on the coast at Emden. The leading Protestant reformer there was the Polish nobleman Jan Laski (John à Lasco), whose theological penetration was sufficient to discern the difference between Menno's gospel and that of the Münsterites, and his integrity sufficiently great as to admit the fact. As a result, he pleaded with the Countess Anna to find more creative ways than burning to suppress the growth of Menno's people, an action that counts as humanitarian in the sixteenth-century context.

All the same, Menno was forced to move on to the temporary shelter afforded by the diocese of Cologne, which was in a state of flux – always the best conditions for Anabaptist growth – due to the Archbishop's attempts to protestantise the area. When these hopes were dashed by the military defeat of the Schmal- kaldic League of Protestant princes, the diocese of Cologne returned to Catholic jurisdiction and Menno was obliged to remove himself once more.

The last fifteen years of Menno's life (1546–61) were spent in Holstein, north Germany. He wrote voluminously, but his style is simple and direct, generally devoid of classical – or even patristic – allusions, and was clearly pastoral in intent. Where he defends his own theological distinctives or those of Anabaptism in general, he does so in a homely manner that addresses the literate, rather than the educated. His first writing, naturally enough, was directed against the Münsterites. *The Blasphemy of John of Leiden* was written in 1535, around the time of his conversion, but before his formal repudiation of his Catholic priesthood. It was his *Foundation of Christian Doctrine* (1539–40), however, which established his reputation with its felicitous summary of Anabaptist beliefs and practices. Other writings take up pastoral matters – the new birth, baptism, church discipline, excommunication, the nurture of children, meditations and prayers for mealtimes, letters of consolation and encouragement to individuals – as well as dealing with doctrinal issues and differences: the already-noticed tract against Jan van Leiden, two writings on the incarnation, two against the followers of David Joris, a letter to the Amsterdam Melchiorites, an affirmation of the Trinity, and replies to the Reformed teachers Gellius Faber and Martin Micronius. Even in most of the latter category of writings, Simons' aim is pastoral, attempting to keep the flock from error, or to win over those who had already strayed.

Dirk Philips was also involved in this enterprise. His *Enchiridion* or *Handbook* was published in 1564, but elements of the work undoubtedly originate much earlier in his career. The book consists of eighteen sections, covering a range of topics of concern to the Dutch and north German Anabaptists, but which in their totality give something like a complete picture of their faith. The section *Concerning Spiritual Restitution* is generally reckoned to have been written in the early 1560s, but the ideas expressed relate to the Münster crisis.[14] Unless Dirk was mirroring his brother Obbe, who did not write his mature reflection on the whole affair until about the same time, then the thoughts behind the words (if not the words themselves) must date from a much earlier period.

Dirk's burden in this writing was to refute the claims of Bernhard Rothmann, whose *Restitution of true and sound Christian Teaching* had been written in 1534 to justify the revolutionary theocracy. Philips sought to show that Acts 3:20–21 did not refer to a restoration of a this-worldly kingdom, hence the emphasis of his title; the restitution was to be spiritual. Just as the Old Testament people of God had fallen away through Jeroboam, so the church had done through the papal Antichrist. Similarly, just as the temple had been restored in the Old Testament, so the true church was now being restored through the work of the evangelical Anabaptists. Philips provided a list of specifics:

> a true penitence, faith in God, the true knowledge of Jesus Christ and of the Holy Spirit, Christian baptism, the true Lord's Supper, the godly life, brotherly love and trust among all the saints, the evangelical separation or the ban.

---

[14] D. Philips, *The Writings of Dirk Philips*, eds. Dyck, Keeney and Beachy, pp. 54–5.

So concerned was he, however, to minimize any millenarian implications of the restorationist ideal that he all but severed the biblical connection between this restitution and the second coming of Christ; the former was to take place 'until his return', rather than as a sign of the imminence of that return. [15]

Differences between the various radicals which would later be set in concrete remained somewhat fluid during the late 1530s and early 1540s; all of the non-violent Melchiorites remained at least on terms with one another as they sought to evade persecution and keep going in the dark period after Münster. But during the course of the 1540s fundamental doctrinal differences emerged, necessitating the use of what was to become the most characteristic ecclesiastical tool of the evangelical Anabaptists: the ban.

The first set of disputes occurred with the Davidjorists. Nikolaas Meyndertsz van Blesdijk was one who had begun to move in their direction. Originally, he had been a supporter of Menno and Dirk, but by the mid-1540s he had come under the spell of Joris and, perhaps, also of Joris' eldest daughter, whom he married in 1546. The same year at Lübeck, in debate with the evangelical Anabaptist leaders, Blesdijk defended, amongst other Davidjorist views, the practice of Nicodemism (after Nicodemus in Jn. 3, by whose name the art of dissimulation to avoid persecution has generally been dignified).

The decision to ban Blesdijk was taken by Menno and Dirk in conjunction with two leaders, Giles of Aachen and Adam Pastor, whom they had ordained in 1542. The second of these now began to provide some trouble for the brethren on his own account. He had been one of the emissaries sent out from the city of Münster during the siege but, once free of the madhouse, he had defected to the pacifist evangelicals, in whose bosom he had remained through all the trials that followed. He had never accepted the peculiar Christology of Melchior Hofmann, however, and this put him increasingly at odds with Menno, who was by now the leading Anabaptist bishop, and who did accept this teaching. (Hofmannite Christology, it will be remembered, taught that Christ did not take his flesh from the virgin Mary, but brought

---

[15] *Ibid.*, pp. 341–2, 344–5, 347.

it with him from heaven.) Pastor rejected this downplaying of Christ's humanity to the point of actually denying his divinity, and the doctrine of the Trinity for good measure.

Disturbingly for Menno and Dirk, Pastor did not find himself without significant support. Nonetheless, he and those who stood by him were banned by the larger body of North German and Dutch Anabaptists from 1547 onwards, although a reconciliation was attempted, fruitlessly, at Lübeck in 1552. Pastor took his support mainly from the Rhineland area around Münster and Cologne, but it does not appear to have been so well organized as to have outlived him; by the late sixteenth century, his following seems to have evaporated.

The final struggle of Menno's career seems to have been over the issue of the ban itself. Both he and Dirk were inclined to a strict view, namely that a member who had been shunned, whether for reason of heresy or because of unrepented sin, was not to be eaten with by fellow-Christians – even when that meant the shunning of a wife or husband. This was a hard teaching indeed, but not so hard as to prevent Leonard Bouwens, the Anabaptist bishop with responsibility for the congregations in Holland, from making it yet more severe. According to Bouwens' exposition, refusal to eat with those under the ban should be extended to cover all social intercourse. When one woman in Emden refused to shun her husband, who had in any case been banned under questionable circumstances, Bouwens threatened to ban her as well. This process amounts to what might be called secondary separation: not only are the ostensibly godless to be shunned, but so too are those who refuse to shun them. (The process is obviously capable of infinite extension, to tertiary or quaternary separation etc., a technique perfected by some exclusivist groups in more recent centuries.)

Bouwens' behaviour provoked a crisis, the final result of which was the withdrawal, from the 1550s onwards, of a large group of Mennonites from the wider fellowship. Living mostly in the area of Waterland in North Holland, they were consequently known as Waterlanders. These took a more liberal (some might say, less mean-spirited) view of the ban, and eventually came to tolerate even the possibility of marriage with outsiders and the acceptance of public office, as long as the latter did not involve the use of lethal force. This last view was perhaps more practical in the *de facto* pluralist society of the Dutch republic than it would have been elsewhere, but nevertheless marks a serious departure from what was coming to be perceived as Mennonite orthodoxy.

The South German Anabaptists were also less inclined to the excessive rigour concerning the ban which was exhibited by many of their brethren in the north, and this issue, along with their dissent from the northerners' Hofmannite Christology, created diplomatic rifts which were not easily smoothed over.

One of the more picturesque – or cinematographic – of the many disputes which clouded Menno's later years was an incident in 1553. Mary, the Catholic daughter of Henry VIII, had come to the throne of England that year, bringing the protestantising enterprise of her younger brother Edward VI (or rather, that of his uncles and guardians) to an abrupt conclusion. When a shipful of refugees from the newly ascendant Catholic government in London sought refuge in Denmark, however, they found that any ecumenical sentiments which the Lutheran king, Christian III, might have possessed did not extend to harbouring those of the Reformed persuasion. Forced to sail on, their vessel became trapped in the ice off the coast of Wismar, and they were only rescued – and fed – by the efforts of a particularly hospitable group of local people. These, they found to their horror, were Anabaptists. For most of them, this could mean only one thing: the spectre of Münster. Nevertheless, their throats remained unslit, their wives unravished, their goods unmolested. The wickedness of their hosts did extend, however, to engagement in theological controversy. Even this started amicably enough at first, though it later became more acrimonious. The main point at issue was Menno's Hofmannite Christology, which Simons debated with Martin Micronius, one of their Dutch leaders. When it was all done, the guests went on their way, but the whole debate was reproduced in print (in variant versions, one by each of the respective participants, plus reflections and parting shots) two years later, in 1556. The result, *Reply to Martin Micron*, is one which even John C. Wenger, a modern Mennonite contributory editor of Simons' works, allows to be 'tedious and tiresome'.[16]

---

[16] M. Simons, *Complete Writings*, p. 836.

It was, however, the unedifying internal debate over the application of the ban which consumed Menno's last years, and many of his later tracts and letters are related to this vexed question in which, perhaps sadly, he inclined to the rigorist view which the southern brethren rejected and which was eventually to be repudiated even by the North Germans and Dutch after his death.

His wife had died in the mid-1550s, and when Menno himself died on 31st January 1561, one daughter and his only son had also predeceased him. He was in his mid-sixties, and for almost exactly a quarter of a century had eluded all the efforts of state and ecclesiastical authorities, both Protestant and Catholic, to capture him. His constant pastoral work, teaching and writing had brought the shattered remnants of the Melchiorite move-ment from the disaster of the mid-1530s, through recuperation, past the snares of spiritualism and Arianism, to a place of stability. The Anabaptist creature he left was rigid, perhaps, and legalistic, with a growing ghetto mentality which, in the long run, would dent the daring evangelistic thrust of the early years. But at least it was alive. And in the harsh climate of sixteenth-century Europe, that was no mean achievement.

Pilgram Marpeck

One other figure demands our attention in respect of reconstruct-ing the mess which had befallen so much of Anabaptism within a few years of its birth. Although he has received less historical recognition for it, Pilgram Marpeck played in some respects as significant a rôle in galvanizing evangelical South German Anabaptism as Menno did for that in the north. Perhaps the relative historical neglect is understandable. The situation that needed to be retrieved in the south was less catastrophic, less impressively awful, than that which the Münster calamity had bequeathed to such fragments of the Dutch and Low German Anabaptist movement as survived it. Even so, the persecution in Switzerland and the south had a drastic effect.

In 1528, Ludwig V, Elector Palatine, had instigated moves against religious radicals within his realms on the grounds that they were opposed to all secular, as well as religious, authority. Three hundred and fifty people, at a minimum, lost their lives in the wave of executions that followed, and when news spread that Jakob Hutter and his Tyrolean brethren had begun to establish Anabaptist communities in territories to the east, the possibility opened up of fleeing there. Faced thus with a choice between premature removal to heaven or a judicious one to Moravia, about twelve hundred Anabaptists from Ludwig V's territories chose – temporarily, at least – the latter. However, some Anabaptists returned instead, slowly and quietly, to the state churches, often after periods of less and less frequent Anabaptist meetings.

Persecution was not the only pressure. Many in south Germany had been followers of Hans Hut, who had prophesied a glorious – and probably violent – deliverance for the people of God within three and a half years of the Peasants' War. When this failed to materialize, many were disillusioned. The deaths, not only of Hut (who perished in prison in 1527), but also of a whole generation of leaders, evangelical and heterodox alike – Grebel, Mantz, Blaurock, Sattler, Hubmaier, Müntzer, Denck – between 1525 and 1529 could hardly have failed to discourage their various followers. When Hut died, however, the South German radicals were particularly badly affected. Not only did his prophecies fail to come true, but rather too many successors emerged to replace him and, although some of these were closer to biblicist evangelicalism than their predecessor had been, such a proliferation of leaders could not fail to make the movement increasingly disparate and disunited.

In the spring of 1528, the Augsburg authorities acted decisively against the movement there. When a remnant gathered in a field outside the city late in the summer, they agreed to suspend their meetings 'since the time was past during which God sufficiently revealed and verified true baptism'. As one historian comments, 'This action constituted, in effect, the official dissolution of the South German Anabaptist movement in the area.'[17] One might add that the wording of their decision is indicative of a spiritualist

---

[17] W.O. Packull, *Mysticism and the Early South German-Austrian Anabaptist Movement 1525–1531*, p. 127.

direction of thought; the 'true baptism' that had been on offer was, after all, not necessary.

Some, at least, of those who fled to Moravia found Jakob Hutter's fractious experiment in communal living which they found there so unlike heaven that they returned westward, and sought shelter in the Rhineland and in southern Germany. Thus it was that a new and different, more sober and chastened form of Anabaptism emerged in Augsburg and elsewhere during the 1530s and 1540s. Its relationship with the earlier movement was, perhaps, not so much one of 'direct evolution' as 'a new permutation'.[18] One of its most important leaders was the mining engineer Pilgram Marpeck.

Marpeck had been born about 1495 and brought up in Rattenberg, in the Austrian Tyrol. His family was wealthy, though not noble, and he had once lent the Archduke Ferdinand I a thousand guilders at 5 per cent interest *per annum*, as well as losing real estate to the value of 3,500 guilders when this was confiscated in 1528 because of his Anabaptism. Marpeck had come under suspicion for refusing to aid the authorities in their search for heretics among the local miners, over whom he was the magistrate.

It is possible that he had previously been influenced by Lutheranism, and certain that he later rejected it because of its 'fleshly liberty'.[19] His departure from the Tyrol was doubtless prompted by prudential considerations following the execution of a local leader, Leonhard Schiemer, on 15th January, 1528, and he made his way, like many another Anabaptist in trouble, to Strassburg. Here he stayed for four years, living openly as an Anabaptist and protected partly by the tolerant climate in the city, and partly by his value to the local economy as an engineer. Even so, he was imprisoned briefly in the autumn of 1531 for opposing infant baptism and for encouraging citizens not to take the oath of allegiance to the city. In the spring of 1532 he was banished, and his whereabouts for the next twelve years remain as much a mystery to historians as they did to contemporaries. He seems to have spent his time wandering around the southern German-

---

[18] *Ibid.*
[19] P. Marpeck, *The Writings of Pilgram Marpeck*, eds. Klassen and Klaassen, p. 22.

speaking lands, encouraging Anabaptist groups wherever he found them. It was not until 1544 that he found a permanent domicile in Augsburg.

The city appears to have done a tacit deal with Marpeck; in return for his invaluable abilities as a mining engineer and at least some degree of circumspection in his religious behaviour, the civic authorities would simply turn a blind eye to his Anabaptism. This somewhat irregular arrangement held for the remainder of Marpeck's life (he died in 1556). Sometimes a councillor or official who was too principled, or who was ignorant of this particular application of *Realpolitik*, would make a protest and the city council would dutifully relay its displeasure to the chief engineer, as happened on at least four occasions. But always action was limited to a verbal rap across the knuckles. The engineer was too precious to the city's wellbeing to expel or imprison; Marpeck's survival was a triumph of indispensability over principle. And as a resident of Augsburg, he was able to lead and guide the Anabaptists, not only of that city but, through his writings, many far beyond.

Although it may be argued that Marpeck's thought 'was more indebted to German mysticism and [the spiritualist] Hans Denck than to the Swiss or Schleitheim', the effect of his work was nevertheless to strengthen evangelical Anabaptism in an area where it had been gravely weakened by division, persecution and the discouragement of failed prophecies and disappointed apocalypticism.[20]

His first works were written in 1531, while still resident in Strassburg. These were directed against the spiritualists' insistence that 'because of the death of the apostles, there is no longer any command or witness of the Scriptures concerning ceremonies such as baptism and the Lord's Supper' and that consequently 'these practices fall away'.[21] Marpeck urged the evangelical line that it was not only possible, but urgently necessary to restore the true church.

In Marpeck's view, his own day was a mirror of the days of Ezra and Nehemiah; just as the Jews had been taken into

---

[20]   C.A. Snyder, *Anabaptist History and Theology*, p. 78.
[21]   Marpeck, *Writings*, p. 47.

captivity, and had then returned to restore Jerusalem, so the church had fallen[22] and was now being restored:

> Just as the Israelites, rescued out of Babylonian captivity (Ezra 2), restored the ancient ceremonies, so too does Christ today, through his servants rescued out of the prison of the [Roman] Antichrist, restore and renew his instituted ceremonies (Acts 3) by means of His inner command and His bestowal of the certainty of His Spirit.
>   Similarly, because of the apostasy of the same Jerusalemites (2 Thess. 2), Christ is again restoring the spiritual Jerusalem.

Neither did Marpeck have any of Philips' reticence about locating this restoration, faithfully to Acts 3:21, in eschatological perspective:

> As then, so now, by breathing on his disciples and directing the shining brilliance of His countenance toward His spiritual Jerusalem, Christ will accomplish what He has promised, the revelation of His glory by means of His physical return (Lk. 21). To prepare for His coming, the King, Christ, has already begun to send ahead messengers who will ensure that His temple and the city of Jerusalem are purified and cleansed of all abuses of His commands, laws, and ceremonies. [23]

The whole thrust of Marpeck's first writing, his *A Clear Refutation* of 1531, was against the erring spiritualists who denied 'that restitution is called for at this time'.[24]

The disaster at Münster in 1535 had affected Anabaptists everywhere and of all kinds. For this reason, it is doubly interesting that Marpeck was not afraid to borrow extensively, for his major work on baptism and the Lord's supper, from Bernhard Rothmann, one of the theological architects of that ill-fated New Jerusalem. Rothmann's book *Bekenntnisse* had been published in 1533, a few months before the takeover by Jan Matthijs and his accomplices. About two-thirds of Marpeck's *Admonition* of 1542 is, in fact, taken (though often amended) from Rothmann's work. Certainly Marpeck held no sympathy for Rothmann's cause; he considered that 'Satan raised up' the Münsterites 'in

---

[22] Luther had evoked this biblical image with the title of his tract *The Babylonian Captivity of the Church*. His vision, however, was of renewal or reformation of the existing structures of Christendom, rather than of a restoration of the primitive church.

[23] Marpeck, *Writings*, pp. 46–7.

[24] The authorship of this work has been questioned, but there is now general agreement that it is by Marpeck. See *ibid.*, pp. 43–4, 569.

order to confuse and disrupt the true baptism of Christ'. True Christians should be pacifists: 'There need be no external power or sword, for the kingdom of Christ is not of this world. Thus, no true Christian needs to occupy or defend either city, land or people.'[25] Perhaps Marpeck considered Rothmann's reasoning on the sacraments in the *Bekenntnisse* to be sound enough, and had no more concern about using such a tainted source than he would have had about 'meat sacrificed to idols' (1 Cor. 8).

But Marpeck was no small-minded legalist in any case. He wrote sharply against the Swiss Brethren for their illiberal use of the ban, urging that Christ has made people truly free, and then had to defend himself – predictably – against the counter-charge that he was encouraging Christians to behave exactly as they pleased. One of his illustrations was directed against overly rigid observation of the Sabbath.

* * *

As with Menno, so with Pilgram. His ministry was more consolidatory than visionary. The day of revolutionary rhetoric and sudden growth was past; stability was at a premium. It is to Marpeck's credit that he helped salvage much of what remained of South German Anabaptism and escaped, more successfully than his counterparts in the north, the tendency to excessive legalism. The fact that, unlike Menno Simons, he left no great movement bearing his name should not obscure the importance of his achievement.

At least five thousand Anabaptists were put to death for their faith during the course of the sixteenth century. Hounded and persecuted, the Mennonites tended to move eastwards, some reaching the area around Danzig as early as the 1540s. Towards the end of the eighteenth century, many accepted the invitation of Catherine the Great to settle in Russia, where many became quite prosperous farmers.

The situation in the Netherlands eased after that country won its independence from Spain in a long and bitter war, which lasted from the 1560s until 1648, with a twelve-year intermission

---

[25] *Ibid.*, p. 209.

from 1609 to 1621. The circumstances of the war forced the Dutch to allow, in effect, religious toleration, and by the early decades of the seventeenth century some areas had as much as 25 per cent of the population adhering to Anabaptism.

The easing of persecution in the Netherlands afforded the possibility of leisure for, among other things, a more exact recording of the times of trial. The Anabaptists' sufferings had been recorded before, during the heat itself, but Thieleman van Braght (1625–64), a Mennonite elder of Dordrecht, built and improved upon these in producing his monumental *Martyrs Mirror* in 1660. This immense work was compiled, like the work of the Englishman John Foxe, from original correspondence, civic archives and court records. However, unlike Foxe's *Acts and Monuments* (better known as the *Book of Martyrs*), van Braght was writing some time after the central acts of the dramas he portrayed, and after the heroic age of Anabaptist martyrdom was past, in his own country, at least. Certainly his book has a strong Dutch orientation and, apart from the early years, is little concerned with Swiss or South German martyrs. It is an irony, perhaps, that van Braght's haven of peace produced such an enduring classic of Christian witness and suffering.

An alternative destination for those Anabaptists elsewhere, who continued to endure pressure from the authorities, was to remove to the New World. Their first permanent settlement was in Germantown, Pennsylvania in 1683, and numbers grew thereafter. Many Swiss Anabaptists, eventually accepting the 'Mennonite' label, came around 1700, and later settled parts of Canada and the American Midwest. In the nineteenth and twentieth centuries, they were joined by their brethren from Russia.

Today the Mennonites number slightly over one million adherents, under half of them living in North America. If such statistics leave the heirs of the Anabaptist vision in possession of only a modest numerical presence on the world stage, it is nevertheless a lot more than the bare survival for which Menno and Pilgram laboured. And when one bears in mind that Anabaptism continues to have a moral and theological influence well beyond its own ranks, then the magnitude of that legacy becomes more impressive still.

Chapter Seven

'Men sitting upon their Ale Benches': Radicalism in Mid-Tudor England

We now turn to the vexed question of whether or not Anabaptism made any impression upon England. Both the facts and their interpretation are matters of dispute. A number of recent historians claim to discern Anabaptist influences upon Elizabethan separatism and upon the genesis of the different species of English Baptists in the seventeenth century. Other scholars reject such findings as so many clouds in the coffee. But these questions are dragons to be slain in future chapters. What concerns us here is whether Anabaptism was present at all in sixteenth-century England – and, of course, in the most literal sense, it was.

In the 1530s, many Dutch Melchiorites had fled to England, a fact we have already had occasion to notice. However, the nature of the welcome that awaited them had encouraged many, like Anneken Jansdochter, to flee back again. Twenty or so were arrested in London in 1535, about half a dozen of whom were burned. As early as 1532, a 22-year-old Dutchman, Peter Franke, was burned at Colchester for his Anabaptism; both his martyrdom and the life that preceded it appear to have made a deep impression on those who witnessed them. [1]

The Dutch radical presence in England seems to have persisted throughout the century. Indeed, any other state of affairs would have been surprising; the wool trade across the channel had been the country's chief export business for centuries, and the Dutch and Flemish expatriate communities in London and the south-

---

[1] J. Bale, *A Mysterye of inyquyte*, Hvi^v-viii^r.

east counties were quite large. The existence of these communities necessitated that the Protestant governments of Edward VI (1547–53) and Elizabeth I (1558–1603) permit the establishment of 'Strangers' Churches' (in communion with, but distinct from, the Church of England) in order to meet their spiritual needs and to keep their Protestanism within uniform bounds. Even so, such churches tended to be more full-blooded in their expressions of Reformed Protestantism than the insipid variety on offer in the parish churches, and a succession of English governments felt it necessary to insist that such services were for the benefit of the expatriate community only.

But even among the crowd of Reformed Protestants of the sort English governments more or less approved, there always lurked, as the ecclesiastical authorities justly feared, a number whose Anabaptism or radicalism threatened to infect the native population. Martin Micronius, one of the superintendents of the officially sanctioned Dutch church in London in 1550, thought it 'a matter of the first importance . . . to guard against the heresies which are introduced by our countrymen'.[2] Yet, a quarter of a century later, on Easter Day 1575, the Elizabethan authorities in London still found themselves rounding up Dutch Anabaptists. Twenty-five were apprehended, of whom five were persuaded to recant, fourteen women and a young boy were deported (the latter after a public flogging) and the remaining five kept in prison under threat of burning. Of these one, Christiaen Temels, died after a week in the filthy and verminous hospitality provided for them, and two, Jan Pieterss and Hendrick Terwoort, were burned in Smithfield on 22nd July.[3] When these latter were told of their impending fate and asked if they wished for postponement (the authorities preferring recantations secured by terror to unnecessary combustion), Terwoort answered laconically that, if they had to be burned, his persecutors should 'make haste in the matter, for we would rather die than live, that we may be delivered from this dreadful vermin'.[4]

---

[2] H. Robinson ed., *Original Letters Relative to the English Reformation*, ii., p. 560.
[3] van Braght, *Martyrs Mirror*, pp. 1008–24.
[4] *Ibid.*, p. 1010.

But what of actual English Anabaptists, as opposed to Dutch refugees? Against the scholarly proponents of the existence of such an entity, it has to be said that the identification of specific examples is notoriously difficult. Arrested along with the group in 1575 was one Englishman, known to us only by his initials as 'S.B.'. He appears to have been a hanger-on, however, rather than a fully integrated member of the group. Indeed, it is not even certain that he had actually been baptized as a believer though, by the same token, one might argue with equal justice that there is no evidence that he had not been so baptized.

Back in 1532, when two Flemish Anabaptists had been arrested in London for importing 'books of the Anabaptists' Confession' (Schleitheim?), six Englishmen had been seized along with them, though what became of them is unknown. At least one of the Flemings and one of the Englishmen were discovered to hold 'strange' and 'damnable' opinions concerning the incarnation, references probably best understood as the response of baffled authority confronted by defenders of Hofmannite Christology.[5]

Although it is certain that imported ideas, notably the deviant Christology peculiar to the Dutch variety of Anabaptism, took root amongst English radicals, examples of actual indigenous Anabaptism are much harder to verify. The problem is compounded by the confusing tendency of contemporaries to use the term with reference to radicals generally – regardless of whether or not the people in question actually practised or espoused believers' baptism, or even denied the validity of infant baptism. In the mouths of mid-sixteenth-century English people, the term 'anabaptism' denoted simply a form of religious profes-sion more radical, or 'left-wing', than the speaker approved of or felt comfortable with. In that sense, it was similar to a word like 'fundamentalism' today, which originally had a specific meaning, but which since the 1970s has simply been a term of abuse denoting a form of religious belief more conservative than that of which the person using it approves.

Those of us studying the picture from a vantage point four and a half centuries removed may note the propensity of

---

[5]   J.S. Brewer, J. Gairdner, R.H. Brodie eds., *Letters and Papers, Foreign and Domestic, of the Reign of Henry VIII*, 1, i., p. 809.

contemporaries to bandy the word 'anabaptist' around in this declamatory fashion, but we do ourselves no service by following their usage. Unless, of course, we wish to identify more 'Anabaptism' in mid-Tudor England than could possibly be held to have existed otherwise.[6]

The most we can say is that there were in England a fair number of fellow-travellers with continental Anabaptism. The following was neither particularly large nor organized, and what there was tended to centre around various local leaders, almost none of whom were educated beyond the level of basic literacy. Jean Veron, a French reformer in London in the 1560s at the behest of the Elizabethan government to assist the newly re-protestantised national church, felt able to dismiss all radicals contemptuously as 'these men sitting upon their ale benches'.[7]

The theologies of the various groups of English radicals were, to say the least, somewhat inchoate, not to say inconsistent. What they do demonstrate, however, is a willingness on the part of some ordinary people to overturn ecclesiastical domination and to make their own decisions about Christian life, doctrine and church polity. Most importantly, the general drift of those decisions pointed in the direction of a believers' church, that is, away from the concept of Christendom, and towards the idea of church as (in the sociological sense) sect.

The majority of the mid-Tudor radicals seem to have been offshoots of native English Lollardy, or even internal developments within the various existing Lollard groups. Many Lollards were unimpressed by the Reformation that was being introduced by the English state; they had grown accustomed over more than a century to a sectarian existence as a scattering of gathered churches, and as such were ill-disposed to the kind of compromises – not to mention the theological sophistication – that inevitably attended state-sponsored religious changes designed to carry along the bulk of the population. Theological theory has

[6] Already, alas, I am betraying my own interest in these disputes; my book on this subject, so little known as to be almost confidential, *Between Known Men and Visible Saints*, examines the mid-Tudor radicals in more detail than can be given here. My assessment of their treatment at the hands of my fellow historians is dealt with there on pp. 228–34 and elsewhere.

[7] J. Veron, *An Apologye or defence of the doctryne of Predestination*, Bviii^v.

a habit of catching up, sooner or later, with established practice, and this phenomenon was certainly observable amongst the *de facto* sectarians who constituted late Lollardy; an emphasis upon practical discipleship and the following of dominical precepts had long since displaced Wycliffe's insistence on predestination and the control of the church by the prince as the dominant religious concerns of ordinary Lollards.

Henry Hart and the Freewillers

Perhaps these developments are best exhibited by the group – or groups – who found their leadership and inspiration in the character of Henry Hart, a moderately prosperous tradesman of Pluckley, in Kent.[8] Collectively known as the freewillers, or free-will men, Hart's associates were drawn almost entirely from areas of established Lollard strength in the Kent and Essex villages and small towns connected with the wool trade. His immediate circle was drawn from the triangle of mid-Kent determined by the towns of Maidstone, Faversham and Ashford, and flourished from the late 1530s until his death in 1557 or 1558. Undeterred by his prosecution in 1538 for holding conventicles, Hart continued to operate and, when the harsh régime of Henry VIII was replaced in 1547 by the more determinedly Protestant governments of the young Edward VI and his caretakers, he ventured into print.

Neither his first effort, *A godly new short treatise* of 1548, nor his second, *A consultory for all Christians, to beware lest they bear the name of Christians in vain* of the following year, was ever intended to be judged on its literary merits. Both works are rambling and tedious. It is unrealistic, perhaps, to expect sixteenth-century sentences to conform to the pattern of internal coherence that obtained in English prose for several centuries down to the 1960s, before 'improvers' got to work on our schools.

---

[8]   C.J. Clement offers evidence (*Religious Radicalism in England 1535–1565*, pp. 185–6) to suggest, very plausibly, that Hart may have been a carpenter based, for long periods of his life, in Westminster. If correct, this hypothesis would explain a number of biographical details.

In that sense, Hart might almost be a product of the current education systems in English-speaking countries: sentences are long and rambling, without any grammatical structure, and tend to lose themselves in a labyrinth of clauses and subsidiary points. There is no structure or logical progression in his argument; as the reader emerges, dripping with verbiage, from the final page, the most that he or she would be able to report about Hart's mind is that he wished his readers to live godly lives for the sake of their souls. To be sure, I have marked worse essays than Hart's, but only a few.

The very mediocrity – or worse – of Hart's writings, and his apparent inability to press home any specific theological point with consistency, spared him the danger of trouble with the authorities on account of them. What could not so easily be overlooked was his persistence in holding illegal religious gatherings, or conventicles. At Christmas, 1550, along with a goodly number of his followers from Kent, he travelled to visit a like-minded group of people in the Bocking area of Essex. But when sixty of them crowded into the house of a cloth merchant, Thomas Upchard, for worship and discussion, detection was relatively simple, and a number of them appeared the following month before the Privy Council (effectively the government of England) to answer for their activities.

It is at this hearing that the distinctive doctrinal emphases of the group – and of Hart's influence upon them – become apparent. One after another, the arrested conventiclers testified that 'Henry Hart said . . .', before going on to describe some complaint against established religion and its doctrines. The most important concerns to surface were anti-intellectualism and free-will.

According to the arrested men (no women had been kept in custody on this occasion, although they had been present in Upchard's house), Hart maintained that no faith was to be built upon human learning, for all errors were brought in by the learned. Apart from vindicating his own ignorance, this emphasis had the effect of keeping control out of the hands of an educated élite. Possibly this worked in the direction of egalitarianism and the active participation of all (the faithful gathered in Upchard's house are recorded as having debated amongst themselves); possibly it simply delivered control into the hands of those who, like Hart himself, were possessed of personal charisma.

The Reformed doctrine of predestination was a prime case in point of the sort of thing to which Hart and his fellows objected so strongly. It was a philosophical proposition which, despite having a certain intellectual appeal, was clearly repugnant to common-sense morality. It had also been given recent prominence by the officially sponsored – and learned – protestantisers of England. One of the conventiclers held that it was a doctrine more suitable for devils than for Christians, and Hart was said to have taught that there was no man so chosen that he could not damn himself, nor any so reprobated but that he could not keep God's commandments. Another conventicler, Humphrey Middleton, said that all the people in Adam's loins were predestined to be saved and that there were no reprobates.[9] This, of course, implied a denial of Augustine's doctrine of original sin, a point made explicit by one of the most highly educated members of the group, Thomas Cole, a Cambridge graduate and the first headmaster of Maidstone Grammar School, who some two years later was pressured by the authorities into preaching a sermon of recantation before Archbishop Cranmer.[10]

One phrase used by John Plume, from the Kentish village of Lenham, makes the group's Lollard background abundantly clear: he affirmed that it was a general doctrine of the group that 'they ought not to salute a sinner or a man whom they know not'. (Special greetings were to be reserved for 'known men'.) Another man, Nicholas Young, said that they 'would not communicate [i.e. take communion] with sinners'. These last two remarks clearly reflect the essentially sectarian self-image of Hart's group; it was to consist of the committed alone. In this, their concerns run parallel with Anabaptism, a movement which was also generally opposed to Reformed doctrines of predestination and to Augustinian conceptions of original sin.

---

[9] C. Burrage, *Early English Dissenters*, ii., p. 1–4.
[10] T. Cole, *A godly and frutefull sermon*; M. Pearse, *Between Known Men and Visible Saints*, pp. 36–9.

Hart himself appears to have eluded arrest, although it is by
no means clear how he did so; his home village was well known
and Cranmer (if he had a long enough memory) would have
known of Hart's previous brush with the authorities, for he had
mentioned him in that connection, in a letter of 1538, to Thomas
Cromwell.[11] Several of them were sentenced to prison where one
of their number, John Ledley, was dead by the following
August.[12] However, Hart and several of his followers were to
surface again in the even more hostile climate of Mary I's reign.

During this latter spell in the limelight, Hart's place was
supplanted to some extent by John Trew of Sussex. Trew and a
group of other freewillers had been arrested in 1555 and kept
in the King's Bench prison in London, where Bishop Bonner
and his officials sought to persuade them, mostly by threats of
incineration, to recant. (Bonner was to feature as the arch-
villain in Foxe's *Book Of Martyrs*, after the Bible the most-read
book in Elizabethan and seventeenth-century England, which
meticulously chronicled Catholic persecutions of Protestants.)

In prison the freewillers encountered their erstwhile opponents,
the Reformed state-church Protestants of Edward VI's reign. Both
sides were presented with a dilemma: should they have nothing to
do with one another, as befitted their previous relationship as
persecutors and persecuted? Or should they put up a show of
Protestant unity so as not to give encouragement to the Catholic
authorities who were now persecuting all 'heretics' without
distinction?

In the main, the two parties tried to do both things at once,
putting up a front of unanimity to their inquisitors whilst arguing
furiously amongst themselves. The results would have made an
excellent Hollywood drama. The bishop and his officials were
hardly deceived, and even less likely to have been converted from
popery by the unedifying prospect of their captives blatantly lying
to them regarding their own internal divisions. The two parties
wrote tracts and letters, both to one another and to their supporters
outside the prison walls, made attempts to patch up their differences, and came within a hairsbreadth of organizing joint com-

---

[11] T. Cranmer, *Works*, ii., p. 367.
[12] M.T. Pearse, *Between Known Men and Visible Saints*, p. 28.

munion before Christmas 1555. But then the whole argument started off again with mutual recriminations of bad faith.

This time the core of their argument was concerned with predestination and free-will. The Reformed argued that the radicals were effectively Pelagian; that is, they were effectively seeking salvation by works. This argument was plainly unfair in respect of John Trew and many of the others, who repeatedly stated their belief in justification by faith in quite unequivocal terms. But the accusation was hardly wide of the mark when applied to Henry Hart himself.

Hart was in danger of being reduced to the status of a bystander during all this furore. For some inexplicable reason he had evaded capture, even though Bishop Bonner had learned from an informant precisely where in London the leading freewiller was lodging. However, Hart kept in close contact with the radical party in prison and was drawn into debate with John Bradford, the former royal chaplain and easily the best man on either side of the unseemly squabble.[13] By this means, by his contacts with other prisoners in Newgate, and perhaps by his drawing up of a confession of faith of thirteen articles (now lost), Hart succeeded in maintaining his position as 'the principal of all those that are called free-will men'.[14] He may also have been helped in retaining his predominant position by the removal from the scene of John Trew, who escaped from the King's Bench in the summer of 1556, an action that was considered discreditable by his opponents.

Although a number of his fellows became martyrs, Hart himself was never so much as captured, though a warrant was issued for his arrest in the early months of 1558. When an attempt was made to enforce it in Pluckley (had he returned from London?), the official wrote a terse comment in the margin to the effect that Hart was already dead. He had indeed died intestate, and his son John was named that March as the administrator of his property (though he himself was to die within fifteen months).

---

[13] A complete edition of Bradford's writings, notable for their gentle spirit and charity, was published by the Parker Society in 1848 and 1853, and it is these two volumes which have been reprinted in recent decades by the Banner of Truth Trust.

[14] J. Foxe, *The Acts and Monuments*, viii., p. 384.

Hart's group of radicals died with him. The severity of the persecution under Mary and the constant pressure from state-church Protestants who, being educated, could usually outwit them in debate, was more than such a small and unsophisticated group could withstand in the long run. Nevertheless, Hart certainly made an impact upon the public consciousness of the age in which he lived. Official opinion seems to have regarded him as more dangerous than any other single radical with the exception of Joan Bocher. And to the story of this remarkable woman we now turn.

Joan Bocher

The year of Joan Bocher's birth is not known. From the fact that she was described as 'Mother Bocher, widow' at the time of her first arrest in 1527, we may conjecture a date sometime in the 1480s since, though the misfortune of widowhood might occur at any age, the quasi-respectful epithet 'Mother' would hardly be appropriate to a woman much under forty. At that time she was living at Steeple Bumpstead, in an area of Essex long known for Lollardy, and had been holding conventicles in her house. She was accused of all the usual Lollard stuff: heresies against the sacrament (denying transubstantiation) together with the denunciation both of pilgrimages and the issuing of pardons by the church. William Bocher was arrested at the same time. If he was her son, then Joan's widowhood had been caused by a previous bout of persecution, for William's father is reported as having been put to death for similar heresies. On this occasion, she recanted, as Lollards frequently did . . . before returning promptly to their own practices and beliefs.

The next time we hear of Joan, in 1541, she was living in Frittenden, Kent, and had been arrested for breaking the Easter fast, according to which no meat was to be eaten. Clearly a woman of iron constitution, she had been consuming a calf's head. She had also been criticizing other aspects of traditionalist religion in a way typical of old Lollardy and new Protestantism alike.

Henry VIII's later years were characterized by an increasing insistence on traditional Catholic practices, even though the country had formally broken with Rome a decade before. Henry may have wanted to be master in his own house, but he was no Protestant, and the would-be reformers who had helped him in his ecclesiastical enterprises had to bide their time and smile sweetly in the hope that an opportunity for real Protestantism would come about in due course. In the meantime, they tried to shield Protestants and Lollards of whatever type – as long as they were not explicitly Anabaptists or Christological deviants – from the wrath of official policy. They did so now. Archbishop Cranmer and his commissary Dr. Nevinson blatantly twisted the rules to get Bocher released in 1543, much to the fury of the conservative Kentish gentry, who saw her as a troublemaker.

By the time of these disturbances in the early 1540s she had remarried, although apparently continuing to be known by the name of Bocher. She had been at a friend's house when discovered perpetrating her culinary indelicacy, with her husband apparently nowhere around. Indeed, he even gave information to one informant of a nature which could have harmed Joan's efforts to be released. When she was finally let out she stayed, not with him, but with friends in Canterbury. One wonders what sort of a marriage this was.

It is from this period of her activities that she picked up the name frequently used of her by enemies: Joan of Kent. Although her name was seldom bracketed with his, the sphere of her operations overlapped to such a large degree with that of Henry Hart that it is almost inconceivable that the two never met (notwithstanding the absence of any direct statement that they did in fact do so). It is certain that they had friends and contacts in common.

The events that established Joan's fame – or notoriety – were those which led up to her death, in May 1550, as one of only two radicals to be executed for their opinions during the reign of Edward VI. (We have noticed above, however, that John Ledley died as a result of his imprisonment and so counts, perhaps, as a third.)

In 1549 she was arrested in London, along with a number of others, on a charge of holding heretical opinions concerning the

incarnation. These amounted to a version of Hofmannite Christology, which raises the whole question of where she had come by
such views. The only hesitation in ascribing them to Anabaptist
influence must come from the fact that there had been isolated
incidents of similar teaching before the Reformation, both
amongst English Lollards and in the Netherlands. However, one
of those captured with Joan (and who later recanted) was a Dutch
butcher by the name of Michael Thombe, who also stood accused
of denouncing infant baptism. From the fact that Bocher was not
charged with the latter opinion, we can be certain that she had
not advanced to actual Anabaptism; there would have been no
question of leaving such a stone unturned.

As it was, she refused to recant the Christological heresies of
which she stood charged. Numerous attempts were made to
persuade her to recant, and some of the leading Protestant
churchmen in the country disputed with her in private. She
withstood them all and, on 2nd May 1550, she was burned at
Smithfield. One Catholic polemicist, writing a few years later in
Mary's reign, says that she denounced the official preacher at her
execution and claimed that there were a thousand Londoners in
her sect.

This last point is often repeated, especially by those who wish
to 'talk up' the strength of radicalism, and to take at face value
contemporary hyperbolic descriptions of Joan Bocher as an
'anabaptist'. The remark attributed to her, however, may well be
entirely apocryphal. But even if she did make it, the figure of a
thousand is itself likely to have been hyperbole. What is certain
is that no large organized sectarian grouping of that size existed
in the capital or anywhere else. It is entirely likely that there were
several hundred sympathizers with radical opinions in
Edwardian London, but that radicalism was multi-faceted and
uncoordinated. If we were able – and we are not – to add up the
Dutch and other immigrants who may have adhered to one or
other of the varieties of Anabaptism, their English fellow-travellers, and groups of Lollard background such as Hart's and
Bocher's, the total would certainly run well into three figures,
and perhaps to the requisite four. Nevertheless, the spectre of a
thousand organized and united radicals in the mid-sixteenth-
century capital is a bogeyman – useful to officialdom in justifying

the urgency of speedy repression, useful perhaps to radicals exaggerating their own strength, and, finally, useful to romantically inclined historians, who may wish to discern a more significant Radical Reformation presence in England than, however sadly, was really present.[15]

Robert Cooche: a Genuine English Anabaptist

If we cannot even give a name to those (possible) English Anabaptists who were arrested with their Dutch fellow-workers in the 1530s, and are ignorant of anything more than the initials of the 'S.B.' who endured imprisonment in 1575, there is at least one English Anabaptist about whom we have considerably more information. Even in the case of Robert Cooche, however, his birth and death dates remain hidden in a shroud of mystery, as do his place of origin, his education and his early career. What is known is that he worked in the wine cellar of Queen Catherine Parr, Henry VIII's last wife, and that he later became a singer in the royal chapel, probably that of Edward VI, and certainly that of Elizabeth I. This was, of course, extremely unusual for an Anabaptist; not only was he in a position of great danger, but even his attendance at – let alone his active participation in – the rites of the established church entailed a certain degree of compromise, to put the matter at its mildest.

Whether or not Cooche had a following of any size may be questioned; the only evidence for it is the vague references to 'your bewitched scholars' and 'certain unlearned simple men' made by a Church of England clergyman.[16] Assuming that he did have a number of followers, they do not appear to have been highly organized or particularly numerous, having left no records and eluded the authorities. One suspects that, if Cooche was known about by prominent people such as William Turner, the Dean of Wells, his show would quickly have been closed down if it had attained any size or solidity. In fact, Cooche appears to

[15] For points mentioned here – especially contentious ones – concerning Joan Bocher, see M.T. Pearse, *Between Known Men and Visible Saints*, pp. 81–97.
[16] W. Turner, *A preseruatiue, or triacle*, Gvij[r], Mvij[v].

have been little more than an idiosyncratic maverick, and as such little threat to established order.

A professed Anabaptist who had no objection to singing in the royal chapel was an unusual enough specimen. This one does not appear to have had contacts with immigrant radicals or to have had any interest in the dissident Christologies which held such a fascination for the Dutch branch of the Anabaptist movement. It may be that Cooche was very much a lone operator.

Our first knowledge of Cooche comes from a letter written to him, in December 1551, by Pietro Martire Vermigli (known in English as Peter Martyr), the Italian Reformed scholar who had been appointed Regius Professor of Divinity in Oxford. It is clear from the contents that Martyr was replying to a previous missive from Cooche, in which the latter had queried the practice of infant baptism, and that the correspondence was a continuation of a debate they had had orally at a previous meeting. The debate was on a very high level relative to what was usual amongst the English radicals: the evidences of early church history were freely deployed by both sides, and the merits of contemporary theologians were discussed. Martyr's main point in favour of infant baptism was the doctrine of original sin.

It seems that Cooche was swayed by the logic of Martyr's argument, but not in the direction the latter would have wished. When Cooche next comes to light, in early 1552, we find him in dispute with William Turner, the Dean of Wells, and this time he is attacking both infant baptism *and* original sin. On this occasion, Turner appealed to the Reformed doctrine of predestination as a defence against Cooche on both counts. If Cooche was the author of a tract written later in the decade, during Mary's reign, entitled *The confutation of the errors of the careless by necessity*, an authorship which most historians have assumed,[17] then he had been moved by Turner's logic in the same way as he had been affected by Martyr's, for the work is an attack upon Calvinism as the creed of coercive state churches, and also an inducement to lax morals. Cooche's slow

---

[17] There is no direct evidence that Cooche is the author, but the circumstantial evidence is, perhaps, not unreasonable. See my arguments in *Between Known Men and Visible Saints*, pp. 127–8, 132–5.

progression in doctrine is, perhaps, further evidence that he was not in contact with the foreign Anabaptist mainstream, for had he been so he would have taken on board such ideas as a package, without the need to have his theology developed for him on these issues by the pressure of polemics from his opponents.

Cooche's Anabaptism, in any case, does not seem to have endured. John Parkhurst, the Elizabethan Bishop of Norwich, wrote to Rudolph Gualter, the Zürich reformer, in 1575, describing Cooche as having abandoned his heresies 'a few years ago'.[18] He still, however, continued to raise all sorts of religious queries (for example, about the proper method of celebrating communion) in a manner that appears to have been designed to show off his own erudition as much as anything else.[19] Unfortunately Cooche, the sole identifiable English person whose Anabaptism was unequivocal (rather than mere name-calling), seems on closer inspection to have been something of an odd-ball, rather than a representative of some noble and sacrificial underground movement.

John Champneys

John Champneys, a native of Somerset who had moved to London, is rather harder to categorize than Henry Hart and Joan Bocher, who were clearly coming from a background of Lollardy, or than Robert Cooche, who was a maverick attracted by Anabaptism. Champneys does not fit neatly into either camp and, were it not for the fact that a number of people were prepared to put up a fairly substantial amount of bail for him when he was arrested for having presumed to criticize the Edwardian Protestant church in print in 1548, we might be justified in assuming that he was an isolated individual of radical opinions.

The title of his book, *The Harvest is at Hand*, indicates an apocalyptic expectancy on the part of the author. Such an

---

[18]   C. Burrage, *Early English Dissenters*, ii., p. 8.
[19]   H. Robinson ed., *The Zürich Letters*, ii., p. 236–7.

expectancy is indeed present, but it is not the only, nor even the main, theme of the book. Above all, Champneys was outraged that so many clergymen who had served the Roman Catholic church before the Reformation, or Henrician Catholicism up until the death of the old tyrant in 1547 – and had hence persecuted Protestants – should now be permitted to continue in office. The Edwardian Reformation went neither far enough nor fast enough for Champneys. In that sense, he could be dismissed as a Puritan-before-Puritanism, a sort of lower-class equivalent of John Hooper, the forthright Edwardian Bishop of Gloucester, who similarly anticipated the kind of protests that would break out on a larger scale during Elizabeth's reign. Champneys, however, advocated a number of doctrines that were hardly compatible with a state church at all, and therefore deserves to be classified with other true radicals.

In the first place, Champneys declared that the real meaning of Scripture is revealed only to true believers on the basis of its 'true literal sense'. He profoundly mistrusted the application of learning to the study of the text so as to bring forth an exegesis apparently at odds with its plain meaning; indeed, he mistrusted the application of learning for any purpose whatsoever. He spoke of the imminent appearance of the Lord to destroy the godless. He also believed (in a manner not dissimilar to Wesley some two centuries later) in an experience of sanctification subsequent to faith, an experience which could lead on to a sinless life.

Most important of all, he believed that 'the gospel has been much persecuted and hated ever since the apostles' time, so that no man might be suffered openly to follow it', and that the saved, whose identity was discernible, were 'but a small number in comparison to the multitude'.[20] Such teachings clearly pointed in the direction of Christianity as a minority ethic and away from any notion of its being an inclusivist form of social regulation. And if the author could not see this point, Archbishop Cranmer could. Champneys was arrested within weeks of his publication appearing, and was forced to recant. As part of his penance he was required to do his utmost to retrieve all copies of the book and yield them up to the authorities for destruction. Fortunately,

---

[20] J. Champneys, *The Harvest is at Hand*, Bii[r], Dv[r], Ciii[r–v].

he proved unequal to the unwelcome task, and at least three copies have survived down to the present.[21]

Champneys survived into Elizabeth's reign (how he passed the years of Catholicism under Mary I is unknown) and in 1561 he published a work attacking the predestinarianism of Jean Veron. Champneys was familiar with the sort of official welcome accorded to authors who expressed their opinions without permission of the censor, and so, on this occasion, he published his book anonymously. But somehow, the printer was caught and Champney's identity divulged. Veron dashed off an indignant defence of the divine decrees, replete with mocking excoriations of 'this high divine'. 'Who would have thought so much divinity to be in Champneys', he asked, as to be able to engage in theological controversy at all?[22] But although he now stood in danger of arrest once again, no record survives of Champneys' actually having been apprehended; on this occasion, he appears to have got clean away.

Perhaps it was because the destruction of the offending tracts was not, this time, left to the author that no surviving copy remains. Doubtless Champneys had indeed written, in essence, what Veron said he had, but our ability to assess the strength of his arguments or the literary merits of his work fails us.

And, with his escape from a second arrest, Champneys himself eludes our grasp as well. Nothing further is known about his career, or of the time and circumstances of his death. Like Robert Cooche, like 'S.B.', like so much of the English Radical Reformation, Champneys took his leaf from Melchizedek and has left nothing more than a few salient details about his spiritual career; those of us who come after must glean what we can, and will, if we are wise, avoid building too many large theories on so slender a foundation.

---

[21] Although – if one might be permitted an acidic comment – the succeeding genera - tions of curators and librarians might as well have spared their efforts; most historians who mention Champneys have made their pronouncements solely on the basis of the legal charges drawn up against him, and appear to have left the book itself to gather dust. C.J. Clement (*Religious Radicalism in England 1535–1565*, pp. 73–94), however, provides an excellent commentary.

[22] J. Veron, *An Apologye or defence of the doctryne of Predestination*, Evi[r].

'The Secret Land' of Hendrik Niclaes: the Family of Love

No survey of the Radical Reformation in England would be complete without saying something about the Family of Love. From the late 1570s (when the ecclesiastical authorities first began to pay attention to the group's existence) until the first decades of the seventeenth century, the Familists were held up as a phantom to frighten others; they were dreaded for their deviousness and skill at eluding detection, at giving evasive answers, and for their downright mendacity.

Certainly the Family of Love appears to have been the largest single sectarian grouping in Elizabethan England. Lying as they did well beyond the bounds of theological orthodoxy, the impulse to ignore these Moonies *avant la lettre* is understandable. The Familists' numerical strength, however, makes their inclusion in our history a matter of integrity; in any case, their very similarity to modern cults is itself highly illuminating.

The actual beliefs of the Family of Love are, when it comes down to it, extremely difficult to describe, not so much because of a paucity of information available to historians, as because of the cloudy and elusive nature of the beliefs themselves. In essence, they amounted to an extreme form of spiritualism: the Bible was not to be understood literally (except where it suited their purposes); outward ceremonies and institutions were a matter of indifference (although the Catholic church was to be preferred to Protestant ones); the mutual anathemas of the Catholic and Protestant churches were uncharitable and led to confusion and strife (but Hendrik Niclaes, a merchant of Delft, in Holland, was the real messiah, and all who failed to recognize the fact and join his Family of Love were lost).

Legal records dating from 1561, just two and a half years into Elizabeth's reign, reveal a congregation in Surrey holding a rag-bag of unorthodox views – anti-Trinitarianism, perfectionism, mortalism, antipædobaptism – and which later moved into the Familist network.[23] The group had connections in Berkshire, Devonshire, the Isle of Ely, Essex, Hampshire, London and Sussex, and some of this circle seems to have moved in the same

---

[23]   J.D. Moss, *Godded with God*, pp. 70–74.

direction as their Surrey brethren; the Isle of Ely proved to be an ants' nest of Familism by the time Bishop Richard Cox began tending that corner of his vineyard in earnest in 1579.

Over against traditional understandings of doctrine, Familism tended to emphasize internal experience. 'Heaven' and 'resurrection' were to be understood as internal realities; their importance in eschatology or in history was downplayed, a shift which both required, and was facilitated by, a spiritualizing interpretation of Scripture. Most of the Anabaptists and radicals emphasized practical sanctification, but amongst the Familists in particular, righteousness had to be experiential or it was nothing. The Protestant notion of imputed righteousness *via* the death of Christ was not looked upon with enthusiasm. In all of these respects, though not in others, the Family of Love anticipated the Quakers in the following century, so perhaps the later Quaker strength in the Isle of Ely was not entirely coincidental.

Niclaes himself had been a friend of David Joris and had come to share with him, not only his spiritualism, but also his messianic pretensions. He had been born in 1502 in Münster (of all places) but had left that city in 1530, some three years before its brief and catastrophic rôle as the New Jerusalem began to unfold, and had moved to Amsterdam, where he began to style himself 'H.N.'. The designation might be thought reasonable enough for someone with his name, but the initials were actually intended to be understood as *homo novus* or 'new man', arguably nothing more than an idiosyncratic way of asserting that he was a regenerate individual, but in fact part of a claim to messiahdom.

Most of Niclaes' writings are similarly an exercise in studied ambiguity. No doctrine or point of view is expressed in such unequivocal terms that it could not, if necessary, be explained away to the agents of ecclesiastical authority. When Niclaes' following in England became at least as significant as that in the Netherlands, his works began to be translated by his chief spokesman there, the joiner Christopher Vitel, into an English so mysterious that one critic expostulated at the absence of 'matter in the author [Niclaes] that may be drawn into argument'.[24] Certainly Niclaes' status as messiah was not placed 'up front' for

---

[24] J. Rogers, *The Displaying of an horrible secte of grosse and wicked Heretiques*, Bij^v.

acceptance by neophytes. Rather, as John Bourne, a glover of Wisbech in Cambridgeshire who was arrested in 1580, pointed out, the 'obscureness of the doctrine must not be declared unto them by any conference with men, but revealed unto them from God, and to be found and understood among themselves'. [25]

That is not to say, however, that the content of the proselyte's 'revelations' were left to chance; William Wilkinson, who spent some time in the 1570s investigating the sect, was told by members that new recruits had their Bibles taken away for a while, and were given Niclaes' writings instead. [26] The effect, of course, was to ensure that Scripture, when access to it was permitted once again, would be read through the lens of Niclaes' own teachings. One of the leading Familist elders, known only by his sect-name of Tobias, warned that 'no man without [i.e. outside] the fellowship of H.N. or without the obedience of the requiring of his doctrine' would be able to come to God. [27]

All of these amount to classic cult tactics, and all are used, in one form or another, today. 'Heavenly deception', a euphemism for lying, is practised by one prominent modern cult, which also tends to insinuate (rather than claim openly) the messianic status of its leader, so that new recruits can 'discover' it for themselves. The endless web of secret teachings (a way of guaranteeing the continued fascination of some), complete with degrees of initiation, is used by another well-known movement. The exclusive identification of the cult with 'God's organisation' is frequently employed by yet another. Most are only too eager to ensure that Scripture – or some special version thereof – is read only in conjunction with suitable study guides, to point out some particular preferred meaning.

Artisans, the equivalent of what might today be called the lower middle class, made up perhaps the bulk of the Family in England. Like Gnostic groups before and since, Familism appealed to the esoterically inclined amongst the middle classes. The present writer confesses to the (possibly unspiritual, and certainly 'politically incorrect') conjecture that most Familists

---

[25]   J.D. Moss, *Godded with God*, p. 76.

[26]   W. Wilkinson, *A Confutation of Certaine Articles*, Piij[v].

[27]   Tobias, *Mirabilia opera Dei*, A2[r].

were in the second quartile of the IQ range; people of less than average intelligence would have paid no attention to such complex and non-commonsensical beliefs, whilst the seriously intelligent would immediately, or at least very quickly, have recognized them for the utter piffle that they were. If some of the Familists were indeed possessed of serious intelligence, then they lavished it all upon their perfidious dealings with their opponents.

Many had had a chequered religious history before becoming Familists (although in fairness, given the frequent changes of régime in mid-sixteenth-century England, the same might be said of the entire population). Certainly a number had dabbled in one or another type of religious radicalism. Thus, in the first year of Elizabeth's reign,[28] Christopher Vitel, who was either Dutch or of Dutch dissent, had been forced to recant Arian heresy in London.

Official persecutors had long lamented the traditional willing-ness of Lollards to recant their heresies when caught and then return to them once released, but the Familists improved upon this: they were willing to lie and equivocate about the nature of their beliefs in the first place. Although religious persecution was 'a lamentable thing', Niclaes' spiritualism allowed him to claim that martyrdom was no virtue, because God was not 'appeased with an elementish body'; what was required was the laying down of the self-life.[29] When the flood of Familist books began to circulate in English from the mid-1570s onwards, the authorities were alerted and put into motion the wheels of repression, but Familist deviousness made detection difficult, and securing a prosecution even harder. No wonder the bishops, brought up to see religious sectarianism as a recipe for anarchy, and all radicals

---

[28] J. Rogers, *The Displaying, Diij*[r]. Indeed, Vitel had not been alone in his Arianism. Georg van Parris, a Dutchman, had been burned for this heresy in Edward VI's reign, and John Assheton, the minister of Shiltelington, had been forced to recant the same heresy. John Bland, parson of Adisham in Kent, might perhaps have toyed with the same opinion, and John Philpot, the Protestant martyr during Mary's reign, was shocked to encounter Arians sharing his prison accommodation in 1555. See my *Between Known Men and Visible Saints*, pp. 146–54.
[29] N. Niclaes, *Evangelivm Regni*, 78[v]; H. Ainsworth, *An Epistle Sent Vnto Tvvo daughters of Vvarwick*, p. 61.

as would-be Münsterites, viewed the followers of Niclaes as particularly unnerving agents of the devil.

They need not have worried. The Familists were entirely non-violent and, despite official propaganda to the contrary, were not given to licentiousness. Neither was their occasionally apocalyptic rhetoric the prelude to attempts to overturn the social order; as with Familist teachings generally, the dawning of the age to come referred, to the internal spiritual condition of Familists themselves not to the imminent destruction of episco-pal palaces.

England's nearly-Anabaptists

The world of mid-Tudor radicalism was not a particularly large one but it certainly was variegated. Biblicism, mysticism, apoca-lypticism and Christological heresy of various types were all represented. Most of the roots of England's Radical Reforma-tion can be traced to Lollardy, but there was an undoubted injection of new ideas and vigour from continental Anabaptism. The latter movement was represented mostly by Dutch emigrés, but their influence on English people only very rarely extended beyond the passing on of teachings such as Hofmannite Christ-ology to the transmission of actual Anabaptism itself. Only in the case of the wholly unorthodox Family of Love was there any large-scale conversion to a specific movement of foreign origin and leadership.

The common elements amongst the various dissenters which qualify them for inclusion under the heading 'Radical Reforma-tion' are, on the one hand, their opposition to the theology of the emerging Protestant state church and, inextricable from this on the other hand, the drift of their ideas towards a concept of church as 'gathered' and voluntary. Moreover, all of the radi-cals mentioned here were united in their castigation of the loose morality attendant upon the Reformation; not only had the advent of Protestantism failed to raise the standards of behav-iour of the populace as a whole above those which had obtained under the Roman Catholic church, but the very nature of Reformed theology (especially the doctrine of predestination) seemed to them to encourage fatalism and, with it, a relaxed attitude towards experiential righteousness.

Most radicals tended to assume, and some explicitly to teach, that the church should consist only of the personally committed. Their rejection of both Roman Catholicism and Reformed the-ology made a drift in the direction of Anabaptism inevitable – even if only a very few of them actually arrived there.

Chapter Eight

'The Letter kills': the Spiritualism of Denck, Franck, Schwenckfeld

Not all of the sixteenth-century radicals were as sanguine as Conrad Grebel, Menno Simons, or even their more scatter-brained English counterparts such as Henry Hart, that the one true church could be restored on the basis of the biblical revelation alone. What is more, not all who rejected a straight biblicism were convinced, as Melchior Hofmann had been, that a veritable avalanche of new prophecy would somehow make good the legitimacy that had been lost by the apostasy of the fourth century (or, according to some expositions of history, by the apostles' immediate successors). Such people found themselves in an unhappy situation.

Convinced by the radicals' critique of the Middle Ages, and persuaded also of the inadequacy of the Reformers' attempts to settle Christendom on an improved basis, they were nevertheless too deeply ingrained with Catholic notions of apostolic succession and historical continuity to allow that the Anabaptists had a right to establish churches of their own from scratch. If the church had fallen, it could not be restored except by a new dispensation. The conflicting – and rapidly proliferating – expositions of Scripture on offer by various groups provided ample demonstration that a simplistic appeal to 'what the Bible says' was no solution to anything. This being so, the best option was to cultivate the inner spiritual life on the basis of minimal doctrinal affirmations, to share fellowship with all who were truly devout and to submit to nobody's insistence that theirs was the only true church.

Merely to describe such a view is to make an almost irresistible appeal to the postmodern mind. In the sixteenth century, however, such opinions (which consciously drew short of closure on many key issues) tended to be confined to the quite well educated, and so to bypass both the poor and the artisans. Those who held views of this sort are generally designated 'Spiritualists' by historians, a category which has nothing in common with modern 'churches' that go by that description. Caspar Schwenck - feld von Ossig (1489–1561) and Sebastian Franck (1499–1542), the prime exponents of this standpoint, tended to exalt 'spirit' and to denigrate 'flesh', rather in the manner of much theology – and heresy – of the second to fifth centuries, which had been strongly influenced by Neoplatonism. A crucial forerunner of both men was Hans Denck.

In January 1525 – the same month that the first believers' baptisms were taking place in Zürich – Denck insisted to the Nuremberg council that

> immediately after the apostles' death, there appeared very many divi - sions or sects all of whom armed themselves with Scripture badly understood. Why badly understood? Proceedings headlong according to their own presumption, they acquired a false faith before desiring from God a true one.

Appealing to 2 Peter 1:20, he argued that no Scripture is a matter of one's own interpretation; it belongs to the Holy Spirit.[1] The primitive fall of the church, then, had come about because of precisely the kind of fragmentation that was so evident in the 1520s. The plan for its restoration, however, was given an indi - vidualistic twist by an appeal to the Holy Spirit, of whose voice 'everyone must beforehand be certain in himself'. Scripture could not, of itself, dispel human darkness, since it was humanly written, transmitted and received.[2]

The first indisputable date in Denck's biography is his ma - triculation at the University of Ingolstadt in October 1517, just a fortnight before Luther's posting of 95 theses in Wittenberg launched the Reformation. The date of his birth has to be deduced from that of his matriculation, and scholars vary in their estimates from 1495 to 1500. After his studies in Ingolstadt, Denck served briefly as a schoolmaster in Regensburg, by which

---

[1] H. Denck, *The Spiritual Legacy of Hans Denck*, ed. C. Bauman, pp. 58–9.
[2] *Ibid.*, pp. 56–7.

time – at the latest – he had acquired Lutheran opinions. A spell in Basel, where he studied under the reformer Oecolampadius (and possibly also under Erasmus), completed his education, and in September 1523 he returned to schoolteaching, this time in Nuremberg, a city that was in the throes of gradual reformation.

It was the sojourn in Nuremberg that first saw Denck advancing toward a radical position, and in the process he got himself into serious trouble. During the autumn of 1524, a variety of radical opinions were aired in Nuremberg, and both Thomas Müntzer and Hans Hut visited that September, the latter staying in Denck's house. When a painter who was on trial for sacramentarianism mentioned to the authorities that Denck was a sympathizer with Karlstadt's views on the eucharist, Denck found himself hauled before the council. However, he gave such slippery oral replies that Osiander, the city's leading reformer, evinced his biblicist's confidence that texts were susceptible of only one meaning by requiring Denck to submit a written statement of his theological opinions on a variety of key doctrines, including baptism.

These, when they were forthcoming, exhibited the spiritualism that was to mark Denck's career as a radical. Concerning baptism, he concluded that infant baptism was useless, since water could no more wash away sin – a characteristic of the object being washed – than it could wash away the redness of brick or the blackness of coal. Its efficacy was not in itself but, as indicated in 1 Peter 3:21, in the covenant for a good conscience with God. Though he conceded that baptism taking place within such a covenant – that is, with one who was already truly penitent – was good, he stressed that it was unnecessary for salvation. It was the inner baptism that was necessary.[3]

Here was the classic spiritualist position, albeit in embryo: if any party was in the right concerning baptism (or the church, or true faith, or Scripture) then the Anabaptists were right. But in fact even their teachings were superfluous, since outward ordinances and expressions of Christianity were rendered virtually redundant by the spiritualists' own stress on inner realities and on the need for the experience of the Holy Spirit.

---

[3]   *Ibid.*, pp. 60–63.

It was the same with the Lord's Supper: he who 'eats the living invisible bread' and 'drinks from the invisible chalice the invisible wine', by placing his own will in God's will, is strengthened and empowered. 'One can live without this outer bread', like Moses on Sinai or Christ in the desert, but 'without the inner [bread] no one can live', for 'the righteous live by faith'.[4]

On 21st January, the day on which Grebel, Mantz and Blaurock were baptizing one another in Zürich, Denck was formally banished from Nuremberg and ordered never to return. Like many another, he now found himself cast adrift in the midst of the Peasants' War. His whereabouts are unknown, though the summer found him visiting the Swiss Brethren in St. Gall during the excitements there. By the autumn, he had settled in Augsburg, a city of internal political instability, and therefore an ideal sanctuary for those prone to persecution everywhere else. His friends in the city included those who were connected to both Caspar Schwenckfeld and Sebastian Franck. It was probably at this point that Denck submitted to believer's baptism, perhaps at the hands of Balthasar Hubmaier, who was passing through the city in the spring of 1526, *en route* from his ignominious forced recantation in Zürich to his new fields of labour in Moravia.[5]

The Augsburg period represented perhaps the greatest fruition of his ministry. Here he led a fast-growing fellowship of Anabaptists that included wealthy merchants and city patricians, as well as humbler folk. Here too he published his most important writings, chiefly rebutting Lutheran positions. His book *Whether God is the Cause of Evil* was aimed against the Wittenberg reformer's intemperate *On the Bondage of the Will*, which had been published the previous year. In this work, Denck argued that mankind does have free will, and that Luther's position made God the author of all the evil and suffering in the world, and indeed of the very sins for which man stands condemned by God. Denck was thus adopting a position similar to that of Erasmus, against whom Luther had been writing.

---

[4] *Ibid.*, pp. 64–7.
[5] G.H. Williams expresses some doubt on the matter. *Radical Reformation*, 3rd edn, pp. 255–7.

His second work, *Concerning the Law of God*, was an attempt to demonstrate that the Law was not simply set aside by the Gospel as Luther claimed it was. Christ came to fulfil the Law, not abolish it – though it is, to be sure, now internalized in the lives of those who truly follow him. Denck's concern here was to act as a corrective to magisterial Protestant teachings, which had started as a critique of Roman laxity but which, with their stress upon unconditional grace and forgiveness, had actually encouraged a decline in general levels of morality.

The last of the three works, *He Who Truly Loves the Truth*, highlighted forty paradoxes – or perhaps contradictions – in Scripture (e.g. 'God does not tempt [Jas. 1:13]; God tempted Abraham [Gen. 22:1]').[6] The purpose was to give pause to the biblicists – radicals and Protestant scholars alike – in their insistence upon simplistic or scholarly-authoritative doctrinal pronouncements. Reading it might give pause to their equivalents today. The Scripture, claimed Denck, could no more be understood by a person unenlightened by the Holy Spirit than animals could comprehend human speech.

Denck's influence spread throughout the cities of southern Germany, and meetings in Augsburg occasionally attracted more than a thousand attenders. It was only in the autumn of 1526 that Urbanus Rhegius, the (apparently very unobservant) chief reformer of Augsburg, finally realized that Denck, who was admittedly tactful to the point of elusiveness, was actually an Anabaptist. His indignation perhaps fuelled by embarrassment, he blustered that 'John Denck has hidden his teaching from me and denied it in front of me for more than a year; in the meantime he has nonetheless taught in corners and baptized'.[7] Rhegius arranged a disputation in front of the city council, but Denck knew the purpose of such exercises well enough and made his departure the same night.

For a couple of months he stayed in Strassburg, another centre of political instability and a magnet for radicals of all hues. There again he came to the attention of the authorities, and this time was cornered into a debate with Martin Bucer in front of four

6   C. Bauman ed., *Spiritual Legacy*, pp. 168–9.
7   *Ibid.*, p. 12, f. 18.

hundred leading citizens over the weekend before Christmas. Bucer was not smitten with Denck, whom he dubbed 'the pope of the Anabaptists'; if one had to deal with Anabaptists at all, then Sattler was more to his liking. Denck seemed devious in debate and reluctant to make his real views plain. When the wily debater protested that he could not make himself clearer than he already was, Bucer asked for – and obtained – a banishment order against his, by now, much-travelled opponent.

Thus it was that Hans Denck left Strassburg on Christmas Day 1526, to recommence his wanderings. During 1527, he stayed briefly in Worms, Basel, Zürich and Ulm, before attending the 'Martyrs' Synod' (most of the leaders attending were arrested, though Denck himself escaped) in Augsburg that August. Reaching Basel again in October, he was pressured into writing a recantation – though in fact its clever wording retracted almost nothing – and died of the plague there in November. He was, at most, in his early thirties.

Sebastian Franck

But Denck's successors were already in the making. One of his literary opponents had been a young parish priest of Lutheran persuasion by the name of Sebastian Franck, who had first ventured into print with a translation of a Latin work attacking Denck's *He Who Truly Loves the Truth*. However, Franck found himself less than entirely convinced by his own arguments, or by those of the original author. Indeed, he amended the text of the work he was translating, making concessions to Denck's position. Catholics had been 'Werkheilige' (those who tried to sanctify themselves through good works), but now Protestants were 'Wortheilige', thinking that the mere repetition of the words of Scripture – or a mental acceptance of its doctrines – would serve to put them right with God. All things considered, Franck's translation and editorial comments in respect of this book, *Diallage*, reveal him as ill at ease with the emergence in Germany of what he called the 'Landgott', a sort of tribal god, with religion being determined by the governors of the state in which one happened to live. That said, he could hardly reconcile himself to the Roman church, whatever the universal claims it made for itself; in his eyes, as for so many of his generation, it now stood permanently discredited.

He had been born in 1499 to a family of weavers in Donauwörth, Bavaria, educated at Heidelberg and then, in the 1520s, made a parish priest in the Franconian margraviate of Ansbach-Bayreuth, aligning himself with the Lutheran reform. However, the moral laxity wrought by the preaching of solafidi-anism increasingly troubled him. When his plea that the civil authorities should permit the excommunication of people living in open and unrepented sin was rejected in 1528, he concluded that the uncompromised advocacy of a holy life was more im-portant than serving the interests of the 'Landgott', and he resigned the ministry. Christendom was hopelessly split into innumerable factions, and so now, shunning all external ceremonies and organized churches, he advocated Spiritualism.

Franck rejected any attempt to restore the primitive church, though he shared with Anabaptists and other radicals the conviction that it had indeed fallen. He agreed with one of his correspondents, John Campanus, whose book was modestly entitled *Contra totum post apostolos mundum* ('Against all the world since the apostles'). Franck assured him that 'thou hast done rightly', for 'the outward church of Christ, including all its gifts and sacraments, because of the breaking in and laying waste by Antichrist right after the death of the apostles, went up into heaven and lies concealed in the Spirit'. He professed himself 'quite certain' that no true church or sacrament had existed for fourteen hundred years. As soon as the apostles had passed away, everything had been corrupted: 'Baptism was changed into infant baptism; the Lord's Supper into misuse and a sacrifice'. Clearly he accepted some, at least, of the Anabaptist critique of Catholicism. Indeed, he considered the Anabaptists to be 'intelligent people', though he rejected their assertion that the church had fallen at the time of Constantine in the fourth century; instead, he believed that the fall had occurred immedi-ately after the apostles. Such pre-Constantinian Fathers as Clement of Rome, Irenæus, Tertullian, Origen and Cyprian were but the 'wolves' and 'antichrists' which it had been predicted would fall upon the flock of Christ (Acts 20:29 and 1 Jn. 2:18).[8]

Given that he held such drastic views, it comes as something of a relief that Franck ascribed to himself no quasi-messianic rôle in rescuing the true church from this grim scenario. His pretensions were scholarly and spiritual, not prophetic. There was to be no reconstruction or restoration in which Franck could play a starring part. Instead, God himself 'fed, gave to drink, baptized and gathered the faithful', even though 'all outer transactions' had passed away. This spiritual church – to become visible only at the return of Christ – was composed not merely of true Christians from all of the different confessions, but also of the godly before the coming of Christ and even of devout and sincere pagans and Muslims who, unknown to themselves, had the spirit of Christ. Thus was Franck not only a prophet of modern ecumenism, but a forerunner of the twentieth-century Catholic theologian Karl Rahner, with his concept of 'anonymous Christians'.

Literal Scripture was 'the sword of Antichrist' which kills Christ; 'heresies and sects come from the literal sense of the Scripture'.[9] He came to believe that Scripture was 'sealed with seven seals', so that the spiritually enlightened alone could discern its meaning. His book of that title, *Das . . . mit sieben Siegeln verschlossene Buch* of 1539, picks up on the very themes of scriptural paradox and contradiction that he had written and translated against in Denck over a decade before.

In contrast to Anabaptist literalism, Franck saw God as revealing himself through history. A lifelong passion for the German past was reflected in perhaps his most important work, the *Chronica, Zeitbuch und Geschichtsbibel*, which purported to give a history of the world from the creation to his own day. The Emperor Charles V and his forebears emerge poorly from the second part of this work, the popes even worse from the third. Erasmus (to that scholar's great indignation) found himself lumped together with late medieval figures whom the Roman

---

[8]   G.H. Williams and A.M. Mergal, *Spiritual and Anabaptist Writers*, pp. 148–52.
[9]   G.H. Williams, *Radical Reformation*, pp. 696, 698.

church had found to be heretics, such as Wycliffe and Hus. The fact that Franck approved of all of them was no consolation to the great Dutch humanist!

In emphasizing the individual's relationship to truth, rather than to hallowed church institutions, Franck could hardly have failed to upset many people. It was the exclusivism of so many different churches that drove him to his own distinctive position. His exposition on this point bears quoting at some length:

> For it is impossible that the one undivided God with Christ, grace and the sacraments should be in such different churches. Because of this, if Luther baptizes, Zwingli with his church does not baptize; if the Pope and the Baptist Brethren validly baptize, no one else would really be baptizing – none, that is, who did not belong to their conventicle or church, but instead he would be lost, since he would not be one of them. . . .
>
> Therefore either none of all the churches baptizes or only one. If only one, where, my friend, is this church? Perhaps in India, Greece, Germany, Armenia, at Rome, in Saxony, or in the mountains. But I believe nowhere. Instead they all run uncalled and enter into the sheep[fold] unsent.[10]

The similarity to some popular modern antichristian attitudes is striking: Franck argued from a situation of *de facto* pluralism to a personal response of agnosticism. But there are differences too. Moderns tend to equate the two statements 'All religions are basically the same' and 'They cancel one another out'. Franck, however, refused to trivialize the differences between the various confessions; he saw them for what they were, and took them very seriously. And although he felt unable to adjudicate between them, he nevertheless responded with a distinctive brand of piety, rather than seizing the opportunity for godlessness; his agnosticism was ecclesial, not absolute.

Franck spent a life in constant transition for his opinions. Moving from Nuremberg to Strassburg in 1529, he was imprisoned there in 1531 for the publication of his *Chronica*, and expelled at the end of that year. After fifteen months of travelling, he succeeded in ensconcing himself in Ulm, but was pressured to leave in 1539. From thence he went to Basel, where he died in 1542.

---

[10] G.H. Williams and A.M. Mergal, *Spiritual and Anabaptist Writers*, pp. 153–4.

A man of his opinions can hardly have expected to leave an institutional, rather than a literary, monument. Nevertheless, through his writings he continued to influence many who were travelling in a spiritualist direction.

Caspar Schwenckfeld von Ossig

Of the spiritualist leaders, it is only Schwenckfeld who has left a lasting movement, and even that is modest enough. The Schwenckfelder church today numbers only a couple of thousand and is mainly located in the United States, descendants of the two hundred or so who fled persecution in Silesia for the freedom of Pennsylvania in 1734. Nevertheless, the influence of Schwenckfeld and the other spiritualists was widespread in the sixteenth century, and has affected the thinking of a variety of others since.

Caspar himself was born in 1489, the son of a Silesian noble family, and along with his brother he inherited the family estate at Ossig in 1519. Although he felt constrained to leave Silesia in 1529, the estates continued to provide him with an income which kept him, if not wealthy, then at least with the wherewithal for existence. His outlook remained quite aristocratic, and his following relatively genteel, qualities which mark him out from the run of radical reformers.

He studied at the universities of Cologne and Frankfurt-an-der-Oder and then, still as a young man, served as courtier to various German princelings. If his social background was distinctive in this way, Schwenckfeld's early spiritual biography was typical of so many others whose stories concern us in this book.

He came under the influence of Lutheranism as early as 1518, and later said that he began to live a truly Christian life from 1521 onwards. Schwenckfeld was instrumental in persuading his prince, Duke Friedrich II of Liegnitz, to declare for the Reformation, and later acted to dissuade his patron from evicting Anabaptists from the area. The poor moral behaviour encouraged by Protestantism troubled him, however, and in the mid-1520s he began to drift away from what was coming to be understood as Protestant orthodoxy. Like many another Protestant of radical tendencies, he questioned the Lutheran insistence on the real presence of Christ in the bread and wine of communion. A letter of August 1525 to the great reformer in Wittenberg, in which he outlined his own views, brought no response at all. When Schwenckfeld ven-tured to visit Wittenberg to debate the subject, Luther received him cordially enough, but two months later sent a sharp letter advising Schwenckfeld to

> stop misleading the people. The blood of those you are misleading must be upon your own head. In brief, either you or we must be the bondsmen of the devil, because we on both sides boast of having the Word of God. [11]

The implication as to which side were the 'bondsmen of the devil' was clear; if Luther evaluated him like this it is perhaps not surprising that Schwenckfeld determined to plough his own furrow. In his own estimation, 1526 was the year in which he had a further 'divine visitation', similar to his conversion in 1518, but which now called him to advance further.

From his conversations with his own tenants, he came to the conclusion that ordinary, uneducated people perceived the sacrament as a kind of infusion of grace to cancel out their sinful behaviour during the week. This was no better than purchasing pardons on pieces of paper, the kind of abuse against which Luther himself had protested when the Reformation started in 1517. As he saw it, Luther's 'high' sacramentalism was thus directly connected with the superstition and the low moral standards among the masses of the population. He saw his own ideas, by contrast, as offering a middle way 'between the former hypocritical life' (he meant Catholicism) 'and the present carnal liberty', which he saw Lutheranism as having encouraged. [12]

Schwenckfeld gathered a following in his native Silesia, though when the prince died in 1529 and was succeeded by one less sympathetic, he decided to leave in order to make life easier for his supporters there. He was never to return; his remaining thirty-two years were largely spent in travelling and writing. He died, probably in Ulm, in 1561.

---

[11] cited in S.G. Schultz, *Caspar Schwenckfeld von Ossig*, p. 98.
[12] *Ibid.*, p. 104.

Schwenckfeld's thought is spiritualist in several senses. In the first place, he considered the spirit more important than the letter of Scripture. The 'inner word' was the true word of God, while the Bible – for all its importance and inspiration – was the 'external word', a kind of sign or deposit of the inner word that had been communicated in the past to prophets. The inner word was incommunicable except through direct experience of God, whether in action in the world, or through his voice speaking to one's spirit. 'For Schwenckfeld, literalism was the way of bond-age and death to Christianity. . . . He always remembered that the actual event comes before anything is written about the event.'[13] The Anabaptists were too literalist for his taste. He likened the Bible to the swaddling clothes of the infant Jesus. [14] Many might argue that Scripture can be used, like the swaddling clothes, either to present Christ or to obscure him. Certainly both tendencies have made themselves apparent in Christian history, seldom more so than in the sixteenth century.

In the second place, Schwenckfeld saw the true church as a mystical body of all those who have true faith, regardless of what outer church they belonged to, or indeed whether they belonged to any at all. In this respect, he was taking Augustine's doctrine of the 'invisible church', which had been fashioned to bolster inclusivism and the Christendom ideal, and turning it in an anarchic direction which made light of particular church bodies and emphasized inward faith over its ecclesial expression. The Schwenckfelder movement he founded was non-separatist, although he preferred his followers not to take communion in their parishes. Like the Anabaptists, he disapproved of the Constantinian alignment of state and church.

Thirdly, his Christology was somewhat Platonic. Though he was orthodox in seeing Christ as both divine and human, he nevertheless felt that, since Christ's flesh redeemed us, there must be an intrinsic difference – beyond the simple absence of sin – between that flesh and ours. He therefore concluded that the

---

[13]   J.R. Rothenberger, *Caspar Schwenckfeld von Ossig and the Ecumenical Ideal*, pp. 54, 57–8.
[14]   I am grateful to Ruth Gouldbourne for this point, and also for a number of others in this section on Schwenckfeld.

Catholics were right in holding to the immaculate conception of Mary. Not only was Christ's Father divine, but his mother was sinless. The reality of Christ's humanity was not denied, but Schwenckfeld was not much interested in the Saviour's earthly life. His interest was much more with his status now – in heaven at the Father's side.

In the fourth place, his views concerning the eucharist went beyond the usual sacramentarian denial that mere earthly elements can become, in any sense, the body and blood of Christ, or that they can convey grace. A 'visitation' or revelation in 1527 or 1528 revealed to him the key to the words 'this is my body' spoken by Jesus at the Last Supper (Mt. 26:26). This key was to be found in John 6:35, 'I am the bread of life'. It is not that the bread represents Christ's body, but rather the reverse: Christ's body represents a sort of bread to us; we need to feed on him spiritually. The one thing needful was (to borrow the English *Book of Common Prayer*'s phrase) to 'feed on him in your hearts by faith'. Schwenckfeld found himself unpersuaded by Luther's literalist exegesis of 'this is my body'.

A 'Stillstand' on celebrating communion was declared for his followers in 1526. Communion was seen as so important that it was better not to celebrate it at all – especially since the believer could in any case feed inwardly upon Christ by faith – than to get it wrong. This 'Stillstand' was only reversed by his followers in Pennsylvania some three centuries later, in the mid-nineteenth century. Similarly, though he rejected infant baptism and sympathized with Anabaptist arguments on this issue, he believed, in point of fact, that baptism was an unimportant outer work; what mattered was the baptism of the Holy Spirit.

Like the evangelical Anabaptists, Schwenckfeld denied that faith without works could possibly be saving faith. But if he shared similar emphases – or had only moderate differences – with them on a number of points, there were also sharp divergences in other areas, and Schwenckfeld sought to distance himself, especially from the Anabaptists' biblicism. He was less concerned than they with the imitation of the earthly life and ministry of Jesus; 'In correction of the Anabaptists, he stresses Christ's glorified nature, seated at the right hand of the

Father'.[15] He saw believers as committed to defending the honour of Jesus, rather as liege knights defend their prince. This honour did not extend, however, to taking bold stands for one's beliefs; he felt that the Anabaptists unnecessarily courted martyrdom.

Unsurprisingly, such an ethos had less appeal to the artisans and the lower middle classes than did, say, the preaching of a Menno or a Michael Sattler. Schwenckfeld's strongest appeal was to the more prosperous urban merchant classes, who saw in his teachings an affirmation of high culture and Renaissance rationalism, along with a slightly esoteric spirituality. These followers frequently met informally for prayer and discussion, and often did not separate from their parish churches.

* * *

Spiritualism was to be an ongoing problem and challenge for the Anabaptists. To be sure, it posed little danger of offering a rival church movement, since its very logic made external organisation of so little account. The overwhelming reason for spiritualism's appeal to so many of an Anabaptist direction of thought was because of the shared 'basic premise that spiritual realities, not physical tokens, were of the essence'.[16] Spiritualists could agree with the radical critique of the 'Christendom' ideal offered by Sattler, Menno or Marpeck because both shared an emphasis on the inward reality of spiritual life and the worthlessness of church institutions that did not reflect such reality. But the spiritualists, for their differing reasons, tended not to believe in the possibility of a restoration of the true church, or to consider such a project to be of any value even if it were possible. Their stress on spiritual inwardness was taken to the point of a dualism which was not without its attractions. It avoided the prickly dogmatism and biblicism of the Anabaptists, and thus short-circuited many tricky exegetical questions. This undogmatic approach implied an absence of abrasiveness and an inclusiveness that were foreign

---

[15]   E.J. Furcha, *Schwenckfeld's Concept of the New Man*, (Pennsburg, Pa., 1970) p. 93.

[16]   C.A. Snyder, *Anabaptist History and Theology: an Introduction*, p. 38.

to the Anabaptist programme of sharply delineated gathered churches. And these were qualities amenable to many people who had imbibed the optimistic air of pre-Reformation Erasmian humanism – including its critique of the Catholic church – and who were now appalled to find that optimism giving way to a new age of division, religious warfare and mutual anathematizing. The somewhat scholarly, mystical, occasionally even esoteric, nature of spiritualism limited its appeal, of course, and if the more prosperous and literate urbanites fell within those limits, yet the nature of the beliefs themselves meant that, except for the Schwenckfelders, no lasting ecclesial movement was bequeathed by them to posterity.

Chapter Nine

'Come out from among them': the English Separatists

A Church Insufficiently Reformed

To be an informed and discerning Protestant in the England of
the 1560s was both a disturbing and a confusing experience.
Those Protestants who were prone to naïveté partook of a more
consoling existence than their less sanguine brethren, as they
doubtless still do. They at least could continue to hope, during
the 1560s, that the young Queen had meant what she appeared
to imply in her 1559 Act of Uniformity. According to that Act,
the ornaments of the church and clerical vestments (so unsatisfactory from a Protestant standpoint) were to be enforced only
'until other order shall be therein taken'. [1] The Queen, surely, had
introduced such a despicable Protestantism-and-water merely as
an interim; once the bulk of the English population had grown
to accept the permanence of the break with Rome and – what
was harder for most peasants to accept – the break with the mass,
then the Reformation would be completed, and the Church of
England would become a more full-bloodedly Protestant affair.
On this view, then, the Reformation was a process, of greater or
lesser duration, in which England would more nearly approxi-
mate itself to the Reformed paradise which those English Protestants who had spent the Catholic Queen Mary's reign in exile

---

[1] G. Bray ed., *Documents of the English Reformation*, p. 334.

in Zürich, Strassburg or (especially) Geneva believed themselves to have experienced.

It is this assumption which accounts for much of the rhetoric used to describe England's protestantisation in the first half of Elizabeth's reign. Many contemporaries commented on the slowness of the process, but all of them presupposed that the highest authorities, including the queen herself, actually wanted the church to follow through Protestant doctrine with more unambiguously Protestant practice – particularly in ceremonies – just as soon as this could safely be achieved.

Popular twentieth-century misconceptions notwithstanding, English monarchs in the early modern period were unable to do exactly as they pleased in any sphere of policy. The only one to act on the hypothesis that they could was Charles I, who paid for his misunderstanding with the loss, not only of his life but, temporarily at least, of the institution of monarchy itself. Not even modern governments, perhaps, have yet risen to that degree of Orwellian omnipotence that literally any policy can be pursued with impunity. Even Nazi and Communist régimes have been met with resistance movements, sabotage and the long-term enervating effects of a population which simply refuses to work either efficiently or competently. Even they have had to placate the machinery of military and security structures as well as sizeable groups within their state and party organizations.

For Elizabeth I, who had come to the throne of England in November 1558, following the death of her Catholic half-sister, the constraints were very much greater and entailed a vast weight of tradition, law and centuries-old vested interests, outside of which neither she nor any other monarch could sensibly act.

As the daughter of Anne Boleyn – and hence the very living symbol of England's break with Rome – Elizabeth could hardly have been an adherent of the church whose pontiff considered her birth to be illegitimate and her title to the English throne invalid. Any yet Protestantism was a creed which had won the unconditional support of no more than a vocal minority of her subjects. True, her sister's policy of persecution had repelled many in the capital and the south-east of her country, and had, in that sense at least, alienated them from Rome. Mary's attempt at re-Catholicization had also been identified in the minds of many with her hugely unpopular Spanish marriage, which had seemed to threaten the incorporation of the country within the Spanish empire. The unpopularity of such policies might also facilitate moves in a Protestant direction under her successor. Antipathy to Rome, however, and enthusiasm for Protestantism are two different things; amongst most English people the former did not necessarily entail the latter. Religious conservatism and attachment to the mass were strong, particularly amongst the peasantry who made up the vast bulk of Elizabeth's subjects. The opinion of peasants counted only collectively, of course, and even then it was probably less important than the instincts of the 'political nation' – the landowners and officeholders in the shires – without whom, and without whose families, the country could not be governed. These were more inclined, on the whole, to Protestantism – indeed, their purchase of confiscated monastic estates and property under Henry VIII, and of chantry lands under Edward VI, virtually guaranteed at least general anti-papal sentiments from them as a class. Even here though there were exceptions, and the Protestantism of many of the remainder was moderate.

Elizabeth's own predilections were also important. She was not personally very devout, and was given to hard swearing when the fancy took her. But she was an admirer of her father, and of her father's religion, which also inclined her to minimalist Protestantism.

Seen in this light, her decision to pursue a policy of 'lowest-common-denominator Protestantism' hardly ranks as a surprise. The debate amongst historians as to whether the settlement that emerged from the Parliament of 1559 was broadly in line with her own views, or whether Protestant MPs had pushed matters further from conservatism than she quite liked, is one that need not detain us here.[2] What is certain is that the new Church of England was still far too conservative to long placate the zealous

---

[2] N.L. Jones ('Elizabeth's First Year' in C. Haigh ed., *The Reign of Elizabeth I*, pp. 27–53) follows most previous historians, and Protestant contemporaries such as John Foxe, in arguing the former case; Sir John Neale (*Elizabeth I and Her Parliaments*, vol. 1) argued the latter.

Protestants emerging from their exilic or troglodyte existences of the previous reign.

The first target of their attack was, of all things, the vestments required to be worn by clergy when officiating at the sacraments. These garments, especially the surplice, seemed to many Protestants to be but 'the rags of popery', a constant visible (albeit silent) claim that the clergyman was, in some sense, a priest mediating between God and the laity. By 1565 at the latest, the party that took this view was being dubbed 'Puritan' by its enemies, a sarcastic reference to the purity of church ceremonies which they sought.[3] The crackdown by the episcopal authorities began in 1563, and in March 1566 thirty-seven London ministers found themselves suspended from their livings for their refusal to wear the hated robes, or for other infringements of the prescribed forms laid down in the *Book of Common Prayer*. Of these, several refused to capitulate and were ejected from their parishes.

The so-called vestiarian disputes were fought out during the 1560s, and perhaps the most painful element was the disunity they created in Protestant ranks at a time when the bulk of the population was only with difficulty being cajoled into Protestantism of any kind. Elizabeth had, in 1559, reserved the position of Archbishop of Canterbury for her chaplain Matthew Parker, a decided moderate who had spent Mary's reign in seclusion in England, and so was uncontaminated by exposure to the Reformed utopias on the continent. Nevertheless, she had been obliged to appoint a number of bishops from amongst the eight hundred or so returning exiles who were so urgently proffering her rather more Protestantism than she was happy to settle for. Many of these had hesitated to accept, appalled by the anæmic qualities of the church she wished to impose. But the prospect of the positions being offered to more conservative men should they refuse – to say nothing of the subtle allure of holding senior office, no matter how unsatisfactory the circumstances – had persuaded most of them 'not to desert our churches for the sake of a few ceremonies', as Edmund Grindal, the new Bishop of

---

[3]   The first known use was by the Catholic Thomas Stapleton in *A Fortresse of the Faith* (fol. 134v), a piece of polemic written from the safety of exile. See L.J. Trinterud ed., *Elizabethan Puritanism*, p. 7.

London, later explained himself to his Zürich mentor, Bullinger. [4]
Having accepted the posts, however, Grindal and his ilk found
themselves obliged to impose, upon erstwhile colleagues for
whom they had every sympathy, pragmatic regulations and
popish rags for which they had little.

The results were predictable. Accusations of 'turn-coat' and
'traitor' blackened the air, as the unwilling ecclesiastical police-
men sought to justify themselves by resorting to arguments that
the garments were *adiaphora* – things indifferent which were 'not
unlawful in themselves'. [5] In any case, these things might soon be
taken away by Elizabeth who was, they were sure, merely adopting a gradualist programme of weaning the population away
from their religious conservatism. All measures were provisional,
to endure only 'until other order shall therein be taken'. In
making such self-justifications, the bishops inevitably found
themselves becoming more conservative in the process. Neither
the pawns nor the bishops knew it, but this particular chess-game
is called 'divide and rule', and its real winner was that consum-
mate politician, the queen herself.

Within fifteen months of the action to suspend ministers who
would not conform themselves, Grindal found himself interro-
gating a group who had responded by separating from the
Church of England. It seems that the separation had happened
quite early on, long enough for them to have spent some time
meeting in houses before they grew in numbers, thereby necessitating the fateful step of deciding to meet in larger premises.

The Plumbers' Hall had been chosen for a gathering in June
1567, but was discovered and the sheriffs made an appearance.
The seventeen or eighteen arrested were perhaps deemed likely
ringleaders on the basis of a spur-of-the-moment judgement by the
constables. Either that, or they were less fleet of foot than their
brethren, for there had been about a hundred at the meeting. If the
former, then there had been opportunity in the Counter prison

---

[4]   H. Robinson ed., *The Zürich Letters*, i., p. 179.
[5]   *Ibid.* By a 'thing indifferent' both sides understood, *not* a matter of private judgement about which individuals might legitimately differ in opinion and practice, but an
issue about which scripture is not explicit, with the prince therefore having every right
to make up his (in this context, her) own mind, which ruling all were then obliged to
accept for conscience' sake (Rom. 13:5).

further to sift leaders from followers, and it was an elect group of
seven who were presented to Bishop Grindal on 20th June 1567.

They explained themselves by saying that 'all our preachers
were displaced by your law', and they had 'remembered that
there was a congregation of us in this city in Queen Mary's days'. [6]
The radicals' use of 'us' was thus laying claim to the mainstream
Protestant tradition in England, whereby Protestants had separated themselves, during Mary's reign, from an official church
which they held to be no true church at all. Then, however, the
official church had been Roman Catholic. The present church
(whatever its shortcomings) was plainly Protestant: how could
the conventiclers justify making the same response to the one as
to the other? For them, plainly, the English national church was
so insufficiently reformed as to be no more a 'true church' than
its Marian predecessor had been.

Three months later, Grindal spoke to one 'Master Pattenson',
a suspended minister arrested for continuing to preach. Albert
Peel, the eminent Congregationalist historian, reasoned that this
event indicates the existence of at least two separatist congregations in London during 1567, since Pattenson claimed his own
congregation and, had this been identical with the group arrested
at Plumbers' Hall, the fact could hardly have failed to come to
light. [7]

Grindal's interview with the Plumbers' Hall group was repeated in March 1568, after seventy-seven people had been
arrested at a goldsmith's house in Westminster. Six of the original
leaders were again amongst those taken into custody. This latest
trawl included four or five parish ministers, although actually the
separatists ordained their own. Indeed, they also appointed their
own elders and deacons, administered their own sacraments and
excommunications, and would not allow their members to attend
the services of the Church of England, even for the purpose of
hearing Puritan preachers. In all, there were about two hundred,
including more women than men, meeting sometimes in private
(presumably large) houses, sometimes in fields outside the capital, and sometimes in ships moored on the Thames.

---

[6] E. Grindal, *Remains of Edmund Grindal*, ed. W. Nicholson, p. 203.
[7] A. Peel, *The First Congregational Churches*, p. 9.

However provocative their actions, it was difficult for the episcopal hierarchy to forget that they were, in many cases, dealing with people who had risked or suffered imprisonment, or even endured exile, for their beliefs during Mary's reign in exactly the same way that they themselves had. John Bolton, one of the separatist ringleaders, had been in Geneva. Indeed, one of the principal practices of the group was to use the Genevan service book in their meetings, a fact which served as a constant reminder to the half-embarrassed enforcers of ecclesiastical order of the churchmanship to which they themselves had once so enthusias-tically aspired. On this occasion, the privy council took a firm line and had the leaders imprisoned, though they were released the following April at the request of the still sympathetic, or possibly conscience-stricken, bishop.

The disturbances continued, however. In 1571, a separatist congregation had the temerity to address a petition to the queen, imploring her to allow 'the word of our God . . . to reign, and have the highest place', and to cease using 'the manners, fashions, or customs of the papists, but contrariwise utterly to destroy them'. They declared that they were 'a poor congrega-tion' (eighteen of the twenty-seven signed themselves with a mark) 'whom God hath separated from the churches of England and from the mingled and false worshipping therein used'. As well as gathering every Sunday in houses there was a meeting every Wednesday for prayer (*plus ça change?*) and, they added, menacingly, 'to exercise discipline upon them which do deserve it'. The petition complained that the minister of their 'Privy Church', Richard Fitz, a deacon and two members had all died of 'long imprisonment' at the hands of the authorities.[8]

The Ideal of a Church Reformed

There is one absolutely crucial point that must be made concern-ing these radicals: they clearly supported the concept of a state church which forcibly embraced the population as a whole, and had no intention of forming gathered churches of true believers

---

[8]   C. Burrage, *Early English Dissenters*, ii., pp. 15–18.

only. The latter would have been impossible anyway, for their Calvinist theology declared that it was impossible to know who was, or was not, in a state of salvation. The mistake that is so frequently made by present-day students of this period is to confuse the separatists' sectarian circumstances with sectarian principles. They were, perforce, living a sectarian existence in Elizabeth's reign; they were illegal and, as such, could force no one into their meetings who did not choose to be there. But that does not mean that this was their ideal. Their whole existence as a group was a protest against the particular national church which obtained at that moment; they did not criticize national churches as such. Indeed, they aspired to be such a church themselves, to supplant the present Church of England (or even simply to reform it, if Elizabeth would only let them) and to turn England into their ideal of a godly church-state. To misunderstand this point is to misconceive their whole *raison d'être*, and to impose upon the separatist past the 'denominational', pluralist ethos of modern Congregationalism, its linear descendant.

That having been said, the sectarian existence which formed the daily, lived reality of these separatist groups could not but have a creeping effect upon their ecclesiology. Even as the petitioners of 1571 proclaimed that it was the duty of 'the magistrates' and 'the queen's highness' to 'bring home the people of God to the purity and truth of the apostolic church', they yet saw themselves as those whom God had separated from the false Church of England, 'saying "Come out from among them, and separate yourselves from them, and touch no unclean thing" '.[9]

The separation was, of course, from a church made false by its adherence to popish ceremonies and priestly garments – not by the convertedness or otherwise of its members. Nevertheless, the rhetoric of separation (combined with decades of sectarian existence) was to cloud the issue in the minds of many separatists so that, with the passing of the years, they were tacitly to view themselves as the company of saints and their church as a believers' church.

---

[9]   *Ibid.*

Indeed, the existence of a church covenant in Fitz's congregation was perhaps the first sign of such a creeping and implicit voluntarism. Each member was required to declare that the 'relics of Antichrist' in the Church of England were 'abominable before the Lord our God', and that 'I have joined in prayer and hearing God's word with those that have not yielded to this idolatrous trash, notwithstanding the danger for not coming to my parish church'. The vestiarian disputes, which had been the starting-point of the quarrel before anyone had taken so drastic a step as separation, also continually surface in the declamations required of Fitz's members: 'I will not beautify with my presence those filthy rags. . . . I come not to them because they should be ashamed, and so leave their idolatrous garments'.[10]

It is necessary here to note the relationship between separatism and the Puritan movement and, before we can do that, we must make explicit the use we are making of the term 'Puritan'. The precise content of the word has been endlessly debated.[11] For reasons that cannot be entered into here, the definition that recommends itself strongly to the present writer insists on two points. In the first place, Puritanism was a protest movement concerned with ceremonies and, on its more radical wing, with church government – not a movement concerned with doctrine. Puritanism was indeed all but exclusively Calvinist but, until at least the 1620s, when Charles I started promoting an English type of Arminianism, it had no monopoly on that within the English church. The hierarchy itself, indeed, was moderately but very firmly Reformed. In the second place, the term 'Puritan' refers to people *within* the Church of England and is inappropriate, in its English context (though not necessarily in its American), to describe those outside that institution. Puritanism wished, quite literally, to 'purify' the Church of England from those residues of popery which its exponents discerned there. Consequently it is almost meaningless to apply the epithet to sectarians who had left it.

---

[10]   *Ibid.*, ii., pp. 13–15.

[11]   See, for example, C. Hill, *Society and Puritanism in pre-revolutionary England*, ch. 1; R.L. Greaves, 'The Puritan-Nonconformist Tradition in England, 1560–1700, *Albion* 17.4 (Winter, 1985), pp. 449–86; C.H. and K. George, *The Protestant Mind of the English Reformation, 1570–1640*, pp. 117–73; M.G. Finlayson, 'Puritanism and Puritans: Labels or Libels?', *Canadian Journal of History* 8 (1973), pp. 203–23.

This leaves the separatists we are considering here in an ambiguous position. They certainly did wish to see the Church of England reformed, but their credulity – or their patience – had been stretched beyond measure and, in the meantime, they had left that institution. If they held a wait-and-see attitude towards possible future reform of the existing national church, then they did so by way of mental reservation from their much more obvious tactic of denouncing it, in the present, as a false church. It was this latter activity to which they devoted their main energies.

Our definition of 'Puritan' is perhaps open to objections. It is, nevertheless, the meaning which does least violence to sixteenth- and seventeenth-century usage, whilst retaining some degree of objective and rational delimitation. It is, therefore, probably wisest to exclude separatists from the category of 'Puritan' altogether. Indeed, following the logic further, it should be said that Puritanism is a subject which does not primarily concern us in this book, for we are telling here the story of the sectarian radicals. There remains, of course, an indirect interest; most of the English and American dissenters might be accounted spin-offs or by-products of Puritanism. Our point is though that, however much they retained of the Puritan heritage, they ceased to be specifically Puritan when they passed the point of no return and gave up seeking to purify (by whatever lights) the Church of England.

That said, in its view of the 'marks' which infallibly designated a true church, Fitz's 'Privy Church' was still in line with large sections of the Puritan movement within the Church of England. According to Fitz on the one hand, and to most Puritans on the other, there were three such 'marks'. The first was the preaching of the gospel truly, though Fitz also insisted that this must be 'not in bondage and subjection, but freely', implying that that criterion was hardly met by the Church of England. Secondly, the sacraments had to be ministered purely. Again, Fitz's church demanded that this be 'only and altogether according to the institution and good word of the Lord Jesus, without any tradition and invention of man'; it must have been almost impossible for those directly involved to read such words without generating a mental picture of the hated surplice in the mind's eye. These first two 'marks' of a true church were uncontentious amongst Protestants, and it was only the third 'mark' which divided the episcopal authorities from their Puritan and separatist critics.

According to Fitz's Privy Church it was necessary to have, 'not the filthy canon law', which had been inherited by the Church of England from the Catholic Middle Ages, 'but discipline only'. [12] The separatists' church order document had implied that the Church of England barely met the first two criteria for being a true church; there was no doubt in their minds that it wholly failed to meet the third. Non-separatist Puritans leaned towards ambivalence on this point: discipline was highly desirable, perhaps essential, and the present position was highly unsatisfactory. Upholders of the hierarchy, however, would have been more likely to counter that it was not an actual criterion of church-hood at all. The former response demanded a degree of equivocation, and this polemical weakness of the Puritans was to be the separatists' strength in the years to come.

What, in any case, did Puritans (or indeed Fitz's separatists) mean by 'discipline'? In effect, they were arguing for the rôle of moral policeman to be given to each parish minister, perhaps assisted by lay elders, so that the notoriously ungodly (or the notoriously un-Protestant) could be excommunicated, and thereby forced into line. The sanctions of existing canon law, by contrast, were used primarily against administrative offenders – including, most notably, Puritan agitators – rather than as a punishment for moral or doctrinal misbehaviour. In any case, the canon law machinery was administered at diocesan level and above, rather than parochially and pastorally by clergy. Ideally, many of the Puritan ministers (especially those who, from the early 1570s onwards, were inclined to support a presbyterian system of church government) wished to examine their parishioners before admitting them to communion.

The real differences between this insistence upon the third 'mark' and the practice of the Anabaptists, who also strongly advocated church discipline, were twofold. In the first place, the English Puritans envisaged a weeding out of a few unworthy

---

[12]   C. Burrage, *Early English Dissenters*, ii., p. 13.

people from amongst the much larger group comprising the bulk of the population, with the aim of forcing the recalcitrant to an amendment of life.[13] It did not amount to a belief in a believers' church, which they considered unattainable on the grounds that God's judgements are inscrutable to us. Discipline, then, was to be directed at outward behaviour and geared toward securing outward conformity to the demands of the church. Anabaptist concepts of church discipline, by contrast, envisaged a similar treatment of individuals, but were predicated on the basis that most people would be permanently excluded. They were working, as it were, from a zero-base, with the godly being the minority in society, and churches consisting of committed disciples only. Unencumbered by Calvinist dogma, they had no doctrine of an 'invisible church' which had to be distinguished sharply from actual, visible churches.

In the second place, both Puritans and their more impatient cousins, the separatists, wanted the forcible imposition of this discipline upon the population as a whole. This is not so much a criticism of them, as an observation about the essential nature of their ecclesiology. The continental Anabaptists, by contrast, sought to discipline only their own members. Neither is this to praise them; the use of the ban amongst the Dutch and North German Mennonites could be extremely harsh. It was, however, of the nature of their ecclesiology that such discipline had to be voluntarily embraced by members who were not (indeed could not be) forced to remain part of the church that imposed such behaviour upon them a moment longer than they chose to belong.

Having stressed the differences, it is finally important to stress how they began to break down. Under the circumstances of a prolonged sectarian existence, the separatist model of church discipline (which they took from their Puritan background) was capable of transmogrification into something much closer to the Anabaptist 'zero-base' model. With this metamorphosis was to come something as close to the Anabaptist idea of a gathered church as Calvinist theology would permit.

---

[13] See P. Collinson, *The Elizabethan Puritan Movement*, pp. 346–55 for a discussion of this topic.

The concept of 'visible sainthood' was to become prominent in English radical thought.[14] In essence, it conveyed an idea almost opposite to that which it might suggest to the modern mind. The identity of the true saints is not visible to us, since God alone knows whom he has predestined to salvation. Nonetheless, those who are neither ignorant in religion nor scandalous in life might (to a charitable judgement) be thought to be among the elect; as such, they are to be accounted visible saints.

On this logic, it is only the persons who are actually visible, their sainthood being merely apparent. The church could not judge of eternal things, but only of apparent, temporal realities. It made no claim to discern who was converted, only who was godly. If their theology would not allow them to countenance a church which distinguished the saints from the lost, they at least began, with the passing of the years, to separate *visible* saints from the ungodly.

Reformation without Tarrying for Any

The most radical separatist in the years that followed was Robert Browne, which is an unfortunate circumstance for a number of reasons. In the first place, his ideas constitute the only major exception to at least some of the points we have just been outlining. In the second place, he eventually deserted the movement, recanted and became a schoolmaster, and then later a clergyman. Finally, as the first major writer thrown up by the separatist movement, it was thenceforward named after him by its enemies, to the great embarrassment and perpetual irritation of its proponents, who saw him, not unnaturally, as a turncoat. So persistent was the unwelcome eponym that the separatists of 1596, in writing their confession of faith for public consumption, felt obliged to publish it as a statement of those things which 'we . . . falsely called Brownists do hold towards God'. How else, otherwise, would people have known who they were?

Browne was born in Rutland about 1550 and educated in Cambridge where, like many of his class and generation, he was

---

[14]   See E.S. Morgan, *Visible Saints: the History of a Puritan Idea*.

radicalized in his religious opinions. In his case, the major influence came from Thomas Cartwright, the Lady Margaret Professor of Divinity, whose lectures in 1570 on the Acts of the Apostles propounded presbyterianism, and who shortly after-wards found himself jobless as a result. The young Browne graduated in 1572 and spent the next few years as a schoolmas-ter. From about 1580 he started working with his more cautious and moderate friend Robert Harrison to establish separatist congregations in the Norwich area. These took definite shape in 1581. He was arrested, however, and only released after the intervention of Elizabeth's chief minister, Lord Burghley, who was a distant relative and an occasional rescuer of Puritans in trouble.

Following this brush with authority, Browne and Harrison led such of their flock as would accompany them to the safety of the Netherlands, where the circumstances of a Protestant-led war of national liberation against Spanish rule and a freewheeling enterprise economy based on international trade combined to allow *de facto* religious toleration to all who were not actively hostile to these ends. In their refuge at Middelburg, Zeeland, the exiles hoped to establish a church order along lines that seemed to them to be indicated by Scripture. In this, their hopes were remarkably similar to those of the eight hundred or so Protest-ants who had left their native shores during Mary's reign. In their own minds, at least, the analogy was an obvious one. Perhaps the sequel, a return home in triumph to a changed régime, would be their reward also.

Like many radical Puritans (including, almost by definition, those who had been influenced by presbyterian views), Browne had ceased, from his university days, to regard the English bishops as a legitimate authority in the church. However, it was not until about 1580 that his reasons for this rejection had become sufficiently radical as to lead him into separatism.

In the first place, he reasoned that, if episcopal authority was invalid, then so too must be the ministerial authority of parish ministers ordained by bishops. And since faith comes only from hearing 'the preaching of those which are sent by the Lord' then, as one historian has nicely put it, 'preachers who submitted to episcopal authority did not, by definition, fall into this category';

the setting up of separatist congregations was, therefore, a matter of urgency.[15] Secondly, Browne had come to believe that authority from Christ is passed down, not from one person to one other (as in the 'apostolic succession' concept of episcopacy), but in a constantly broadening stream, so that it is effectively vested in the body of Christ as a whole, rather than in bishops. By this reasoning, the leadership of a church is subject to its membership and not the other way around. Although this teaching was greatly modified in later separatism, it was to have an abiding influence amongst the Baptists. At the very least, it had to follow that members should elect their own pastors.

The tendency of such teaching was to put the spotlight on the membership; Browne held that the way to build the church of Christ was 'by gathering the worthy and refusing the unworthy'. Justifying himself by reference to the parable of the mustard seed, he reasoned that 'the kingdom of God was not to be begun by whole parishes, but rather of the worthiest, be they never so few'.[16] If Browne's intention was separatist, his emphasis upon a membership confined to the 'worthy', who controlled their own churches, was anabaptistical.

It is possible to square Browne's call for the church to desist from forcing 'both papists and careless worldlings . . . to build the Lord's sanctuary' with the usual separatist demand that membership be not restricted further than to the simple insistence upon basic Christian knowledge and a tolerable approximation to Christian behaviour. Nevertheless, Browne's tone suggests a closer approximation to the Anabaptist ideal of a church of committed disciples only.

It was in Middelburg that Browne was to produce some of the most important writings of his career. One in particular deserves our attention here. *A treatise of reformation without tarying for anie*, published in 1582, is Browne's best-known work, and one of his most radical. The title alludes to the notion of a progressive reformation, the lingering hope amongst many

---

[15] B.R. White, *The English Separatist Tradition*, p. 47.
[16] R. Browne, *The Writings of Robert Harrison and Robert Browne*, eds. Peel and Carlson, pp. 402, 404.

that Elizabeth would promote further reforms 'when the time was right', and insists that such a process was much too slow. (Karlstadt had used very similar language in respect of the Wittenberg reformation, in his tract of 1524 *Whether one should proceed slowly*.[17]) Those who wish to reform the Church of England should not wait for permission from the secular magistracy, as the Puritans were doing, but should simply proceed straight away, with or without permission, as he, Browne, had done. For 'if they [civil magistrates] be for them [reformers of the church], there is no tarrying: and if they be against them, they are no Christians, and therefore also there can be no tarrying'. The logic would seem flawless, but only Anabaptists had ever argued that a controlling assumption for Christians should be that magistrates are not (*ex officio*, as it were) in a state of salvation.

If, however, the magistrates 'be not Christians, should the welfare of the church or the salvation of men's souls hang on their courtesy?'[18] It was a fair question but, again, one which only Anabaptists had hitherto been disposed to ask. If, on the other hand, the magistrates truly were Christians, they must be 'under a pastoral charge' (like any other Christian) and as such ought to promote, not impede, the progress of the faith they professed. Browne asked how a pastor, who supposedly had the oversight of the magistrates in his flock, could possibly allow himself to be so overseen *by* the magistrate as to go cap in hand seeking his permission to reform the church.

Browne had put his finger on a crucial issue. There was a conflict of assumptions in Elizabethan Protestantism (indeed, in magisterial Protestantism generally) which, despite being buried by use of a common language, was increasingly contriving to emerge into the light of day. Broadly, this conflict was between the 'godly party' of Puritans and would-be reformers

---

[17] 'May one steal until the thieves stop stealing? . . . Each congregation shall make up its own mind what is right and shall do it without tarrying for any. . . . Because of the weak, they say, one should delay. . . . But is that not the same as if they said that we should allow the council to determine . . . to what degree we should serve God?' see Karlstadt, *Battle*, ed. R.J. Sider, pp. 52, 56, 64.

[18] Browne, *Writings*, eds. Peel and Carlson, p. 164.

who assumed religious faith to be an end in itself, indeed the chief end of human existence, and those more Erastian-minded[19] Protestants, who assumed religious polity to be a means to a social end. Both parties tended to speak a language appropriate to the former assumption, even as they distributed ecclesiastical power on the basis of the latter, with results that constantly frustrated the godly. The appearance of the Presbyterian movement in the 1570s had seen this common language begin to disintegrate; Browne's questioning took the process a good deal further than even the most radical Puritans had hitherto ventured.

'For most of them dare not charge the magistrates, but only closely [i.e. secretly, or implicitly], and with many flatterings, that they might still be exalted by the magistrates.' To the magistrates themselves, he did not flinch from pointing out that the existing church-state relationship had favoured those who, whether they recognized it or not, had assumed religious polity to be a means to a social end: 'The Lord's kingdom must wait on your policy, forsooth, and his church must be framed to your civil state, to supply the wants [i.e. needs] thereof.'[20]

A call to dispense with waiting on the permission of the magistrate for ecclesiastical reform could only be seen, of course, as a path to social anarchy, a fear which Browne did little enough to allay. 'We may not be servants to the unlawful commandings of men', he told his readers, 'and this freedom have all Christians. . . . Therefore the magistrate's commandment must not be a rule unto me of this and that duty, but as I see it agree with the word of God.'[21] The horror that such a claim was bound to evoke he hoped to disarm by emphasizing, in the opening passage of his book, the civil authority of the magistrate. But this was clearly no more than a pitch for some semblance of respectability; his

---

[19] 'Erastian' is a term referring to the views of Thomas Erastus, a Zwinglian theologian who famously argued, at a disputation in Heidelberg, that the church should be firmly subject to the secular authorities of state. Since the disputation took place in 1589, the term is, strictly speaking, an anachronism by a few years in this context. Nevertheless, subject to caveats about loose usage, the term retains a good deal of usefulness.

[20] *Ibid.*, pp. 154, 167.

[21] *Ibid.*, pp. 158–9.

central ideas would have made even – perhaps especially – the most radically presbyterian ears burn.

Browne argued unashamedly for voluntarism, and that, not from the New Testament, but from the Old: 'The Lord's people is of the willing sort. They shall come unto Zion and inquire the way to Jerusalem [Jeremiah 50 is the reference in the margin], not by force nor compulsion, but with their faces thitherward.' He appealed to Psalm 84, which stresses that 'the Lord's people shall come *willingly* in the day of his assemblies'. The Puritans, on the other hand, 'cry for Discipline, Discipline, that is for a civil forcing, to imprison the people, or otherwise by violence to handle and beat them, if they will not obey them'. His exegesis of the Old Testament is occasionally rather strained – as when he attempts to argue that the kings of Judah did not attempt to force their people to receive the church government – but Browne's forcing of the text reveals all the more clearly his passion to establish that 'it is the conscience and not the power of man that will drive us to seek the Lord's kingdom'.[22]

Browne's writing was certainly a polemical triumph, but it did not rescue either him or his group from the problems of internal dissension which so bedevilled religious exiles. One of the main groups of the Marian exiles, whom they were in some sense emulating, had themselves been rent asunder by disputes in Frankfurt in 1554–5. But it was the views expressed in Browne's own writings which, to no small extent, were responsible for the fierce quarrels which ensued amongst the English separatists at Middelburg.

According to his more moderate co-leader, Robert Harrison, Browne's *Treatise of reformation* contained 'manifold heresy'. Harrison did not even agree with the contention that the Church of England was not a true church, since there were within it many 'true worshippers'. On this point, at least, it was Browne and not Harrison who was more in line with what was becoming the central separatist tradition. Harrison, however, was more ortho-dox (by separatist lights) on the issue of voluntarism. According to him, the magistrates did indeed have the right and duty 'to strike with their sword everyone which, being of the church, shall

---

22 *Ibid.*, pp. 156, 162.

openly transgress against the Lord's commandments'.[23] These and other, personal differences rent the fellowship, and Browne left for Scotland, with a small band of his own followers, where they arrived in January 1584.

The ecclesiastical arrangements in Scotland should, theoretically, have been at least a little more to Browne's liking than those in England. The hated bishops, at least, were not in evidence. But the use of state power to silence discordant voices was; Browne swiftly found opportunity to compare the prison accommodation on offer north of the border with that provided in England. The experience did not endear presbyterian ideals to him, for the Scots acted 'more wrongfully than any bishop would have done'.[24] Later that year, he returned to England.

In 1585 he was arrested; a royal proclamation had been issued two years before, banning his writings, as a result of which two men had already been hanged for circulating them. The principal author of separatist disturbances was now in the hands of the authorities, but his life was spared by a second intervention of his highly placed kinsman, Lord Burghley.

On 7th October 1585, Browne signed a document, declaring that 'I do humbly submit myself to be at my Lord of Canterbury's commandment, whose authority under her Majesty I will never resist nor deprave, by the grace of God'.[25] The following year Browne was made master of St. Olave's School, which had been founded in 1568 and was situated then, and for four centuries afterwards, in Southwark.[26] He almost certainly continued to minister secretly to separatist gatherings in the capital, notwithstanding his massive loss of credit with the main separatist leadership resulting from his apostasy. Clearly committed to a double game, he felt able to accept the rectorship of

---

[23] *Ibid.*, pp. 149, 120.

[24] *Ibid.*, p. 519.

[25] *Ibid.*, p. 507. The document is known only from its later citation in Stephen Bredwell's anti-separatist book, *The Rasing of the Foundations of Brownisme* (1588), p. 127. However, since the fact of Browne's apostasy was acknowledged on all sides, there seems no reason to dispute the detail.

[26] The present writer – by coincidence – was once a pupil of this august establishment. He does not, however, have any recollection of attending religious instruction classes taught by our hero.

Thorpe-cum-Achurch, Northamptonshire, when it was pro-
cured for him in 1591 by his usual guardian angel in high places,
the queen's chief minister.

A quarter of a century's silence then descends upon Browne's
tempestuous career, before he was in trouble again in 1617 – and
by this time he was in his late sixties – for failing to use all of the
ceremonial prescribed in the *Book of Common Prayer*. He died
in Northampton town prison in 1633, to whose care he had been
confined for assaulting the local constable, thus proving as ec-
centric in his manner of death as he had been enigmatic and
provocative for so much of his life.[27]

Henry Barrow's case against the Puritans

With Browne discredited, and Harrison dying in 1585, the
separatist cause was potentially at a low ebb. But, not long after
Harrison's death in Middelburg, another separatist church was
being organized in London. Its leader was John Greenwood, like
his predecessors a Cambridge graduate, who had been deprived
of his benefice in Norfolk and had made his way to the capital,
where he had either found or founded what was to become
known as the 'Ancient Church' in St. Paul's churchyard. It was
almost impossible for someone of his occupation to remain at
large for very long; he was arrested in October 1587 and, apart
from a brief spell of freedom in 1592, spent the rest of his short
life in custody.

His companion in leadership and in prison was Henry Barrow,
yet another Cambridge scholar, who had been converted from a
life of frivolity around 1580 and had become involved with the
underground radicals who, in truth, were anything but frivolous.
A few weeks after Greenwood's arrest, Barrow visited him in the
Clink, but found himself staying on the premises longer than he
had anticipated when Archbishop Whitgift, the disciplinarian

[27]   F. Ives Cater, 'The excommunication of Robert Browne and his will', *Trans. Cong. Hist. Soc.* 4 (Jan., 1912), pp. 199–204; D.C. Smith, 'Robert Browne, Independent', *Church History* vi (1937), pp. 338, 344–6, cited in M. Watts, *The Dissenters*, vol. 1, p. 33.

occupant of Lambeth Palace since 1583, ordered him to be detained.

Neither captive was left in peace by the ecclesiastical authorities; both were visited at intervals by Puritan clergy, at the behest of John Aylmer, Bishop of London, in order to convince them of the error of their ways, and persuade them to relapse into mere Puritanism. In this way they would have become eligible for release. Needless to say, these visits resulted in some lively discussions.

Thus it was that Henry Barrow, on 14th March 1590, found himself considering the extraordinary claim by the bishop's latest ambassador that 'I know none wicked in all my parish'.[28] Thomas Sperin was rector of St. Mary Magdalen Church, on Milkstreet, and up to this point he had, by and large, been getting the better of the argument. But now things were starting to go badly for him, and this incautiously optimistic assessment of the morals of his parishioners did not help his cause. It had been goaded from him by the need to insist, on the one hand, that the Church of England was not a free-for-all in which communion was given to the openly wicked, and that discipline was indeed imposed, and on the other hand, by the requirements of strict honesty, for in actual fact there was scarcely a case in his own parish where the theoretical power to exclude the ungodly had been enforced. To those on their right, Puritans had traditionally complained of the church's laxity in implementing 'the discipline', but Sperin was here locked in combat with an opponent on his left. Better, then, to claim that discipline was sufficient, at least in those parishes where Puritans held control.

Barrow, however, had recovered from his poor start, and was beginning to relax; at least, we can infer as much from his gently mocking reply to Sperin's claim: 'What, not one wicked all this while? Sure you then have a more excellent church than ever was on the earth. But trow you are none wicked in all the land, with whom you stand one body (for all are of your church); will you justify also all the parishes of England?'

---

[28]   J. Greenwood, *The Writings of John Greenwood 1587–1590*, ed. L.H. Carlson, p. 187.

What to do? To answer in the affirmative was to invite ridicule. In any case, the Puritan paradise was a universally enforced Reformed discipline, with all of the people properly instructed in their Christian duties and faith; the present situation on a national level, with large numbers of absentee clergy and ignor- ant parsons who could not preach, offended Sperin nearly as much as it did Barrow. So he carefully waded just a little deeper into the mire.

'I will justify all those parishes that have preaching ministers', he declared. 'And what of those that have unpreaching minis- ters?' 'I think not such to be true churches', replied his opponent. Mr. Sperin was then asked to put this in writing and sign it, but something must have jogged his memory concerning the bishop, and he declined.

Perhaps the indiscretion played on his mind, for a few moments later he retraced his steps to claim of parishes with non-preaching clerics that 'if they make the same profession of faith, then I hold them churches also'. Barrow countered that, 'All the parishes of England have the same confession . . .', a judgement from which his antagonist did not dissent. [29]

In their struggle with the church hierarchy, the Puritans had long enjoyed the advantages of consistency. It was they, and not their opponents, who were seeking to follow through Protestant doctrine with Protestant practice. It was they who had been able to seize the high ground of principle, and to make their episcopal foes squirm in the quagmire of pragmatism, forcing them to fall back on arguments about *adiaphora* and the commands of the prince. It cannot have been pleasant, therefore, for Sperin and others of a Puritan direction of thought to have Barrow and his ilk point out to them that they, the Puritans, were themselves trying to have things both ways. If the discipline was indeed being truly enforced, then why, if all the inhabitants were admitted to communion, were not all the inhabitants also godly? If some parishes were not true churches, however, then why should the godly not separate from them?

Again, what was the validity of the Puritan preachers' own ministry, when their appointments and very licences to preach

---

[29]   *Ibid.*, pp. 187–8.

had their authorization from a source they held to be unscriptural, namely the bishops? Sperin, after prolonged needling from Barrow, was eventually flushed out of his hiding place on this point also. At first, Sperin claimed that his own ministry was 'from God, with the approbation of the assembly of the church where I am'. But Barrow pointed out that this 'approbation' was merely an after-the-event consent (and a consent they had no real power to withhold) to the appointment made by the patron and the bishop. When Sperin insisted that 'I will not stand to justify the calling of [i.e. by] the bishops; I have a better calling than the calling of the bishops', Barrow enquired what he thought of the bishops' appointive power. Sperin confessed it 'to be unlawful'. Barrow had caught him again; when invited to put this on paper, with his signature, Sperin complained that there was no purpose in such an exercise but to bring himself into danger.[30]

This, for Barrow, was the real point of the whole discussion. His opponent had not the courage of his own supposed convictions. A moment later, Sperin thought to have turned the tables when he asked, 'Why, then you affirm that the queen and the parliament do wickedly in giving this power and authority unto the bishops. Will you write that?' Disappointingly, his tormentor replied in the affirmative and the debate assumed a more acrimonious tone, until Barrow began to preach at him. 'Christ crucified you all abhor, you can not abide by his cross, you will not suffer or abide by any truth, but daily seek new cavils, distinctions and evasions to hide any truth which bringeth danger, or to avoid the cross of Christ, and therefore you shall not reign with him.'[31]

So that was it. The Puritans were having their morality on the cheap. They were not prepared, in their struggle against sin, to 'resist unto blood' (Heb. 12:4). It was the separatists' basic conviction, that they themselves were following the Puritan direction of thought through to its logical and consistent destination, that sustained their own thinking.

Events were to prove that the trajectory of thought was capable of reaching a goal yet more distant than the separatists were prepared to countenance, but such problems lay in the future. In

---

[30] *Ibid.*, pp. 188–90.
[31] *Ibid.*, pp. 190–4.

the meantime, neither Barrow nor Greenwood were found wanting in their willingness to suffer for their beliefs. In 1593 both
men were hanged, along with John Penry, the Welsh Puritan
agitator and separatist sympathiser who had been implicated in
the production of the notorious Marprelate tracts of 1588.

It should be pointed out that none of these men suffered for
heresy, for their actual theological beliefs were not, according to
the Church of England, actually heretical; they were executed for
subversion and for circulating seditious writings. The statute
under which they suffered had originally been directed against
Roman Catholics, whose loyalty to a 'foreign power' (the pope)
made them *ipso facto* subversive. (For this reason, none of the
three hundred or so Catholics who suffered death during
Elizabeth's reign died as heretics, either; the Elizabethan régime
insisted – rather perversely – that they were not suffering for
specifically religious causes at all.) The distinction may seem a
fine one – and quite irrelevant, perhaps, to those whose twentieth-century notions about 'tolerance' are outraged by any deaths
in the cause of imposing an official 'conscience' on society – but
at least it made the difference between hanging and a more
lingering death by fire, a fate reserved for Anabaptists, anti-
trinitarians and witches.[32]

As Henry Barrow and John Greenwood went to their deaths,
a new leader was already emerging within the ranks of the
harassed and fragmented separatist movement. The pastorate of
Francis Johnson was to prove decisive for the future: separatism's definitive confession of faith was to emerge, even as its
position of fragmentation, impotence and marginality was confirmed. The question of whether the Church of England was, or
was not, a true church was to be urgently reassessed in the light
of the baptism question – and separatism stood revealed as no
less a halfway house than Puritanism or the Elizabethan settlement had been. To this, the crisis of English separatism and the
emergence of the General Baptists, we must now turn.

---

[32] It should be remembered, however, that the fate of a minority of Catholic martyrs
– one thinks of the Jesuit Edmund Campion – who were arraigned as actual traitors
and so were hanged, drawn and quartered, was at least equally terrible as burning.

Chapter Ten

A Further Parting of the Ways: Francis Johnson, John Smyth and the General Baptists

Francis Johnson was no separatist in the spring of 1591. As pastor of the Congregation of English Merchant Adventurers in Middelburg he was a man of Puritan, indeed, presbyterian sympathies.

He had been expelled from his position as fellow of Christ Church, Cambridge for giving voice in a January 1589 sermon to the opinion that each congregation should be governed by elders, and that neglect of this principle had been the cause of 'ignorance, idolatry and all disobedience'.[1] The university authorities had taken the view that, on the contrary, the neglect of which Johnson complained constituted obedience, his sermon the disobedience; he had swiftly been consigned to accommodation appropriate to his case.

From his cell in Cambridge prison, Johnson's options had been limited. A colleague arrested with him had taken the line of least resistance and recanted, but Johnson was made of sterner stuff. He had appealed to Burghley, but Johnson was no relative of the chief minister's and had to sit out his time until someone, somewhere deemed him to have learned his lesson. Upon his release, he had felt it best to leave the country.

The Netherlands provided a number of congregations to which wayward clergy of persuasions similar to Johnson's might minister. There was as large a trading community of English people in the Netherlands as there was of Dutch in London and along the east coast.

---

[1]   B.R. White, *The English Separatist Tradition*, p. 92.

English merchants had been prone to Protestantism even before the Reformation had been adopted by government, and to particularly strident forms of it afterwards, so virtually all of the expatriate English churches were Puritan to some degree or another. Although they did not conform in their worship patterns to the forms prescribed at home in the *Book of Common Prayer*, however, they were not (except for Harrison's and Browne's) separatist; they merely had the convenience to fall outside of the English government's jurisdiction, though they would have accepted – and expected – conformity during any sojourn back in England. In the meantime, they enjoyed the freedom to practise as they saw fit (along the broad lines of Reformed Protestantism approved of by their Dutch hosts) without any imputation of separatism, still less of Anabaptism.

It was a congregation of this sort to which Johnson had come upon his release from custody, and which provided him with the opportunity of experiencing, indeed of guiding, the kind of church polity he found taught in Scripture. Thomas Cartwright, the originator of the English presbyterian ideal, had himself been a predecessor in the post which Johnson now occupied, so he felt quite at home there.

Thus it was that, when Sir Philip Sidney, the English ambassador, sought the co-operation of the Dutch authorities in suppressing the printing of two books by Henry Barrow, Johnson was on hand to demonstrate his loyalty. It was apparently not difficult to smuggle manuscripts out of London prisons (the modern edition of Barrow and Greenwood's writings penned 1587–1593 runs to four volumes), but printing and distribution were more hazardous enterprises. The latter task could hardly be avoided, but the former, at least, could be conducted more safely – perhaps more cheaply even – in the cheerful, business-like anonymity of the 'religious Babel' over the Channel.[2]

---

[2]   K.L. Sprunger, *Trumpets From the Tower: English Puritan Printing in the Netherlands 1600–1640*, pp. 29–32 repeats the estimate of H. de la Fontaine Verwey in respect of the following century that Dutch printers produced half or even more of all the books printed in the world, a lesson on the economic benefits of multilingualism which has yet to be fully grasped by Europe's offshore islanders.

Consequently English diplomats in the Dutch Republic were often occupied, as they were to be for several generations afterwards, in interventions with both central and local government to suppress the printing of English works which Elizabeth (and her Stuart successors) deemed to be subversive.

The English government's interest in the question was obviously that of maintaining religious stability at home, a consideration to which the Dutch authorities were (mostly) inclined to be sympathetic, but their co-operation was nevertheless half-hearted; they were effectively being asked to prevent Dutch nationals from capitalizing on their economic competitive advantage, and to irritate loyal Protestants to boot. In the late spring of 1591, however, they were inclined to be co-operative, and almost all of the printing of two books, one by Henry Barrow and one by John Greenwood, was seized under Francis Johnson's personal supervision and publicly burned.

Curiosity and forbidden fruit are strong inducements, however, and Johnson kept a couple of copies back for his own perusal. If his intention had been to satisfy himself that the writings now lying in ashes were indeed false teaching, then he failed, for he found himself being persuaded by the arguments he discovered there.

In October he drew up a form of church covenant for his congregation, showing influence of separatist thinking (its principles held validity, he claimed, 'as well under Christian princes, as under heathen magistrates'), with the intention that subscription to the aforesaid covenant should be made a condition of membership.[3] These plans, however, were rejected by the church as a whole.

When he visited the English capital in 1592 to confer with the incarcerated authors of the burned books, they were only too glad to clear up, in their own inimitable fashion, his perplexity of mind, with the result that he resolved not to return to his charge in Middelburg, and to take up the pastorate of the underground (one is tempted to say 'extra-mural') separatist church in London instead.

---

[3]   B.R. White, *The English Separatist Tradition*, pp. 92–3.

The sequel was as inevitable as it was predictable: Johnson was arrested in October 1592, almost immediately after having taken up the pastorate. He does not appear to have been held for long, for he was arrested again in December, and this time he was to remain out of circulation for over four years. The following March, fifty-six of his congregation were picked up, but released later that spring on the proviso that they leave the country. By now, separatists knew where to head for, and they reached the Netherlands in July.

It is worth noticing the tenor of the petition they had submitted to Parliament from their cells. This asked for mercy, crowed that there were many of them still at large and meeting for worship, and persisted in claiming the heritage of Marian Protestantism for their own – they had 'as good warrant to reject the ordinances of Antichrist, and to labour for the recovery of Christ's holy institutions, as our fathers and brethren in Queen Mary's days had to do the like'.[4] Once again, English separatists were drawing a parallel between the Church of England and the Roman 'Antichrist', implicitly including the practices of the former in the supposed devilishness of the latter. The title of a book written by Francis' brother George giving a record of the congregation's history from 1594–1600 is, in part, yet another claim to continuity with the persecuted English Protestantism of Mary's reign. Written in 1603, *A discours of some troubles* echoes the title of William Whittingham's account of the English exile congregation in Frankfurt-am-Main in the 1550s.[5]

Johnson and his fellow-elders continued to direct their flock across the Channel. Unlike their peers in the parish clergy, they may not have enjoyed salaries maintained at public expense, but at least their accommodation was. The *True Confession* of 1596, widely held to be a definitive statement of the separatists' beliefs, was penned in full consultation with the imprisoned brethren, though perhaps Henry Ainsworth (1570–1622), a very able scholar and teacher within the fellowship at liberty in Amsterdam, played a larger rôle in producing it than Johnson did.

---

[4] cited in *ibid.*, p. 95.
[5] W. Whittingham, *A Brieff Discours of the Troubles Begonne at Franckford*.

A True Confession consists of forty-five articles, the first six-teen of which are fairly uncontentious from the point of view of the Reformed constituency from which the separatists came. Indeed, these articles might be seen as an attempt to establish their own credentials as good Calvinists. One of the few hints of what is to come in later sections is a statement in the thirteenth that Christ has spoken and speaks 'to his Church in his own ordinance, by his own ministers and instruments only, and not by any false ministry at any time'.[6] Ample demonstration could be given – to the separatists' own satisfaction at least – that the Church of England's was a false ministry, with the inevitable consequence that Christ did not speak through it. A later section emphasizes that Christ governs the saints 'by such officers and laws as he hath prescribed in his word, . . . and by none other'. Confidence in their ability to discern the one true pattern laid down in Scripture was matched only by their certainty that failure to do so led to divine rejection. From section seventeen onwards, the *Confession* is preoccupied with ecclesiology. The Augustinian and Calvinist distinction between visible and invis-ible churches is maintained – hypocrites are sure to be found within the church – but there is also a subtle shift in terminology, almost certainly unrecognized by the authors themselves. Christ is held to have purchased a church for himself, 'separating them from amongst unbelievers', as opposed to separating the ungodly from amongst the church; the experience of a sectarian existence was pushing the separatists towards what we have called a 'zero-base' assumption about the church, in which the godly are the minority separated out from an ungodly mass, rather than the other way around.

Nevertheless, at the more conscious level the separatists were still a state church in waiting: it was 'the office and duty of princes and magistrates . . . to suppress and root out by their authority all false ministries, voluntary religions and counterfeit worship of God', to 'establish and maintain by their laws every part of God's word, his pure religion and true ministry', and to 'enforce all their subjects . . . to do their duties to God and men'.[7]

---

[6]   W.L. Lumpkin, *Baptist Confessions of Faith*, p. 85.
[7]   *Ibid.*, pp. 94–95.

The exiled separatists had had some trouble with the Dutch authorities and had spent some time being moved around, before finally being allowed to settle at Amsterdam, where they were firmly ensconced by 1596. The city was to be their home for over twenty years. Francis Johnson, his brother George, and another elder named Daniel Studley, were only able to join the brethren upon their release – again on condition of exile – in 1597. But the church was hardly inactive in the meantime.

They fell out with one another over a range of issues, including apostasy (apparently a single instance of attending Puritan preaching in a parish church counted as such), alleged embezzlement of money intended for poor relief, and some members having fallen 'into the heresies of the Anabaptists' and consequently requiring to be excommunicated. There was also a crisis, perhaps related to one or other of these issues, whereby the church split down the middle, with one half excommunicating the other, though there was later to be at least a partial patching up of this quarrel. Even so, the church that was left cannot have consisted of more than about thirty-five–forty people.

The arrival of the Johnson brothers and Daniel Studley, in the autumn of 1597, did not noticeably ease the tensions among the exiles. George and Francis cordially loathed one another, and Francis' wife Tomasine was a focus of much of the dispute. According to George, his brother was dominated by her, and she herself dressed far too fashionably for a pastor's wife and an exile. This last point was an opinion shared by a number of other members, not a few of whom were inclined to a serious view of life, but George was the only one to persist in his criticisms. Neither being averse to using the machinery of the congregation to pursue their quarrel, they appealed to the procedure alluded to in Matthew 18:15–17; the congregation found in favour of their pastor and George was excommunicated. The men's father, John Johnson, was also a member, and when he tried to reconcile his sons he found himself likewise expelled in 1602.

Nor was this the end of the church's problems. There were disputes over the nature of the congregation's relationships with other outposts of English separatism in Norwich, London and the West Country. (It is important, not to say consoling, to remember that this most quarrelsome and well-documented of churches was not the sole bearer of the separatist torch.) Thomas White, the pastor of the West-Country church, joined the exiles in Amsterdam for a while, but fell out with Johnson over his (White's) wife, over alleged shortcomings of the exile church (which White insisted on airing in print) and over allegations of sexual misconduct by several individuals including Studley, who certainly seems to have been guilty. A number of members protested that all power in the congregation was being wielded by Johnson and Studley, notwithstanding the democratic princi-ples of separatism. Henry Ainsworth found himself increasingly at odds with Johnson and led a secession of about thirty people in 1610. The separatists had also been less than reticent in their criticisms of the Dutch Reformed church, and had not hesitated to go into print on the matter, so relationships with their Dutch hosts were also less than ideal. When an English Reformed Church (different from, but in communion with, the Church of England) was begun in Amsterdam in 1605 under the leadership, from 1607, of John Paget, a number of Johnson's congregation joined it.

All of this squabbling, seceding and excommunicating may not be excusable, but perhaps the conscientious historian should at least attempt to account for it. Persecution may have its merits in whittling away all – or almost all – but the truly committed, but it also tends to bring to the fore less admirable characteristics. An embattled community needs to know pre-cisely what it is embattled about, and this can lead to unseemly internal wrangles about the extent of permissible compromise. Such things had led to the Novatianist and Donatist schisms in the third and fourth centuries. Among the Dutch Mennonites, moreover, there had been sharp disagreement over the use and application of the ban.

In the case of the English separatists at Amsterdam, the issue surfaced in the form of disputes about who might be described as an apostate. The separatists had emerged from a background, the Puritan movement, which was convinced that there was in the Scriptures but one true pattern for church life: their duty was to discern that pattern and then implement it. Such convictions made each possible variation in theology and practice a likely cause of serious friction, a potential that seems to have been fully realized in Johnson's congregation. In addition, the separatists' self-definition was primarily a negative one; to be separatist is to have separated *from* something, and so to define oneself in relation to a (rejected) externality. The separatists were *not* part of the Church of England, and the depth of that 'not-ness' could not help but foster a certain prickliness that might make any disagreement get out of hand with alarming ease.

Finally, the separatists were people who had broken solidarity with the vast bulk of the population in the country of their birth, and that in an age which valued unity above almost all virtues. The really huge emotional, psychological and social obstacle, that of leaving the church which encompassed all of their fellow-citizens, had already been overcome; breaking thereafter with any of their fellows whom they deemed to be in error would, by comparison, be a relatively trivial step. The experience of social marginality, especially if one has 'plans' for society as a whole, as the separatists certainly did, can lead to fissiparousness, as fascist and communist groups in post-war Western Europe have found; the end result is a sort of murky underground of mutually anathematising fringe groups. It was a slippery slope of this kind on which the English separatists now found themselves.

John Smyth: Separatist

Of all the arguments and disputes that beset the English separatists in the Netherlands, we have, as yet, failed to mention one. To the originator of this, perhaps the most important quarrel, we now turn.

John Smyth was born about 1570, was tutored by Francis Johnson as an undergraduate in Cambridge, and was a Puritan lecturer in Lincoln from 1600 to 1602. A lecturer, in sixteenth- and seventeenth-century parlance, was not the kind of cross between cure-for-insomnia and substitute-for-reading who nowadays makes a living of sorts by holding forth in a university or some other institute of higher education; he was a sort of supernumerary clergyman, whose sole task was to preach. Such posts attracted Puritans, who were not too keen on performing the other tasks expected of normal, beneficed parish clergy – such as celebrating communion whilst wearing the garments of Anti-christ – and were thus happy to have an excuse to elude them. In any case, given that bishops were reluctant to appoint Puritans to parish livings, lectureships were often all that was left to them. Finally, it was primarily Puritan parishes who wished, or could afford, to appoint such extras; town corporations or the godly gentry were the usual sources of finance for posts designed to provide additional preaching. It was, in short, an arrangement that suited both patrons and the Puritan firebrands whom they chose to patronize very well.

But in October 1602 it ceased to suit the corporation of Lincoln. Their employee stood accused of 'personal preaching, and that untruly, against divers men of good place'. Smyth responded that, if individuals had been pricked in their consciences by his words, that had been the Lord's doing and none of his intention. It was a debate which had taken place many times before (one thinks of Chrysostom) and has occurred many times since; men – and women – 'of good place' are notoriously averse to being pricked, by anybody's intention. The following year Smyth lost his licence to preach, and joined a group of separatists meeting in the Trent Valley on the border between Nottinghamshire, Lincolnshire and Yorkshire.

One of his most recent historians, James R. Coggins, places the formation of this group in the context of the post-1604 crackdown on Puritan ministers, according to which all clergy were required to sign their approval of the government of the church by bishops, along with their approval of the *Book of Common Prayer*.[8] Perhaps about ninety ministers were expelled in this way, of whom about twenty were later reinstated. Coggins stresses the extent to which Smyth's separatist congregation contained a number of ejected clergymen and suggests that 'this no doubt helps to account for the strength of the congregational idea among them' – on the logic that few would have been prepared to sit by and fill a pew.[9]

Most historians accept the later recollection of William Bradford (governor of Plymouth Colony in New England, but at this time a mere sapling of seventeen) that the separatists

---

[8] J.R. Coggins, *John Smyth's Congregation*, pp. 29–37.
[9] *Ibid.*, p. 31.

divided into two groups: one meeting near Scrooby, and the other near Gainsborough. Bradford claimed the reason for this was simply one of geographical convenience, but one recent historian suggests a theological motive. On this theory, John Robinson (ca. 1575–1625), the deprived clergyman later famous as the pastor of the Pilgrim Fathers, accepted the lawfulness of continued private fellowship with Puritans within the Church of England, whereas Smyth was inclined to a stricter view.[10] Robinson did indeed believe that 'we, who profess a separation from the English . . . churches, . . . may notwithstanding lawfully communicate in private prayer, and other the like holy exercises'.[11]

Robinson's somewhat more eirenic position was of no interest, let alone consolation, to the authorities; all of the Trent Valley separatists faced harassment for their beliefs and, probably in 1608, they moved to the Netherlands. It has frequently been assumed that, at first, this community joined up with Francis Johnson's Ancient Church, and only left later, as a result of disagreements. Coggins, however, argues persuasively that the Smyth-Robinson group never joined the Ancient Church in the first place.[12]

It was natural, perhaps, that the two groups should meet apart. The newcomers were predominantly from the north-east Midlands, contained a disproportionately large number of clergy and were, by and large, from a slightly higher – and certainly more literate – social stratum than the members of Johnson's church.

Nonetheless, there were initially no significant differences of principle between the newcomers and the more established congregation of separatists in Amsterdam. Furthermore, any theological differences that there may or may not have been between Smyth and Robinson in England did not destroy their fellowship in Amsterdam, until the former began to engage in controversy with Francis Johnson and Henry Ainsworth. Despite all of its own internal wranglings, the Johnson congregation had grown from about forty members upon his first arrival in 1597 to about

---

[10] M. Watts, *The Dissenters: from the Reformation to the French Revolution*, p. 42.
[11] J. Robinson, *The Works of John Robinson*, ed. D.R. Ashton, iii., p. 105.
[12] J.R. Coggins, *John Smyth's Congregation*, pp. 48–50, 60.

three hundred by the time of Smyth's and Robinson's appearance in, probably, 1608, with around one hundred and fifty supporters of their own. Separatists back in England knew there was a refuge over the Channel and, whenever they came under too much pressure, had resorted to it. The Trent Valley group was but the latest and largest of many, even if its size and other differences meant that it could not simply be absorbed by the existing congregation as other newcomers had been.

By late 1608, Smyth found himself sufficiently at loggerheads with the Ancient Church to go into print against it. He then published *The Differences of the churches of the seperation* to elucidate. In the first place, he declared that human books should not be used in the worship meetings of the church. This might be passed over as yet another piece of typical separatist legalism, were it not for the fact that Smyth included in this category translations of Scripture. He had long placed a very high value on each member of the congregation striving to master the biblical languages; only those who had done so would be in a position to follow his latest counsel and translate extemporane-ously in meetings. This proposal has been dismissed as ludicrous by all subsequent commentators (an evaluation shared by the present one), but since we are here dealing with the venerable originator of the worldwide Baptist movement – rather than with some harebrained would-be messiah – it may just be worthwhile examining the possible workings of his mind on this subject.

Superficially, the idea seems like a transparent attempt to keep all teaching within the hands of either himself or those of the former clergy in the congregation who might possess the requisite skills. The justifications, and probably even the real motivations, point in an entirely opposite direction, however. In part, the move was probably a reaction against the set forms of the *Book of Common Prayer*, and so a function of Smyth's hard-edged separatism. Again, we are compelled to note the creeping effects of a sectarian existence. As impatient Puritans, the separatists had begun by objecting, not to prayer books as such, but to the actual one being enforced in England; now, some at least were rejecting prayer books altogether as too legalistic and restrictive of Spirit-inspired participation in worship – a way of thinking hardly compatible with state churches and with religion as a mechanism for social control. If Scripture is inspired, the actual translations of it on offer to Smyth's congregation were, perhaps, rather less so; in this light, their rejection becomes more intelligible. As Smyth said, 'No translation can possibly express all the matter of the holy originals. . . . Hence it followeth that a translation, be it never so good, is mixed with man's devices.'[13]

It was unthinkable that the separatists would use the officially sanctioned 'Bishops' Bible', the translation approved by the English hierarchy, still less the Catholic Douai translation (the Old Testament of which was, in any case, only then in the throes of completion). This left the Geneva Bible, which had been in print more or less continuously since it was first published in 1560 and was beloved by Puritans everywhere. This translation, however, was strongly laced with Calvinism, not only in its translation of disputable phrases, but in its plentiful marginal comments. Whilst the separatists would naturally be disposed to favour such a bias, they were even more desirous of breaking free from external guiding constraints; as Coggins comments, 'It is not difficult to imagine the Smyth congregation, sworn to seek "new light", feeling restricted by such a Bible'.[14]

The second and third issues raised by Smyth concerned church government and the sources of funds. In his view, the distinction made by other separatists and Puritans between the offices of pastor, elder and teacher was a false one; they amounted to the same thing, and the main point was to ensure a plurality of them in each congregation. It was all very well for Smyth to talk; his group contained half a dozen deprived clergy like himself; Johnson's congregation had been left pastorless whilst Barrow and Greenwood were in prison. And it was all very well for Smyth to maintain that Puritans back in England should not be allowed to salve their consciences for staying in an apostate church by throwing money in the direction of those who had had the courage of their convictions. But if the Ancient Church started refusing to accept money from people who were not members, as Smyth insisted it should, it would face greater financial difficulties than would his own congregation, several

---

[13] J. Smyth, *Works*, i., p. 280.
[14] J.R. Coggins, *John Smyth's Congregation*, p. 54.

of whom had owned significant amounts of property back in England.

Smyth also insisted that Johnson's increasingly autocratic style of leading his congregation was inadmissible. Tradition-ally, the separatists had been democratic in their organization. However, Johnson was coming to believe that, once the congre-gation had chosen their elders and pastor, all authority then passed to those officials. After all of the trouble and dissent he had experienced, it is not hard to understand why Johnson should once again have been coming to appreciate the positive aspects of the presbyterian system he had once espoused. As Henry Ainsworth said, 'Christian liberty (which all have) is one thing, the reins of government (which some have) is another thing'.[15]

It is noteworthy that Smyth's congregation already had a more egalitarian thrust. There seems to have been an expectation that a wide variety of people would contribute to worship meetings, and this indeed was the rationale behind his abhorrence of using books, even Bibles. 'The Spirit is quenched by silence when fit matter is revealed to one that sitteth by and he withholdeth it in time of prophesying. The Spirit is quenched by set forms of worship, for therein the spirit is not at liberty to utter itself, but is bounded in.'[16] The Spirit was at almost unlimited opportunity for utterance in the meetings of Smyth's church: there were two meetings (of four hours each) every Sunday, in which four or five speakers might declaim at length, 'as the time will give leave'.[17]

Perhaps we should not be surprised. Those churches with agendas for wider society (Catholic, episcopalian, presbyterian) tend to reflect the emphasis on social hierarchy most favourable to their supporters; the greater a person's ties to a landholding society based on hierarchy – and the greater their stake within it – the more likely, other things being equal, that they will support a churchmanship reflecting a parallel ecclesiastical hierarchy. Within the more limited horizons of sectarianism, however, it is

---

[15] H. Ainsworth, *Counterpoyson*, pp. 176–7, cited in M. Watts, *The Dissenters*, i., p. 44.
[16] J. Smyth, *Works*, i., p. 277.
[17] B.R. White, *English Separatist Tradition*, pp. 126–7.

not unusual to find this picture reversed. Upper-class individuals may favour greater egalitarianism in church life; people of independent means do not wish to be bossed around by leaders any more than they are in secular life, and considerations of keeping order within the wider society are immaterial to them. Sectarians of lower social standing, by contrast, are more used to straight hierarchies of authority and feel more comfortable with the certainties conveyed by them. The phenomenon has been repeated in more recent times. Those who supported Smyth might fairly be designated as the middle-class leftwingers of their day.

In distancing himself from Johnson though, Smyth found himself antagonizing many of the separatists who had come over with him from the Trent Valley. Bluntly expressed, many of them, including John Robinson, found themselves more in agreement with Johnson than they did with the leader from their own ranks. Coggins insists that Robinson's position was mediating, and there is certainly something to be said for this. Robinson was a part of the same group of voluble and articulate people and, like Smyth, felt constrained to emphasize 'the rôle of the whole people of God in the congregation' in such a way that 'caused many "to reproach us . . . and open their mouths against us for popularity and Anabaptistry" '.[18] Nevertheless, he continued to recognize the pattern of leadership found among more traditional separatists.[19]

Even so, Robinson and those who felt as he did decided to split from Smyth's congregation.[20] About a third stayed with Smyth; the other two-thirds went with Robinson. In the early months of 1609 the latter party moved to Leiden, thus emphasizing the severing of connections.

John Smyth: Baptist

The metaphorical distance between the two congregations had been created by something much more significant, however, than

---

[18]   R.T. Jones, 'John Robinson's Congregationalism' (The Congregtional Lecture 1987, Congregational Memorial Hall Trust, London), p. 13.
[19]   *Ibid.*, p. 19.
[20]   J.R. Coggins, *John Smyth's Congregation*, p. 59.

simply Smyth's disagreements with Johnson over degrees of separatism. It had been provoked by John Smyth's conversion, sometime in late 1608 or early 1609, to the view that it was believers, rather than infants, who were the proper subjects of baptism. The logic was simple enough in certain respects.

If the Church of England was a false church, as separatists never tired of proclaiming, then its ministrations were invalid; as the *True Confession* itself expressed the matter, Christ does not act 'by any false ministry at any time'.[21] The conclusion was ineluctable: the Church of England's baptism was no true bap-tism. However, the baptism which the separatists themselves had received had been administered to them, as infants, by their parish clergy. It would, therefore, have to be repeated, for they had not been truly baptized.

In theory, the matter might have rested there, with an ultra-separatist re-baptism; there was logically no intrinsic reason why a congregation which took such a view might not subsequently revert to infant baptism – as long as that baptism was administered by a true church (i.e. themselves). In practice though, the matter could hardly be left there. Once such a drastic step had been taken – which all outsiders would inevitably stigmatize as 'Anabaptism', replete with overtones of Münster – then believers' baptism would (almost inevitably) become normative for the group.

It was just such a step which Smyth took now. And it was this move, with its accompanying radical shifts in theology, which provoked the division in the group and caused two-thirds of them to look to John Robinson for leadership. Many historians have given the impression that the split between Robinson and Smyth happened before the latter came to hold Baptist views. But as Coggins points out, the hypothesis that it was the baptism issue that was the parting of the ways 'makes more sense than assum-ing that Smyth and his associates made such a radical shift virtually without losing any [further] members!'[22]

Smyth baptized himself and then those members who were persuaded by his arguments, about forty persons in all. The first English Baptist church had been formed.

---

[21]   W.L. Lumpkin, *Baptist Confessions of Faith*, p. 85.

[22]   J.R. Coggins, *John Smyth's Congregation*, p. 60.

The magisterial Protestant churches of Europe, the Church of England not excluded, had all had to speak out of both corners of their mouths at once on this, the most delicate of subjects. All declaimed against the Roman Catholic Church as the veritable tool of the devil, with the Pope being cast in the rôle of Antichrist. And yet rebaptizing the populations of those countries which had turned Protestant was neither attempted nor even suggested. They were to rest content with the baptism of Antichrist that they had received as infants, and Protestant reformers theologized accordingly. The alternative was to risk a great ungluing which might lead anywhere, though most suspected that it would, somehow, pave the way to religious anarchy, to Anabaptism and, of course, to that favourite bogeyman, the Münster scenario. After all, if baptism might be reiterated once by a state church, the arguments against sectarian groups doing so again would become very much weaker.

So Francis Johnson was in good company when, in 1609, he reversed his own arguments of the past seventeen years and claimed that the Church of England (and, with it, the Church of Rome) was a true church, albeit a corrupt one. Just as Erasmus had defended Rome against the Protestant reformers on the grounds that it was still, despite its faults, the true church; just as the bishops of the Church of England had defended the Elizabe-than settlement against Puritan critics on the grounds that the essential marks of Protestantism were there, whatever the other shortcomings; just as the Puritans had defended themselves against the separatists by arguing that the essence of their minis-try was not derived from its tainted source at the hands of the bishops but from the calling of their parishioners, and that discipline was enforced, no matter in how unsatisfactory a fash-ion; so Johnson, in a sense, defended all of these positions in order to protect the pæobaptist stance of his own church against the Baptist arguments of Smyth.

The pattern is clear: each group, when attacking those on their right, insisted that 'essence' is, to some extent, determined by 'accidents' (in the philosophical meaning of those words). In other words, the question of whether or not any given institution was a true church was to be decided on the basis of its character-istics, and on that basis they were disposed to find the more traditional institutions wanting. When confronted by critics on their own left, however, each church then reversed those arguments and insisted that unseemly 'accidents' left 'essence' unimpaired. Their own shortcomings as institutions (or the ultimate derivation of their ceremonies or their ministry in a discredited church to their right) did not diminish the fact that they were, nevertheless, true ministers of Christ.

On the far left of these positions, Smyth had come to believe that neither Catholic nor Protestant state churches, nor even the English separatists, were true churches. The exclusivity of his position caused him no small perplexity; he could not ask the Mennonites, of which there were several varieties in Amsterdam, to baptize himself and his followers, for he did not recognize them either.

The fact is a significant one; it should not be supposed, on the basis of Smyth's undoubtedly strong Mennonite connections at a later date, that Dutch Anabaptists must have influenced him to embrace believers' baptism in the first place. For the English Baptists, separatism was their point of departure. They extended its logic, overleaping the (hypothetical, but unoccupied) position of ultra-separatist re-baptism, to arrive at believers' baptism.

That is not to say that this new position could be occupied without the most profound implications for their theology. Shortly after baptizing himself and his flock, John Smyth began renting a bakehouse from Jan Munter, a Waterlander Mennonite, and now the contacts with, and influence from, Dutch Anabaptism began in earnest. Within a few months Smyth was espousing Mennonite positions concerning free will and the denial of original sin. (The conjecture that Smyth picked up the former opinion from contact with the Arminian party in the Netherlands, over whose heads debate was raging at that time, can safely be discounted.)[23] It is possible that Smyth had advanced to a belief in free-will as a result of the Trent Valley

---

[23]   L.D. Kliever, 'General Baptist Origins', *Mennonite Quarterly Review*, xxxvi (1962), 316–7, suggests that Smyth might even have been swayed by the debates in Cambridge in the 1590s concerning Peter Baro, but this seems even more unlikely. As a Puritan at that time, Smyth would have rejected Baro utterly; the possibility of a delayed effect on him after more than a decade seems remote.

group's own insistence that a true church consists of the converted alone. Although John Robinson taught 'that the visible
church must be understood as a company of regenerate people'
and that the regenerate were capable of being 'recognized and
organized into churches', he was virtually unique among Calvinists in holding such views.[24] The standard Augustinian-
Calvinist position was that God's predestination was inscrutable; the separatists never claimed to be able to discern who was
truly converted, only who was outwardly godly. Thus it may
have been – and this is merely speculation, of course – that
Smyth's reflection upon the idea that the regenerate were discernible led him to conclude that Calvinist ideas about
predestination were at best unnecessary and, at worst, unten-
able. Calvinist logic said that the converted could not be discerned; Smyth and Robinson, however, said they could be. For
Smyth, though not for Robinson, it was the Calvinism that
would have to go.

The timing of Smyth's change of mind about this teaching,
however, and the fact that it came together with a shift in his
opinions concerning other doctrines, are strong evidence that it
was the Mennonite connection, at least as much as any other
factor, which swayed his thinking. He even seems to have toyed
with the distinctive Mennonite Christology (inherited from
Melchior Hofmann) according to which Christ did not take his
flesh from the Virgin Mary, but brought it with him from
heaven. At least, Smyth's *Short Confession of Faith in XX
Articles*, whilst remaining orthodox on the point, is nevertheless
carefully patient of such a position: 'Jesus Christ, as pertaining
to the flesh, was conceived by the Holy Spirit in the womb of
the Virgin Mary'.[25]

Whilst he had been under the impression that the Mennonites
were heretics, Smyth had had no qualms about baptizing himself
and his fellows. Now that he had been converted to most of their
views himself, however, he felt that his action had been precipi-
tate. It would have been better, he came to think, to have been
baptized by the Mennonites instead.

---

[24]   R.T. Jones, 'John Robinson's Congregationalism', p. 6.
[25]   W.L. Lumpkin, *Baptist Confessions of Faith*, p. 100.

The Waterlanders were that faction of the movement who had taken the least rigorous line in the ugly disputes concerning the ban which had so disfigured the Dutch and North German movement in the second half of the previous century. He now sought re-baptism (i.e. a third ceremony) at their hands; indeed, his *Short Confession* was penned precisely in order to win the Mennonites' approval and to satisfy them of his orthodoxy. Although about thirty of his congregation stayed with Smyth on this, almost a dozen others rebelled and left him.

The leader of this new breakaway group was Thomas Helwys, a gentleman landowner of Broxtowe Hall. He and several co-leaders wrote to the Waterlander congregation, in March 1610, urging them not to admit Smyth and his followers into member-ship. The terms in which the letter is written are so fraternal that it is clear Helwys' objections were not so much to membership with the Mennonites as such as to Smyth's quest for a yet further baptism. In Helwys' eyes, this was a quest for a kind of apostolic succession. It was no disrespect to the Mennonites to point out that their baptism originated in persons unknown and, *via* the Münster 'apostles', possibly disreputable: 'neither the time, per-son, nor place can be proved to any man's conscience, and so herein we should ground our faith, we cannot tell upon whom, nor when, nor where'. This did not invalidate Mennonite bap-tism, of course, but then baptism was not grounded upon any sacred succession in the first place. Even if the effort were to be made, the succession could not be traced back even as much as a century. But 'John [the] Baptist, being unbaptized, preached the baptism of repentance, and they that believed and confessed their sins, he baptized. And whosoever shall now be stirred up by the same spirit to preach the same word, and men thereby being converted, may according to John's example wash them with water, and who can forbid?'[26]

In taking this stance, Helwys was adopting a *sui generis* (or perhaps a *spiritu generis*) view of the church. In essence, this meant that a true church is formed by the activities of the Holy Spirit in individuals – irrespective of where, how or from whom those individuals had heard the gospel or received ceremonies of

---

[26]   C. Burrage, *Early English Dissenters*, ii., p. 185.

Christian initiation. Thus the perpetuation of the true church does not depend upon any link with some past institution. This stands in contrast with the catholic and episcopalian idea of apostolic succession whereby every ordination has to be carried out by a bishop, who in turn must have been ordained by another bishop, so that (in theory) each minister has been commissioned, *via* a chain of succession, by the first apostles themselves.

The 'commonsense' approach of Helwys and – when he first baptized himself and his followers – also of Smyth is so ubiquitous now, even among those who may have formal ties with traditional, hierarchically structured denominations, that it requires some effort of mind to appreciate that the first English Baptists were being quite radical in formulating it. It certainly injected an element of great organizational flexibility into the Baptist tradition; churches could be started quite spontaneously and with a minimum of fuss and bother, a factor that was to prove of decisive advantage to Baptist growth on the ever-expanding frontiers of the New World.

For it was the smaller group led by Helwys, and not the larger body of Smyth's supporters, who were to form the main stream from which the English General Baptists were to flow. Helwys and his congregation issued a *Declaration of Faith of English People Remaining at Amsterdam in Holland* in 1611, in which they set out what were to be the General Baptist distinctives for most of the rest of the century and, arguably, beyond. This statement adopted some, but not all, of the theological changes made by Smyth since his first enactment of believers' baptism.

The group affirmed that Christ had died for all people – as opposed to the Calvinist view that he had died only for the predestined elect – hence the later nomenclature 'General Baptist' from their belief in a general atonement. This should not be confused with any notions about universal salvation; according to Helwys and company, most people would be damned. All people, however, were capable of being saved – if only they would. No predestination of God held them back from accepting the divine conditions; biblical language about predestination referred only to generalities. God had predestined that all that believe shall be saved, and that all who do not believe shall be damned; which individuals came into each category was left to human choice. Similarly, the group rejected the Calvinist notion that was to be defined in the 1619 Synod of Dort as the 'Perseverance of the Saints' (or, more vulgarly in recent times, 'Once saved, always saved').

Otherwise, however, they were more conservative than either Smyth or the Mennonites whom he sought to join. The General Baptists affirmed a belief in original sin in something like its Augustinian and Reformed understanding. They also explicitly rejected unorthodox Christologies: Jesus Christ was 'the Son of Mary the Virgin, made of her substance'. Furthermore, they refused to discountenance the idea of church members being magistrates (even though this meant a willingness to bear arms) and were willing to 'take an oath by the name of the Lord' if there were just cause to do so. These were views that were anathema to Anabaptists.[27]

In other respects, the new movement was a veritable chip off the old separatist block. There was the same certainty that Christ 'hath in his Testament set down an absolute, and perfect rule of direction, for all persons, at all times, to be observed', with 'fearful judgements' pronounced against any who add to, or diminish from, the one true pattern. But the fierce separatist rigidity was given a new twist: now the church of Christ was 'a company of faithful people separated from the world' who were joined 'unto the the Lord, and one unto another, by baptism, upon their own confession of faith and sins'.

The Baptists were not, like the separatists, a state-church-in-waiting. They were constituted by baptism, 'separated from the world', and restricted to those who could give a confession of their own spiritual experience 'wrought by the preaching of the gospel'. Indeed, far from the separatist insistence that magis-trates had a duty to 'suppress and root out' all 'voluntary relig-ions and counterfeit worship of God', the Baptists warned that 'no prince, nor any whosoever' should tamper with the order of the church if they wished to avoid the judgements referred to at the end of the Book of Revelation.[28]

The net result is a curious mixture: the Anabaptist insistence on a believers' church and the separation of church and state,

27 W.L. Lumpkin, *Baptist Confessions of Faith*, pp. 116–23.
28 *Ibid.*, pp. 94, 119.

coupled with a very un-Anabaptist acceptance of Christian magistracy and the oath, an acceptance combined with a rejection of
pacifism. Such a combination may seem unexceptionable today,
when individuals may participate in the institutions of society,
including politics, on their own terms and without a public
inquisition regarding their religious beliefs. There is, nevertheless, something odd about it, originating as it does in a time when
pluralist societies of a kind that might tolerate Baptists as magistrates could scarcely be imagined. In that context, the Mennonite response of total separation from all the institutions of this
world might be thought to have been more consistent, and even
realistic. The blend actually settled upon by Helwys and company almost certainly owes more to theological compromise and
vestigial shreds of social conservatism than it does to Baptist
prophetic foresight concerning the future direction of Western
societies.

The General Baptist commitment to religious toleration was
absolute, however, a feature which distinguishes them from the
Particular Baptists, with whose emergence in the 1630s we shall
deal in the following chapter. As a separatist, Smyth had written
in 1607 that princes 'must command all their subjects to enter
into' churches rightly established. By 1612 he had changed radically: 'The magistrate is not . . . to meddle with religion, or
matters of conscience, to force and compel men to this or that
form of religion or doctrine, but to leave Christian religion free
to every man's conscience, and to handle only civil transgressions, injuries, and wrongs of men against men.' Helwys agreed:
'Let them be heretics, Turks, Jews, or whatsoever, it appertains
not to the earthly power to punish them.'[29]

John Smyth's application to join the Mennonites was long
delayed and drawn out; he died in 1612 before he and his
congregation were admitted, though the remainder was finally
welcomed into the Waterlanders in 1615. Thomas Helwys and
his (even smaller) group, meanwhile, came to the conclusion that
it was sinful to avoid persecution by remaining in exile; their
Christian duty was to return to the land of their birth. This, in

---

[29] J. Smyth, Works, i., p. 267; ii., p. 748; T. Helwys, *Mistery of Iniquity* (1612), p. 69,
cited in M. Watts, *The Dissenters*, i., pp. 48–9.

1612, they did, willingly embracing the consequences and thus becoming the first Baptist church actually on English soil. A petition to the House of Commons (probably penned by Helwys in 1614) asked for release from prison and pointed out that even Catholics were set at liberty if they would take the oath of allegiance whilst Baptists who took the oath were not. (Had the article in their *Declaration of Faith* about the lawfulness of oaths been a calculated ploy in expectation of a different outcome?)[30] By 1616 at the latest, Helwys was dead; at least, he is mentioned as being so in the will of his relative, Geoffrey Helwys.[31] The Baptist cause in England was to be carried on by others.

In 1620, a General Baptist prisoner in Newgate prison, London, wrote *A Most Humble Supplication* to the king, James I, and to Parliament. The author was probably John Murton, and he complained that he and his fellow Baptists had endured 'long and lingering imprisonments for many years in divers counties of England, in which many have died and left behind them widows and many small children'.[32]

Murton had already written several tracts and had even succeeded in having them printed. These dealt with topics dear to General Baptist hearts: one examined the evil of religious persecution, the legitimacy of baptizing free of considerations of apostolic succession, and the need to remain in one's country and not to flee because of persecution; a second, entitled *Truth's Champion*, does not survive; a third, entitled *A Discription of what God hath Predestinated*, was an attack upon Calvinism as well as a discussion of church organization.

It should not be imagined, from the Baptists' paucity in numbers upon their return to England and their sorry plight in prison during the years that followed, that they were therefore unable to fulfil their mission. By a process unknown to us, they succeeded, despite all obstructions and disadvantages, in planting a number of churches. In 1626, they renewed contacts with the Waterlander Mennonites in the Netherlands concerning the possibility of union. These negotiations broke down over the issues

---

[30] C. Burrage, *Early English Dissenters*, ii., pp. 215–6.
[31] *Ibid.*, i., p. 256.
[32] *Ibid.*, i., p. 265.

of oaths, pacifism and the possibility of Christians serving as
magistrates. (Note that it was these ethical issues, rather than the
doctrinal differences over original sin and Christology, which
were the decisive stumbling block.) From the surviving correspondence of these discussions, it is evident that there were at
least five Baptist churches in England at this time, in London,
Coventry, Lincoln, Salisbury and Tiverton. However modest this
achievement in terms of absolute numbers, given the circumstances – persecution – it remains a notable tribute, in perhaps
almost equal measure, to sectarian tenacity and police ineptitude.

The way to escape the forces of law and order, however, is to
leave few traces of one's existence, and this is a quality which,
though it may have its heroic aspects, is apt to be found less
admirable by historians, who need something concrete to write
about. Admittedly, the absence of documentation has tempted
some writers to indulge in a creative filling of the gaps with a
variety of daresay conjectures and the co-opting of all manner of
imprecisely identified religious dissidents (or the subjects of rumours and local traditions) as honorary Baptists or Anabaptists.
Such conjectures, however, remain precisely that. Our information about the underground life of the General Baptists peters
out at this point. They were to emerge after 1640 into the light of
day, and in that day they were to enjoy a far more glorious
existence.

Chapter Eleven

Separation without Separatism: the origins of the Particular Baptists

The Jacob Church

Whatever the charms of the separatists and the General Baptists may have been, the number of English people prior to the 1630s who were likely to have felt their allure to the point of succumbing was, at best, strictly limited. The trouble with being a separatist was that it did tend . . . well, to separate one. That it separated one from the ritualism and hierarchy of the Church of England was a fact which was not to be minded in the least. That it separated one also from the wider Puritan fraternity was much more unfortunate.

There were, to be sure, all sorts of rhetorical and logical devices and arguments to show that Puritans were worldly compromisers, and that consequently separatism was the right course of action. Deploying them, however, only exacerbated the isolation. The irony was that, at the root, Puritans and separatists wanted the same thing in the long run; at least, they had done back in the days when the first separatists had separated, before the long years of sectarian existence had begun to affect their ecclesiology. Nevertheless, although there remained a few contacts, most Puritans looked upon separatism with horror.

The various churches of English merchants in the Netherlands, such as that led by John Paget, or the congregation led by Francis Johnson before his conversion to separatism, had an entirely different status in Puritan eyes; they were decidedly un-Anglican in their worship but not, in principle, separatist, and so Puritans in England looked upon them with favour and even with admiration. This contrasted sharply with the rejection experienced by the separatists, who had to console themselves with their own rightness. If their numbers grew in the land of exile, this was but poor compensation for their experience of poverty, internecine quarrels and splits and, above all, their certain knowledge of continuing powerlessness. Events in England showed no prospect of moving their way, whilst the very fact of their separatism divided them from the only sizable group – the Puritan party – who might conceivably, at some future point, move things in the right direction.

At least the General Baptists were spared this frustration. As rebaptizers and non-Calvinists, their repudiation by the Puritan fraternity was total and utter; they, however, did not mind. Having cast aside the separatists' continuing attachment to a state church, a godly nation, and the theology that justified it, their task was clear. They aimed to evangelize as widely as possible and to set up a network of Baptist churches, without paying any attention to what the government might or might not do, or to whether the Church of England kept bishops, abolished them, or converted to Islam. Nevertheless, neither concern nor unconcern could alter the fact that the cause of religious radicalism in England – of whatever flavour – was unlikely to make significant progress whilst it was so deeply alienated from its largest principal source of likely recruits, the Puritan movement.

Henry Jacob (1563–1624) was the man who, more than any other, succeeded in remedying this defect. A Puritan clergyman and agitator of long standing, he had been active, in 1603, in stirring up support in London and Sussex for the Millenary Petition, a request by a thousand clergy (and anyone else who could be scraped together) that the new monarch, James I, institute changes in the services of the Church of England.

The petition had succeeded only in prompting the king to call the Hampton Court Conference the following year, which had given him the public forum both to display his own theological erudition and ceremonially to turn down the Puritan requests. Famously, he added the threat that if the Puritan ministers did not conform themselves he would 'harry them out of the land'. This was ominous: those who had already been thus harried had hitherto been confined to separatists. It was not until the 1620s that a larger circle of mainstream Puritans began to feel that they could not live both with their consciences and with religion as officially imposed, and reached for their sea maps.

In 1604, the year of the conference, Jacob found himself imprisoned for a few months for his authorship of a tract advocating congregational government for the Church of England. In essence, the congregational idea of church government had all the advantages, from the Puritan point of view, of presbyterianism at the local level, but without the hierarchy of committees – classes, regional and national synods – that would have accompanied it. Within a general national framework each parish would be loosely self-governing, though the Puritan 'discipline' would be enforced and doctrinal conformity maintained.

The following year, Jacob tried a new tack and petitioned the king for permission to organize a Puritan-style church which, like those of the English merchants in the Netherlands and of foreign Protestants in London, would be different to, but in communion with, the Church of England. There was never the least chance of James acceding to such a request, for to have granted such a permission would have been to open the door to all manner of nonconformity. In 1606, Jacob followed his monarch's advice and allowed himself to be harried into exile, arriving, as tradition almost demanded, on the Dutch coast.

While in the Netherlands, Jacob inevitably came into contact with a variety of English radicals, both exiled and self-exiled, as a result of which he modified his position concerning church government and the nature of a true congregation. His mature views represented what outsiders might consider to be an illogical fudge, or halfway house, between Puritanism and separatism. But then, this was precisely what was needed if advocates of a gathered church were to make significant further inroads upon Puritan opinion in England. Jacob rejected separatism and, although his contacts in the Netherlands with John Robinson did not change his mind on this point, he allowed himself to be persuaded that Christ was the immediate head of each individual Christian congregation. This apparently rather abstract notion,

following as it did quite naturally from his existing congregational convictions concerning church government, had a number
of practical consequences.

It meant, in the first place, that a church did not depend on a
magistrate for permission to exist; Christ was its head regardless.
In the second place, there remained nothing sacrosanct in the
notion of a parish or any other given patch of ground; wherever
two or three were gathered, there the conditions for church-hood
were met. Jacob had long held that the true, visible church could
never be a national body, or indeed a widespread organization
at all; the visible church was the individual congregation. The
catholic church, therefore, was simply their total aggregate.
From his presbyterian days he had experienced the sense that the
conventicles he was attending were in some sense a gathered
church within a larger, wider church consisting of believers and
unbelievers alike; the feeling that gathered churches and national
ones could coexist, and that the former was not equivalent to a
demand for absolute purity of form, was thus already present in
his mind. The main ingredients of the fudge that was to be
semi-separatism were now in place.

In 1616 Jacob slipped back secretly to London and founded
what was to become the most important of the underground
churches during the pre-Civil War period. This was a non-
separatist (or semi-separatist, according to one's definitions)
gathered church. Jacob now believed, not so much in the Puritan
ideal of 'discipline', as in 'keeping forth of the malicious and
untractable without' the church, and restricting membership to
'such people as are not ignorant in religion, nor scandalous in
their life. For only of such Christ's visible church ought to
consist.'[1] He refused to insist that separation from the ungodly
was essential to the existence of a true church. His church's
confession of that year came as close as possible to unchurching
the Church of England for all of its shortcomings whilst deliber-
ately drawing just short of actually doing so:

> We believe concerning mixtures of the open profane with some manifest
> godly Christians, in a visible church, though at once it doth not destroy

---

[1]   as cited in M. Tolmie, *The Triumph of the Saints: the separate churches of London
1616–1649*, p. 10.

essentially, nor make void the holiness of that whole assembly, yet truly it putteth that whole assembly into a most dangerous and desperate estate.

There could be no doubting the identity of the hypothesized 'assembly' yet, as the historian Murray Tolmie so succinctly expresses it, the confession was 'full of separatist language . . . even as it avoided drawing the full separatist conclusion'.[2] Jacob's church repudiated all charges of separatism and recognized parish congregations as true churches 'in some respect'. Though parish ministers' ordinations were void in respect of their having been at the hands of a bishop, they were valid in so far as a congregation 'consenteth to have him, and useth him for their minister', a judgement admirably compatible with that held by Thomas Sperin, the presbyterian Puritan minister who had been so sadly mauled by Barrow in debate a quarter of a century before.

This blurring of principle was not merely a refreshing change among religious radicals in England; it also worked greatly to the practical advantage of the semi-separatist movement. In the first place, it did not alienate the wider Puritan fraternity – or at least not the left wing of it – as much as separatism did, and so enabled links with active connivers within the established church to continue as conduits for mutual support and influence. In the second place, it made it possible for members to avoid detection by the authorities by taking communion in their parish churches occasionally if they so wished. This was less necessary in the teeming anonymity of London than it would have been in a village or small market town though, even in the capital, failure to have one's child baptized by the parish minister could hardly have gone unnoticed. The London separatists of the Ancient Church, who eked out a continued existence in the shadow of arrest, were particularly scathing about this aspect of their new rival's characteristics. To them, it seemed an abandonment of all principle, and certainly of all purity. But then, the semi-separatists did not aim at a pure church – even in principle, like the separatists, let alone in personnel, like the Anabaptists. Pragmatism was to be the key element in their success.

---

[2] *Ibid.*

Of course, from the point of view of the authorities, none of these distinctions, or any of the other issues about which the illegal radicals of London or the diaspora in the Netherlands argued so earnestly, mattered in the slightest. The various grada-tions of separatism and semi-separatism were merely so much irrelevant hairsplitting. All of the groups were completely illegal. All were guilty of holding conventicles. All were disobedient, whatever protestations they might make to the contrary, to royal injunctions concerning religious observance. As subjects, they had failed to conform themselves; as radicals, they must certainly be aiming at the dissolution of existing social and religious conditions, and the setting up of a veritable religious Babel in which each person would act as he saw fit in his own eyes. Jacobites, separatists and Anabaptists alike all threatened anar-chy, and risked being treated accordingly by the forces of law and order.

One of the most remarkable features of the Jacob church though was its latitudinarian attitude on a number of issues, a characteristic rarely met with amongst either the more radical Puritans or the sectarians. Alongside the non-separatist majority, the church contained a number of strict separatists, who could not in conscience communicate in the Church of England at all. Laymen were allowed to preach – a permission that became a necessity after 1622, when Jacob left England for Virginia. A number of women came without their husbands, and servants without their masters, a phenomenon which caused distress and concern to a number of the more conservative members.[3] On this last point, the ambivalence of the Jacob church's position was at its most acute: it was a function of established religion – includ-ing, or even especially, Puritanism – to reinforce social solidarity, particularly families, whereas it has been a historic function of sectarianism, including the early church itself, to accentuate individualism.[4] Here the congregation's theology pointed in the former direction, its sociological situation in the latter.

---

[3]   *Ibid.*, pp. 15–6.
[4]   See, for example, E. Pagels, *Adam, Eve and the Serpent* (London, Penguin 1990); J. Perkins, *The Suffering Self: Pain and Narrative Representation in the Early Christian Era* (London, Routledge 1995).

After Jacob's departure for the New World, lay members preached until another clergyman could be found. For these non-separatists, such a person 'obviously' had to be someone ordained in the Church of England. At least, so much was still obvious in 1624, when John Lathrop was appointed successor. By 1640, however, the church felt no compunction about appointing Praise-God Barbone, a leather-seller of evidently Puritan parentage, to the leadership of that half of the church which met in the western part of the city, alongside the clergyman Henry Jessey, pastor to the whole church since 1637 and thenceforward to confine his labours to the eastern half.

During Lathrop's tenure, in 1632, about forty-six out of the approximately sixty members were apprehended by the authorities and imprisoned for 18 months. But by this time new members were positively flooding in. The church survived, not only mass-arrest, but several breakaways, most of them fairly amicable, and still continued to flourish. Upon their release from custody, Lathrop and about thirty others left for America, whilst Samuel Eaton led a strict separatist secession. John Duppa had led a similar splinter group of about a dozen people in 1630.

Despite the Jacob church's deliberate ambivalence on the point, separatism was becoming a more attractive option to a number of its members from the 1620s onwards, and this at the time when alternative churches in general were exerting a greater appeal to those Puritans who had previously been prepared to put up with the unsatisfactory situation in the Church of England.

No one, after the Hampton Court Conference of 1604, could have harboured continuing hopes that the English Reformation would prove to be a progressive, if extremely slow, affair; no one could think that the Church of England was likely to be further reformed in the foreseeable future. The only rationale, therefore, for continued refusal to separate from an institution that was barely tolerable must now be that Puritan ways might still be found to live within it. Lecturers could provide extra preaching; services could be adapted in quiet corners where the bishops' agents might not be looking, or in the private chapels of Puritan gentry with their private chaplains; there might be private meetings for the repetition of sermons; household prayers might be conducted in Puritan fashion; renewed emphasis might be placed upon Sunday observance which, as the historian Christopher Hill has pointed out, was becoming a Puritan hobbyhorse from about 1600[5].

But even living as a Puritan within the Church of England was becoming less and less easy and, from the late 1620s, downright impossible. The theological disputes in the Dutch Reformed church which surrounded the teachings of Jacobus Arminius (1560–1609) had spilled over into England. In essence, Arminius had undermined the Calvinist view of predestination by asserting human free will. However, in the Church of England a party had arisen which combined this doctrinal deviation with a reversion to an emphasis upon sacraments and sacramentally conveyed grace, upon ceremonies and the importance of hierarchy.

The Arminian doctrines flew in the face of the moderately expressed Calvinism of the English Church's Thirty-Nine Articles, as well as of numerous assertions by even the most anti-Puritan of Elizabethan bishops and archbishops. Nevertheless, Charles I, who succeeded his father in 1625, was strongly committed to the tiny Arminian party, and rewarded them with all of the chief posts in the church. If Puritans had viewed their national church as unsatisfactorily Protestant before, it increasingly seemed hardly Protestant in any sense. To make matters worse, enforcement of conformity was redoubled by Charles and his chief clerical henchman, William Laud, Bishop of London from 1628 and Archbishop of Canterbury from 1633. Faced with this rising tide of apostasy, the response of a number of Puritans was to embrace separation. This might be principled (as in the case of the separatists), unprincipled (the semi-separatists of the Jacob church and similar groups which, as later evidence showed, were already meeting in places as diverse as Bedford and Bristol), or simply geographic (the Dutch or North American options).

Nonetheless, however dark the picture may have seemed to Puritans during these years, the situation had its positive aspects. At least they now had Reformed theology to themselves. Instead of being merely the protagonists of changes in ceremonies and

---

[5] C. Hill, 'The Uses of Sabbatarianism', in *Society and Puritanism in Pre-revolutionary England*, pp. 141–211.

church government, the public appeal of which would always be strictly limited, they were now able to pose as the champions of Protestant orthodoxy resisting a quasi-papist faction at the heart of the body politic. And as Charles and Laud enforced their unpopular religious innovations (and 'innovation' was almost a swear-word in a society conditioned to follow the ways of its fathers), which they combined with equally unpopular secular policies, they were slowly but surely stoking the fires of backlash. That backlash, when it came, was to lead to the Civil War in England in the 1640s and, when that had been won by the pro-Puritan party, to the one-and-only golden opportunity to put the Puritan programme into practical effect.

But these brighter prospects lay in the future. In the late 1620s and 1630s, many members of the Jacob church felt that they could no longer consider the Church of England, with its increasing ceremonialism and its Arminian doctrines, to be in any sense a true church. Whilst they were perfectly welcome to live as strict sepa-ratists within the Jacob church, for many of them this was not enough. They felt uncomfortable sitting alongside people who would quite happily attend their parish churches when it suited them. It was this rising sentiment which resulted in the secessions led by John Duppa and Samuel Eaton, and possibly to a third led by John Green and John Spencer in 1639. However, these separa-tions were amicable in the main, the various congregations remaining in friendly contact with one another.

Not all of the details of the various breakaway groups, the variations in degrees of separatism or semi-separatism, and the realignments of the 1630s are clear. Much remains conjectural, or material for intelligent reconstruction by historians. What can be said is that, by the end of the 1630s, there existed in London a family of churches, originating in the Jacob church begun in 1616, which was latitudinarian and pragmatic in many of its attitudes, Calvinistic in its theology, Puritan in its origin, and characterized by a belief in the independent self-government of each congrega-tion. With the prospect of a satisfactorily reformed national church increasingly relegated to the realms of merely hypothetical possibility, and with their experience of sectarian existence subtly altering their ecclesiological assumptions with every passing year, they, like the separatists of Barrow, Greenwood and Johnson before them, were gradually becoming more ambivalent – or at any rate more confused – regarding whether a national church was desirable at all. It was this family of quasi-separatist, ambivalent, confused and pragmatic Calvinists which was to prove the seedbed for a new type of Baptist church.

'Churches commonly (though falsely) called Anabaptists'

Some among the more radically inclined of the Jacob circle, members of Samuel Eaton's breakaway separatist church, had received 'a further baptism' sometime after 1633. Infuriatingly, the records are silent as to the precise nature of, or the reasoning behind, this baptism, though we may deduce from the fact that some later had it repeated by 'dipping the whole body' that the original was by affusion, rather than by immersion. It may well be, however, that this baptism was simply an expression of the strong separatism of Eaton and his fellows – an insistence that the baptism administered to them in their parish churches had been no true baptism – rather than a genuine believers' baptism.

By 1638, however, there was undoubtedly a congregation ema-nating from the Jacob circle which did practise believers' baptism. It was led by John Spilsbury. Several of his friends had become 'convinced that baptism was not for infants, but professed believ-ers', and these left the mother church, led since the previous year by Henry Jessey, 'the church's favour being desired therein'.[6] Again, the cordiality of the parting, this amicable agreement to differ, is very striking in contrast to the bitter recriminations which had characterized the internal dealings of Johnson's church in Amsterdam. Indeed, in May 1640, the Jessey church itself split, by agreement, into two:

> This congregation being at this time grown so numerous that they could not well meet together in any one place without being discovered by the Nimrods of the earth, . . . they divided themselves equally and became two congregations, the one whereof continued with Mr. Jessey, the other joined themselves to Mr. Praise-God Barbone . . .[7]

6 C. Burrage, *Early English Dissenters*, ii., p. 302.
7 *Ibid.*, i., p. 325.

Shortly thereafter there was another Baptist breakaway from the Jessey church, this time led by Richard Blunt. Once again, the parting was quite amicable. Blunt knew Dutch and had gone to visit the Collegiant Rijnsburgers, an appropriately interconfessional group (Reformed, Remonstrants, Mennonites, though with growing links to the last of these), to see how immersion was performed. Upon his return he baptized his friends. By 1640–1 at the latest, then, the first Particular Baptist church ('Particular' because of their belief in 'particular redemption', i.e. the Calvinist doctrine that Christ had died for the sins of the elect only) was in existence. Despite their later vintage, the Particulars have proved to be the dominant strain in subsequent Baptist history.

The latitude within the Jacob circle of churches was now very impressive indeed. Some of Eaton's congregation had been re-baptized; others had not. Some of the mother church were separatist; others were not. After believers' baptism became an issue, the Jessey church came to tolerate either view, though the Barbone section and the Duppa congregation took a more con-servative view. All of the congregations kept communion with one another except the small church led by John Duppa. It is important to bear in mind that many of the early Particular Baptists were in congregations whose attitude to baptism was highly latitudinarian. It was a practice concerning which Christ-ians might legitimately differ. Several churches continued to contain members who had been baptized as believers and those who had not, though the only one to continue this tradition down to the present day is the Bedford church – now known as the Bunyan meeting after its most famous pastor. For the Particular Baptists, baptism was clearly an issue which could be taken in isolation, rather than the linchpin of ecclesiology and associated theological distinctives, as it was for the continental Anabaptists, and indeed even for the English General Baptists.

By this time the régime of Charles I in the state, and with it that of Archbishop Laud in the Church of England, had reached a point of unprecedented crisis. Entirely at the mercy of a Scottish rebellion he had no military means of defeating, and entirely beholden to a Parliament – which he had now been forced to summon – to vote the taxation with which to provide those means, the hapless monarch could no longer enforce his rule as he insisted he had a divine right to do. Instead, he was obliged to allow the political classes represented in the House of Commons, with the more or less willing connivance of the peers in the House of Lords, to dictate an unprecedented agenda of legislative and religious change as the price of voting – maybe, sometime not too soon – the taxes needed to finance an army with which to quell the Scots. Since it was evident which foot the political boot was now on, the Laudian régime collapsed almost from the very day, in November 1640, when the Long Parliament first convened.

In London at least, Puritan ministers celebrated services with as much or as little of the *Book of Common Prayer* as they pleased, with or without their surplices, and went unpunished. Indeed, there now commenced a *de facto* religious toleration in England that was to last until 1660. Baptists and other sectaries remained every bit as illegal as they had been before, but the episcopal enforcers of ecclesiastical order were so discredited that they were no longer able to exercise their functions, and by the time they were replaced the country had descended into the chaos of civil war, sectaries had grown sharply in numbers (drastically increasing their political leverage) and religious uniformity had become all but unenforceable.

By 1644 there were seven Particular Baptist churches in London, and these combined to produce the *London Confession* of that year. It was transparently a work of public apologetic. The signatories described themselves as 'those churches which are commonly (though falsely) called Anabaptists'.

The charge of Anabaptism was one which they felt compelled to refute. Everyone 'knew' what Anabaptism meant: it meant Münster – anarchy, communism, polygamy, sexual libertinism and slaughter. That was the only meaning ordinary people had ever heard attached to the word (though the religiously informed might be familiar, via polemical descriptions, with at least some of their doctrinal emphases), and so it must be true. And all of these terrible things were perpetrated – or would be if they were ever given a chance – by religious sectarians, especially by those who insisted upon baptizing adults. And what had the Particular Baptists done? They had rebaptized themselves. *Ergo*, they were Anabaptists, and all of the horrors attached to that name would shortly follow, innocent appearances notwithstanding. Everyone knew that, like devils, Anabaptists hid their wicked intentions under a cloak of sincere piety.

Daniel Featley's anti-Baptist tract, nicely entitled *The Dippers Dipt* (the sequel was called *The Dippers Plunged*) included an illustration of believers' baptism: naked men are baptizing naked women in a river, whilst a scornful label of the latter reads 'Virgins of Sion'. That the picture is entirely fictitious is irrelevant; the drawing depicts what everyone 'knew', or thought they knew. No wonder that the *London Confession* complained that

> many that fear God are discouraged and forestalled in harbouring a good thought, either of us or what we profess; and many that know not God [are] encouraged, if they can find the place of our meeting, to get together in clusters to stone us, as looking upon us as a people holding such things, as that we are not worthy to live.[8]

The Confession sought to demonstrate that, on the contrary, the Particular Baptists held none of the Anabaptist tenets, with the sole exception of believers' baptism. It was an attempt to minimize the differences with Puritans, and to demonstrate their own orthodox Calvinist credentials at a time when that mattered, given the recent alarm at the rise of the Arminian party. In short, the purpose was to justify themselves before the world – and especially before the Puritan fraternity – as reasonable people, just like themselves, really. . . .

It was unjust, they pointed out, that they were charged

> in pulpit and print . . . with holding free-will, [the possibility of] falling away from grace, denying original sin, disclaiming of magistracy, denying to assist them either in persons or purse in any of their lawful commands, doing acts unseemly in the dispensing the ordinance of baptism, not to be named amongst Christians.[9]

It was not insignificant that the first two charges could quite legitimately have been laid at the door of the General Baptists (with whom public opinion would, quite understandably, have confused them), while the third point could also have been levelled at the continental Anabaptists. Concerning magistracy, it was a standard charge against those who advocated freedom of conscience that they were undermining civil government, and if, like

---

[8] W.L. Lumpkin, *Baptist Confessions of Faith*, p. 155.
[9] *Ibid.*

the Mennonites, they refused to fight to defend the realm, Protestants and Catholics alike professed themselves satisfied that the
charge had thereby been proved. The Particular Baptists did not
dissent from this line of reasoning, but were not pacifists, and made
no claims at all about the desirable relationship or severance
between church and state.

Ecclesiology, indeed, was the Particular Baptists' weakest
point, but it was an area in which, for pragmatic reasons, they
chose to be weak. A generation ago the historian Glen Stassen
produced a fascinating study into influences on the *London
Confession*, in which he drew very revealing contrasts between
that work and the separatists' *True Confession* of 1596.[10] The
comparison is all the more revealing because the Particular
Baptists' statement consciously uses the work of the exiles as a
basis, which has the effect of highlighting those areas in which
they diverged in favour of their own emphases. Half of the *True
Confession* was copied verbatim by the Particular Baptists; their
changes deleted all references to exclusive purity and all condemnations of other churches. They did not emphasize ecclesiology,
and stressed the significance of baptism in terms of the believer's
identification with the death, burial and resurrection of Christ
(Rom. 6:3–4) rather than in terms of entry into the church. When
propounding the view, in article XXXVI, that each church has
power given it from Christ to choose pastors, teachers, elders and
deacons, this practice was said, in a rather lame phrase, to be 'for
their better well-being' only; the aggressiveness of the separatists
or of the General Baptists – that Christ has ordained this way
and no other – was entirely absent.

Even their distinctive belief concerning baptism was later
modified in its expression. The original edition of 1644 had
maintained that this ordinance should 'be dispensed only upon
persons professing faith, or that are disciples'. After criticism by
their adversary Daniel Featley, however, later editions deleted

---

[10] G.H. Stassen, 'Anabaptist Influence in the Origin of the Particular Baptists',
Mennonite Quarterly Review (1962), pp. 322–48. Stassen's main contention in this
article is that there is some correspondence between Menno Simons' *Foundation Book*
and the Particular Baptists' *London Confession*, a thesis that is perhaps rather less
compelling than his subsidiary point, which is the contrast he demonstrates with the
True Confession.

the word 'only'. Similarly with the mode of baptism: the phrase 'the Scripture holds out to be' was stroked out of the claim that this was to be by 'dipping or plunging the whole body'. Moreover, to counter the popular sexual innuendo of the kind expressed by the illustration in Featley's pamphlet, a marginal note in the confession added that baptism was to be performed 'with convenient garments both upon the administrator and subject, with all modesty'.[11] Verily, the confession of faith was an exercise in the gentlest possible manner of religious assertion.

Stassen's article contrasts the English separatists and the General Baptists on the one hand with the Jacobite semi-separatists and the Particular Baptists on the other. Noting that the General Baptists emerged from separatism, he maintains that, notwithstanding their substantial theological departures, they nevertheless inherited the parent movement's obsession with purity. As he points out, 'separatism describes not merely the act of forming a new church, but the main motif in their theology'. Their central concepts were 'falseness and purity'; their 'spirit was polemical'.[12] The Jacob church and its Particular Baptist progeny, by contrast, were 'Non-separatists' who were 'not concerned to establish a pure church or a pure individual'.

This sums up many of the differences between the two types of Baptists excellently. Both movements had to contend with hostile barracking and with stigmatization as 'Anabaptists'. Whilst the General Baptists more closely approximated to real, continental Anabaptism (in both theology and practice), they tended to take such hostility as a sign of the wickedness both of the world and of the existing social and political conditions. The Particular Baptists, on the other hand, were much more prepared, on the whole, to make a pitch for respectability, to repudiate the charges against them point by point, and to portray themselves, with some justification, as hangers-on of the wider Puritan fraternity. The contrasting attitudes did much to bring about, and indeed to reflect, their contrasting fortunes during the years that lay ahead.

---

[11] W.L. Lumpkin, *Baptist Confessions of Faith*, pp. 153–71.
[12] G.H. Stassen, 'Anabaptist Influence in the Origin of the Particular Baptists', p. 325, f. 11.

Chapter Twelve

'A Swarm of Sectaries': Civil War and the English Republic

By the time the Particular Baptists published their *London Confession* in 1644, the political and religious situation in England had changed almost beyond recognition compared to the outlook in the 1630s. As previously related, not only did the English Arminian régime in the church collapse when the Long Parliament convened at Westminster in November 1640, but the activities of sectaries went largely unpunished. The following twenty years were, in many ways, a golden age for religious radicals in England, and decisive for their future.

As one recent historian has noted, the English Civil War could not have started in the autumn of 1640, because almost no one would have fought for the king.[1] The political classes were all but united in their opposition to the policies Charles had been pursuing in church and state since 1629, and it took the intemperate assaults of the parliamentary radicals over the course of the next eighteen months to fracture this unanimity and to create, by way of alarmed reaction, a party of putative royalists who felt that, all things considered, a chastened monarch – even if he was a crypto-Catholic with aspirations to absolutism – was less frightening than the wholesale reconstruction of the constitution being undertaken by some MPs.

To many, the last-named development seemed to threaten social cohesion, private property and the society of hierarchy and deference which was the only alternative to anarchy that most

---

[1]   J. Morrill, *The Revolt of the Provinces*, p. 13.

people could envisage. Those inclined to this conservative out-look were not surprised to find the sectaries on the side of anarchy. It was yet further evidence that Münster was only just around the corner. Puritan clergymen who sided with Parliament tended to agree with their royalist critics on this last point and, like Daniel Featley, bewailed the ability of the Baptists and others to operate with impunity.

The various sectaries, however, were firmly wedded to the parliamentarian cause; none of them were pacifists and all of them needed as drastic a change as possible from the ecclesiastical conditions that had obtained before the war. In theory, the sepa-ratists might have been content with a sufficiently far-reaching redefinition of the Church of England, but the Baptists were committed to the cause of toleration. The Particulars wanted this for themselves at least, whilst the Generals demanded unlimited liberty of conscience.

With the parliamentarian cause in need of all the help it could get, yet needing at least to make intolerant noises in order to allay fears amongst the middle ground of popular opinion, the situa-tion settled down into one of *de facto* toleration accompanied by sporadic harassment at the hands of local officials and justices of the peace. The collapse in order which came in the wake of civil war meant that, without a large diversion of resources which could ill be spared, repression could not be applied systematically in any case. As a result, the numbers of separatists and Baptists mushroomed.

Fighting between the king and his opponents broke out in August 1642, and within a year the parliamentarian leaders in London were propelled into an alliance with Charles' opponents north of the border. The Scots had recently been in rebellion against Charles on account of his religious policies, and so were inclined to support the parliamentarian side in the English con-flict. Their price was a commitment by the English to introduce Scots-style Presbyterianism in England.

The inhabitants of the northern kingdom had now lived for two generations with a monarchy based in London, and had come to the settled conviction that whoever was in charge there would never be able to resist the itch to bring Scottish practice, in religion and other matters, into alignment with that of the

English. The only way, therefore, to safeguard Presbyterianism in Scotland was to ensure that England was blessed with it as well.

The English parliamentarians, Puritans in the main (though not quite to a man), were less sure. In the first place, the Scots system delivered a lot of power to parish clergy through the system of 'discipline'; an idea that had sounded fine in sermons by English Puritans suddenly seemed less appealing now that it was not, by virtue of its absence, a stick with which to beat the church hierarchy, but an imminent reality. The clericalism of Archbishop Laud's high-churchmanship had been one of the things that had so angered the average English country gentle-man, whose interests the typical MP represented. Would a Pres-byterian moral policeman – a 'pope in every parish' as one critic put it – really be preferable? Those who worried about these questions tended to favour a churchmanship of Presbyterianism-and-water. By all means abolish bishops, because bishops were officious and interfered with the dominance of the gentry in their shires; too many of the most recent batch, moreover, had been officious instruments of Charles' centralizing policies. But let the resultant system be subject to the control of Parliament centrally, and of the gentry locally.

Alongside the Erastian Presbyters who felt this way there grew up, under the pressure of the war, a party for whom Presbyterianism was insufficiently radical. The Independents favoured a loosely organized national church, with each parish governing itself. Indeed, some of the more radical among them, including a little-known MP and increasingly successful cavalry commander, one Oliver Cromwell, were prepared to counte-nance a limited religious toleration. The emergence of such an opinion outside the ranks of the sectarians themselves – an ominous development in the eyes of royalists and conservative parliamentarians alike – marks a turning-point in the situation of religious radicals.

For differing reasons, therefore, many – even most – of the English parliamentarians were less than enthusiastic about the terms upon which Scottish military assistance was being prof-fered. It was certainly a problem that exercised the mind of Sir Henry Vane, an Independent and a member of the delegation of diplomats sent north to treat with the Scots. Vane had an eye for the helpfully ambiguous diplomatic phrase which might prise the required military help from the allies whilst leaving the door open to equivocation over the religious *quid pro quo*.

At his suggestion, therefore, the final agreement between the two parties promised that the demanded religious changes would indeed be implemented in England, 'according to the Word of God'. Who could object to the inclusion of such a sentiment? Which of the Covenanters could allow that their brand of Presbyterianism was anything other than faithful, down to the last detail, to the biblical revelation? And yet precisely what the Word of God does in fact teach had been the subject of some debate for sixteen centuries prior to Vane's suggestion, and he had a shrewd suspicion that, with a little encouragement, divines might spin the discussion out for a few months more. During that time, Scots armies would be doing their work on the battlefields of the English Civil War and, when the victory was won, the more nebulous promise implied by that irreproachably pious phrase might allow far greater leeway in determining the religious complexion of England than the Scots were prepared to countenance from their much stronger bargaining position in the spring and summer of 1643.

The immediate religious upshot of the Solemn League and Covenant, the rather magniloquent title dignifying the Anglo-Scots agreement of that summer, was the famous Westminster Assembly. The historical reputation of this body, and even more of its resultant Westminster Confession of Faith, is so high even today – especially among those inclined to Reformed views – that to make light of it may be seen in some quarters as but one degree removed from blasphemy. The plain fact is, however, that the Assembly was simply a talking-shop; every line of the parliamentary ordinance which set it up makes this fact plain.

The body was to consist of thirty secular political figures and one hundred and twenty-one clergymen, with the quorum for meetings set at the modest figure of forty. They were to seek only 'nearer agreement' between the Churches of England and Scotland, and the duty of members was to 'consult and advise' only of 'such matters . . . as shall be proposed unto them' by the

Lords and Commons. They were to have 'power and authority', but this was merely 'to confer and treat amongst themselves of such matters and things' concerning the Church 'as shall be proposed unto them by both or either of the said Houses of Parliament, and no other'.

There was to be no broadening of discussion by members; the politicians would set the agenda for them. What is more, the Assembly was to submit its advice only when it had been explic- itly requested to do so. There was also a direction 'not to divulge by printing, writing or otherwise' without parliamentary consent; there was to be no use of tracts and newspapers to appeal over the heads of the politicians to London's volatile public opinion, a tactic of populist politics which had been used for the first time by the parliamentarian leaders themselves (against the royal government and its officials) during the months before the outbreak of fighting.

Just in case there could be any lingering misunderstanding about the true status of the Assembly, a final paragraph dispelled all doubts on the point:

> Provided always, that this ordinance, or anything therein contained, shall not give unto the persons aforesaid, or any of them, nor shall they in this assembly assume to exercise, any jurisdiction, power or authority ecclesiastical whatsoever, or any other power than is herein particularly expressed.[2]

In truth, the politicians could hardly have made themselves more clear.

Clarity is not, however, a quality that comes to mind when the twentieth-century reader is attempting to grasp the political implications of the different varieties of Puritanism – or sectari- anism – on the parliamentarian side. In general though, we can say that, the more radical a given religious grouping was, the more uncompromising its political stance. For example, those who favoured Presbyterianism – whether of the Scots or Erastian variety – tended to be the most conservative. Aiming not so much at military victory over the king as at an avoidance of defeat, they wanted a compromise political settlement that would enhance the position of the gentry in post-war England,

---

[2]   J.P. Kenyon, *The Stuart Constitution*, item 74.

and make a repetition of Charles' attempt at absolutist royal government impossible. They fondly hoped that the king would abandon his principles and, as part of the package, allow the enforcement of a presbyterian form of church government.

The Independents to their left found themselves, by 1644, in the somewhat contradictory position of desiring, on the one hand, a resolution of the war by a military knock-out of the royalist forces, with a much harsher settlement imposed upon the monarch, and on the other, of hoping to achieve this with as little help as possible from the Scots army, since any settlement in which the parliamentarians were much beholden to the Scots would oblige an acceptance of the Scottish Presbyterianism to which they had been such unwilling signatories. Because the kind of post-war England they desired was so much more different to anything the king might be expected to countenance than were the relatively moderate demands of the Presbyterians, the Independents *had* to place their faith in an outright military victory if they were to have any hope of obtaining their desires.

This was particularly true of those Puritans who, once the fighting started, had made their way back from the New World to join the parliamentarian forces. Those who had left home and property in England in the years before the war, and had gone into exile *via* a hazardous sea-crossing in which there was no guarantee of safe arrival, had done so only under the greatest duress. Only people who felt the situation in their native country to be completely intolerable could have been induced to subject themselves and their families to such an ordeal. It is not difficult, therefore, to sympathize with the grim satisfaction which such exiles took at the plight of the king now, nor with their determination to ensure that the full penalty would be exacted from him. However, 'the full penalty' should not be misunderstood as a widespread desire to kill the king; none but a few cranks even considered such a thing before the spring of 1648, and those who fought for parliament during the first Civil War always insisted that they contended for 'king and parliament'. (This insistence may have been somewhat disingenuous, but most chose to believe that they were attempting to rescue the king from his evil advisers, and return him to the pursuit of his own best interests.) The penalty which the Independents had in mind at that time was a constitution in which the landowning classes who possessed the vote would have a major say in the rôle of government, with the king unable to make major decisions without the consent of Parliament. They also wanted self-governing parishes and religious toleration extended to various types of godly Protestants who subscribed to basic orthodoxy (though what constituted this last point was obviously a matter of some debate).

In this climate of unprecedented political and religious division, the sectarians were able to flourish. Clearly, the programme of the Independents suited them best, proffering as it did the hope that they might be included in the scope of future arrangements for some degree of religious liberty. In the meantime, they already had this freedom, in practice if not in theory, and they were swift to capitalize on the situation. Their fastest spread tended to be in London and the larger cities, and in the ranks of the parliamentarian army.

The latter institution rapidly took on a political life of its own. The demands of military effectiveness transformed it from being, at the outbreak of fighting, a collection of forces based on the county militias, into a national force – the New Model Army – by the end of the first Civil War in 1646. Instead of serving under their landlords and immediate social superiors as officers, young soldiers found themselves being led by those who had been promoted on merit during the course of the struggle. Pioneered by Oliver Cromwell, this was a very controversial procedure. He had found that godly men, of all persuasions, were the best soldiers; their faith made them unafraid of death and gave them an internal discipline, while their religious commitments made them the most determined opponents of the king and so strongly motivated. Cromwell promoted them, regardless of their social status in civilian society, whenever the opportunity arose, which in warfare was inevitably rather often. As a result, a number of young men found themselves pitchforked from the anonymity of village peasanthood or London apprenticeship into positions as captains and even majors – holding the power of life and limb over the civilian populations of the districts in which their forces were quartered. This provoked the understandable fury of the county gentry, many of whom had resisted royal policies in the 1630s precisely in order to secure unfettered control over their localities. The parliamentarian cause began to break apart; the army became a political player in its own right, and found itself well to the left of the bulk of the MPs who had first called it into being in 1642.

The sectarians inevitably found themselves aligned with the army and the small minority of the most radical MPs. Indeed, the army itself became a hotbed of religious radicals from the mid-1640s onwards. Richard Baxter, the Puritan rector of Kidderminster, was briefly a chaplain to the army and was appalled at the influence given to sectarians by Cromwell: 'by degrees he had headed the greatest part of the army with Anabaptists, Antinomians, Seekers or Separatists at best; and all these he tied together by the point of liberty of conscience, which was the common interest in which they did unite. . . . When a place fell void, it was twenty to one a sectary had it, and if a godly man of any other mind or temper had a mind to leave the army he [Cromwell] would secretly or openly further it.' Though he insisted that radicals were 'not one to twenty throughout the army', yet they were 'the soul of the army' and 'bore down the rest or carried them along with them'.[3]

Clearly, such sectarian involvement with the military was two-edged in its effects. On the one hand, it gave the religious radicals a powerful political base during the period of the Civil War and, after the execution of the king in January 1649, the republic. On the other hand, it seemed to confirm, in the eyes of the traditional political classes and many poorer people as well, the idea that religious radicalism was but the doorway to a new and frightening social revolution: the ghost of Münster once more.

The Levellers

The ghost did indeed seem to have arisen from its grave in the shape of the new political movements that flourished during this period. Even to speak of 'political movements' is at once to enter the discourse of the modern world. To be sure, there had been

---

[3]   R. Baxter, *The Autobiography of Richard Baxter*, pp.49–50, 56.

religious movements aplenty before this time, but not political ones.[4] Politics had been the preserve of the powerful few, and the struggles for control which had taken place among them had been essentially personal. Even where groups had combined to wrest changes from the existing powers-that-be, such as those taken by de Montfort and his followers from King John in 1215, those changes had been essentially *ad hoc* and opportunist rather than programmatic. But the advent of print, the growth of urban populations and the unsettling effects of civil tumult and fighting had combined to make possible the involvement of significant numbers of ordinary people in the political process. The emergence of a national army officered by non-gentlemen as a major political player made that involvement certain.

But what ideology would inform the thinking of the popular political forces unleashed by civil war? It was inevitable that religious radicalism would play a part. Although the Levellers were a secular political movement and emphatically not, as sometimes portrayed by some superficial modern text books, a religious sect, it is nevertheless true that their ranks were filled up in no small measure by religious sectarians of various types. The reasons are not far to seek.

As their name suggests, the Levellers were egalitarian in outlook, and are often hailed as the first modern democrats. Campaigning in the late 1640s, they demanded the vote for all adult males. Although they were not explicitly republican, they wanted the sovereignty of the House of Commons, with Lords and monarch (if suffered to exist at all) as insignificant constitutional appendages, a vision not finally attained for another two and a half centuries.

Twentieth-century westerners, to whom such a programme seems axiomatic and commonsensical, find it hard to understand why all people in all places should not have wanted these very same things; why the Leveller aspirations appealed so specifically to religious sectarians is a question that is well beyond the comprehension of most moderns. A democratic state, however, is one in which large-scale and competing political factions are

---

[4] Unless, of course, one wishes to describe the inchoate fury which vented itself in periodic – and invariably unsuccessful – peasant revolts as 'political movements'.

institutionalized, and the myth of social unity is impossible to sustain. It is a state in which minority opinion must be tolerated, for tomorrow – or at the next election – it may be the majority, and must be given the opportunity to become such. A democracy makes no appeal to divine right as the sanction for its govern-ment, for it is transparently based upon social utility and (tran-sient) public preference. Such arrangements suited those who wanted religious toleration and a complete separation of church and state. The implied free market in ideas also guaranteed freedom for sectarian evangelism.

Members of radical churches had also participated in some-thing which, for pre-moderns, was a novel experience: they had voluntarily entered into an agreement with others to 'be church' together. The contrast with the normative experience of Europe-ans over the foregoing millennium was stark; 'church' had been a datum, a given, an institution into which one was simply born. But if it were possible to covenant together voluntarily with the people of God to form the microcosm of a local church, then why, by extrapolation, might not the process be applied to the macrocosm of the political realm? Might the people of England not also covenant together to form a government of their own choosing, rather than simply receive one – the king – on the authority of heredity, birth and the past? Apostolic succession and the divine right of kings were doctrines which, it could be argued, stood or fell together.

The Leveller movement emerged during 1646, was strong from 1647–50, and struggled thereafter to maintain its existence. Its strengths were in the army and among the London apprentices. Like its religious counterparts, the movement was largely an urban affair, appealing to the literate (but not educated) lower middle classes.

Its foremost leader was John Lilburne (1614–57), the younger son of a minor gentry family from County Durham, who had been apprenticed to a London cloth merchant in the 1630s. He had been imprisoned under the Laudian régime for distributing presbyterian tracts, and his incarceration had radicalized him further. Released by the Long Parliament, he had fought for them against the king's forces, but had resigned in 1645 because, as a separatist, he felt unable to take an oath swearing to uphold the Solemn League and Covenant with the Scots. It was from this period that his forays into uncharted political leftism began.

A superbly inspirational figure, writer of pamphlets, and ora- tor, he had an intuitive grasp of how to catch public attention, and how to pressurize political decision-makers. When it came to orchestrating his supporters, raising petitions and organizing demonstrations, Lilburne had no equals. Loathed by the major- ity of horrified conservative opinion, adored by the vociferous minority who were his adherents, a demagogue with, as one writer has put it, 'an exaggerated sense of his own grievances', Lilburne was the Arthur Scargill (or, in American terms, perhaps the Malcolm X) of the seventeenth century.[5]

Samuel Oates was one of a number of General Baptist leaders to become involved in the Leveller movement. Active as a Baptist evangelist in the East Midlands in 1647–48, he got into trouble for distributing copies of *The Agreement of the People*, a Leveller manifesto whose very title echoed the sectarians' experience of church covenant. Thomas Lambe, a pastor in London, organized support for the Levellers' petition in the spring of 1647, and Jeremiah Ives, pastor of a General Baptist congregation in Old Jewry, also in the capital, went to prison that autumn for the same activity. Edward Barber, another Baptist leader, proclaimed his support for the movement as late as 1649, when its demise was imminent, and Henry Denne, leader of the General Baptist church at Fenstanton, Cambridge- shire, was present at the debacle of Burford in May, when a Leveller-inspired army mutiny was suppressed by Cromwell. The insurgents were surrounded and, after a peaceful surrender, locked up in Burford parish church overnight. Cromwell de- cided to have four of the ringleaders shot *pour encourager les autres*, and Denne was one of those earmarked for this early home call. However, he was pardoned at the last moment in exchange for doing penance in a white sheet and preaching against the cause to his comrades and captors in Burford church, 'howling and weeping like a crocodile, and to make him a perfect rogue and villain upon everlasting record', as one of his captive audience later complained.

---

[5]   H. Shaw, *The Levellers*, p. 27.

However drastic the constitutional changes of the 1640s and 1650s – the sovereignty of Parliament, the overthrow of the episcopalian national church, even the abolition, from 1649, of the monarchy itself and the declaration of a republic – the demands of the Levellers remained unrealistic. Perhaps the irony of their situation is that, even if they had succeeded, they would have failed; any free election in which all adult males had the vote would have resulted in the return of royalists and the re-establishment of the *status quo ante*, if not of the 1630s then of the 1610s and '20s. Most of the population remained peasants, and peasants as a class are profoundly unrevolutionary. An election based on the traditional franchise – or indeed on any gradation between that and the universal one envisaged by the Levellers – would have yielded the same result. Even such support as the Levellers had (outside the ranks of the committed sectarians) was at least partly a consequence of the dire economic circumstances in which England found herself in the late 1640s. These in turn were a consequence of the disorder and dislocation created by warfare and a succession of abysmal harvests. But from the end of the decade political conditions began to stabilize – at least relatively – and the weather improved, developments which delivered a double blow to the Levellers' political prospects, and the movement experienced a rapid decline. Throughout the 1650s a tiny rump of supporters (Lilburne had abandoned the cause) was reduced to plotting with whomever would deal with them, including, bizarrely, some desperate royalists.

No radical movement is without a breakaway group for whom the parent organization is altogether too moderate (or too realistic), and the Levellers were no exception. Thus it was that, in April 1649, Gerrard Winstanley, a tailor from Wigan, and his 'True Levellers' (or 'Diggers') occupied St. George's Hill ('George Hill' in both Puritan and sectarian parlance) outside Cobham, Surrey and established it as the first experiment in communist collective farming.

Winstanley had been baptized as a believer in the 1640s, though whether by Generals or Particulars is unclear. By 1648, however, he had advanced (if that is the right word) to a mystical pantheism which made only 'loose, often symbolic, figurative or metaphorical' use of Scripture.[6] According to Winstanley, 'the great creator Reason made the earth to be a common treasury'; the fall was to be identified with private property. Since every person is 'subject to reason, his maker, [and] hath him to be his teacher and ruler within himself, therefore . . . he needs not that any man should teach him'.[7] Not even, presumably, Winstanley.

Whether the radical individualism and self-determination implied by these remarks could have been squared with the collectivist constraints required by life in a commune was a question that was given little time in which to resolve itself, for in 1650 the local gentry, satisfied that the government in London had finished lurching ever further leftwards, recovered its collective nerve and expelled Winstanley and his squatters.

The Diggers' exercise had never been practical politics; however much their literature vaunted itself as 'a declaration to the powers of England and to all the powers of the world', the episode at George Hill remained a strictly local difficulty, and a temporary one at that. Nevertheless, the home counties pantheists have continued to exercise a fascination for twentieth-century English socialists; in recent years Winstanley's works have been edited by the Marxist historian Christopher Hill.

Winstanley himself had been a failed businessman before his conversion to religious communism, and after the collapse of the Surrey soviet he returned to his capitalist roots and went back into trade. He also became a Quaker sometime after the Restoration of the monarchy in 1660, a fact full of polemical possibilities for Marxists, who like to argue that radical religious movements are the sublimated expression of frustrated economic demands.

The Fifth Monarchists

By contrast with the broadly secular nature of the Levellers, Fifth Monarchism was an intrinsically religious political movement. It

---

[6]   G.E. Aylmer, 'The Religion of Gerrard Winstanley', in J.F. McGregor and B. Reay eds., *Radical Religion in the English Revolution*, p. 95.
[7]   G. Winstanley, *Winstanley: The Law of Freedom and Other Writings*, ed. C. Hill, p. 77.

is possible to argue that, since the latter came to prominence at about the same time as the demise of the former, and that since both movements received the support of religious radicals, the two are different forms of the same thing. Indeed, conservatives of the day were inclined to lump all of the radicals – political and religious – together. All were mad and deluded; all considered that they acted under the guidance of the Holy Spirit; all aimed at the subversion of social order, hierarchy and private property; all were infected with the spirit of Münster. One notes wearily the same tendency at work in our own day; outsiders lump all 'American fundamentalists' – or Middle-Eastern Islamic parties, or nationalist groups – together, and on the basis of their alleged insanity, fail (or refuse) to give serious consideration to their ideas. The penalty for such myopia was the same then as now: an impotent inability to understand the causes and nature of unfolding events.

The truth is that, within the emerging kaleidoscope of religious radicalism, Fifth Monarchism drew upon different strands to those which had given strength to the Levellers. Whereas the Levellers had contended for a secular state, the Fifth Monarchists demanded a religious – even a theocratic – government by the saints (meaning, of course, themselves).

Their name is a reference to the five kingdoms described in the second chapter of Daniel. In this passage, the Old Testament prophet interprets the strange statue dreamed of by the Babylonian king as representing a series of future kingdoms, each replacing its predecessor. The fourth kingdom would be like the legs of the statue, 'strong as iron', though the feet were 'partly of baked clay'. Then, however, 'the God of heaven will set up a kingdom that will never be destroyed. . . . It will crush all those kingdoms and bring them to an end, but it will itself endure for ever'. This fifth kingdom, or monarchy, was the rock which, as the king saw in his dream, 'struck the statue on its feet of iron and clay and smashed them' (Dan. 2:31–45).

This was an apocalyptic vision, of course, and the conclusions drawn from it by a variety of radicals (located mostly among the Particular Baptists, separatists and the most unstable elements of the Independents) constituted a form of what today would be called post-millennialism. This is the idea that the Second

Coming of Christ comes after (*post*) the one-thousand-year reign of the saints on the earth. If this doctrine were true, then the saints would be reduced to ushering in their own reign. That being so, what could be better, reasoned the Fifth Monarchy men, than a little political jiggery-pokery – or even a little military action – to bring it about?

As Second Comings go, theirs was a rather parochial version. The prophecies of Daniel were being fulfilled by the events of the English Civil War. Charles I had proved himself 'one of the ten horns of the beast spoken of [in] Rev. 17:12–15', and a limb of the Catholic Antichrist (indubitably to be identified with the fourth kingdom), by his marriage to a French princess and his re-opening of diplomatic relations with Rome, not to mention by the quasi-popery of his own preferred ecclesiastical régime.[8] To be sure, once the government of England was firmly in the hands of the saints, a crusade was to be launched against 'the Antichrist-ian powers of the world (Rev. 15:2 &c.), whom they may expect to combine against them universally (Rev. 17, 13, 14)', but the powers in mind were clearly France and Spain, and it is impos-sible to envisage the Fifth Monarchists' vision embracing India, say, or Africa, regions of which their society had theoretical cognizance but no mental compass, in the divine plan of events.[9]

. The Fifth Monarchist movement grew upon two main bases. The first of these has been described by the historian William Lamont in his classic study, *Godly Rule*.[10] As Lamont shows, millenarian expectations were far from being confined to the radical fringes of English society during the first half of the seventeenth century, and expectations of the Second Coming rose during the 1640s. Moreover, these expectations generally took the form that we would call post-millennial, a development from the overly optimistic rôle of Protestant military saviour in Europe accorded to Queen Elizabeth – and then by implication to her successors – by John Foxe's vastly influential book, *The Acts and Monuments of the Christian Church*, vulgarly and more excitingly dubbed *The Book of Martyrs*. As the various English

---

[8] A.S.P. Woodhouse ed., *Puritanism and Liberty*, p. 477.
[9] *Ibid.*, p. 245.
[10] W.L. Lamont, *Godly Rule: Politics and Religion 1603–60*.

monarchs pointedly declined to enact the script so considerately written for them by Foxe, so the messianic hopes therein enshrined were transferred to other institutions.

Hopes had run high in some quarters that Parliament would usher in 'godly rule'; presbyterian discipline – for those who liked that sort of thing – had seemed to promise as much. But by the time it was formally instituted as the religion of the country, in the summer of 1646, it had been so watered down as to be little more than a parody of what its most ardent protagonists had desired. Indeed, the country was in such a ferment that there was scarcely a possibility of enforcing so much as a bare conformity, and only a third of all parishes ever came under even the formal control of a presbyterian classis. If the country was ever to be made a truly godly realm – a possibility not discounted by those radicals whose theological roots remained embedded in Puritan-ism, and whose commitment to a gathered church was therefore ambiguous – then deliverance must be sought elsewhere than in the House of Commons.

So it was that on 19th February 1649, just three weeks after the execution of the king and the beginning of the English republic, a group of radicals in Norfolk wrote to Thomas Fair-fax, at this time Lord General of the army and the man with effective power over Parliament, urging him never to 'be instru-mental for the setting up of a mere natural and worldly govern-ment, like that of heathen Rome and Athens', the republics of antiquity. Fairfax was the man whom God had honoured by using him to 'begin the great work of smiting the image on the feet'; it was now his duty to 'comfort his Saints, in whom he reigns spiritually, and by whom he will reign visibly over all nations of the world'. The fifth monarchy predicted by Daniel was at the door, but 'kings, yea parliaments also' must 'be put down, before this kingdom can be erected'. This they hoped the Lord General would do. They urged him to 'consider . . . what right or claim mere natural and worldly men have to rule and government . . .? How can the kingdom be the Saints' when the ungodly are electors, and elected to govern? . . . What a sin it would be to set up the dim light of nature for our law, when God hath given the light of the scriptures, a better law?' Although the chief target which these criticisms seem to have had in view was almost certainly the emerging government of the Rump Parliament, the appeal to natural law had also been an important part of the Levellers' political programme.[11]

By August of the following year, 1650, representatives of the English army in Scotland were declaring, not only the common-place view that the royalist defeat was part of 'the great and wonderful workings of God in these two nations of England and Scotland', but the more novel assertion that 'we [i.e. the army] were called forth by the Lord to be instrumental to bring about ... the destruction of Antichrist and the deliverance of his Church and people'. The rôle of the parliamentarian army was thus seen as a fulfilment of biblical prophecy: following 'the Antichristian tyranny that was exercised by the late king and his prelates', the parliamentarian soldiers had acted out of their 'understanding by the manifold gracious promises of the word of God that a time of deliverance was to be expected by the Church of Christ, and destruction and ruin to Babylon'.

Certainly, almost none – perhaps absolutely none – of the parliamentarian soldiers who had enlisted when the fighting first began back in 1642, or even the vast majority of those who had joined up later, had had any such understanding; the power of such claims lay, not in their faithful reflection *of* the past, but in the fact that they represented the reflections of many *about* the past. They were, to use the postmodern terminology, a product of the religious imagination interpreting their lived experience. Certainly those soldiers who were inclined to Fifth Monarchism saw themselves as spokesmen for 'the people of God', rather than for 'the people of England', as the Leveller-agitators had seen themselves three years earlier. Although God seemed to be an Englishman, and English events were certainly at the epicentre of this particular apocalypse, 'the people of God' were not entirely interchangeable with 'the people of England'; the sectarianism of the Fifth Monarchists, however inconsistent, ensured that the former category would be smaller than the latter.

---

[11]   The Rump was what remained of the Long Parliament, including mostly the more radical MPs who were allowed to continue sitting on the said portion of their anatomy at Westminster after the army leaders had purged the conservative majority in December 1648.

The traditional picture of the Fifth Monarchy men has been, as one historian has humorously expressed it, that of 'brain-sick and bloodthirsty fanatics who aimed to rule in the name of King Jesus'.[12] But not only were the Fifth Monarchists drawing upon sentiments – post-millennialism and the quest for godly rule – widely held in English society, they were not even, as a movement, the most extreme expression of those sentiments. To put the matter simply, their historical reputation has been unduly coloured by the unrepresentative actions of the cooper Thomas Venner who, in 1657, led his circle of London tradesmen and artisans in a foredoomed rising to establish the reign of the saints. Though captured, Venner's life was surprisingly not held forfeit on this occasion, a detail which was not overlooked when he repeated the exploit in 1661 after the Restoration of the monarchy.

But Venner was an aberration. More typical were the Calvinist sectarians and radical Independents who rejoiced when Cromwell, in the summer of 1653, dismissed the Rump Parliament with his soldiers and summoned a Nominated Assembly to act in its place. This assembly, known more widely by its jeeringly appended title of 'Barebones Parliament', lasted for less than six months, but it was the nearest the Fifth Monarchists came to attaining actual power.

Cromwell is sometimes suspected as having been a sympathizer of the Fifth Monarchist cause, but his recorded utterances hardly bear this out. Rather, he made use of cloudy rhetoric of a kind likely to have found favour with senior subordinates like Major-General Harrison, a firm advocate of the cause. Thus he suggested tacit support and at least an open ear toward a (temporarily, as it turned out) powerful group, much as he had done with the Levellers before the time had come to settle accounts with them. This is not to accuse Cromwell of having been motivated by duplicity and manipulation (or not exclusively so). Pliability and indecision are likely to have been at least equally important factors. History knows few finer practitioners of the art of watching to see which way the cat will jump than the great Lord Protector.

---

[12]   B. Capp, 'The Fifth Monarchists and Popular Millenarianism' in J.F. McGregor and B. Reay eds., *Radical Religion in the English Revolution*, p. 165.

This scepticism about Cromwell's alleged Fifth Monarchist inclinations is confirmed by a closer examination of the make-up of the Barebones Parliament. It was popularly named after Praise-God Barbone, the leather-seller and pastor of the non-Baptist half of the Jessey church in London. To the conservative opponents of the assembly, he was an outstanding example of the tradesman-turned-preacher, the base-born radical whom they feared was taking over the country. His first name was the epitome of the kind of barbarous religiosity they detested, and his second made a useful play on words for those who wished to suggest that the institution summoned by Cromwell was a parody of a real parliament (as indeed it was). The assembly was, they insisted, an assortment of wild-eyed fanatics who would not rest until they had overturned all decency, all hierarchy, all private property. Münster again.

In reality, however, Cromwell had been less radical than the presbyterian gentry feared or than the incipient theocrats wished. Barebones contained only a small minority of members nomin-ated by the gathered churches, and only about a dozen commit-ted Fifth Monarchists out of a total of 144. More than a third were gentry of the kind who might have expected to be MPs in an ordinary parliament, and one or two indeed were to be notable crown servants after the Restoration. But as Baxter had com-plained of the sectarians in the New Model Army, it was the activist radical minority who tended to guide the direction of events, this time displeasing Cromwell into the bargain. Perceiv-ing this, the moderates outflanked them on 12th December; whilst the radicals were absent at a prayer meeting, the moderates answered their own prayers by quickly convening, abolishing themselves and repairing in haste to Whitehall to surrender their powers to Cromwell.

Although the Fifth Monarchists refused to lie down and die in the face of this calamity, their moment had clearly come and gone. The movement retained support among a number of (almost exclusively Calvinist) radicals, including the famous Welsh Independents Vavasor Powell and (for a time) Morgan Llwyd, as well as the separatist leader John Canne. Their most prominent spokesman close to the levers of power, Major-General Harrison, was dismissed from the army in December

1653 for opposing the establishment of the Protectorate, with its new constitution and with Cromwell as head of state. The influence of the sectaries over the government of the English republic was by no means at an end (indeed, toleration of them remained one of Cromwell's few consistent principles), but any realistic prospect of them seizing political control had passed.

Chapter Thirteen

The Spirit tried by the Scriptures: English Baptists in the Mid-Seventeenth Century

The General Baptists, 1640–60

'There is one Lambe that was a soap-boiler', wrote the disgusted Presbyterian clergyman Thomas Edwards in 1646, 'and a church that meets in Bell Alley in Coleman Street called Lambe's Church. This man and his church are very erroneous, strange doctrines being vented there continually . . . Many use to resort to this church . . . especially young youths and wenches flock thither, and all of them preach universal redemption'. This description epitomizes the sense of shock with which the activities of the General Baptists were viewed by conservatives for whom, until five years previously, sectarianism had been a mere subterranean phenomenon incapable of mounting an open challenge to officially sanctioned orthodoxies and church structures. Soap-boilers turned preacher; popular enthusiasm led by the young; doctrines of free will. It seemed to Edwards that every sectary was a preacher.

Edwards would have made an excellent columnist for the London *Daily Telegraph*; his tone throughout his book *Gangræna* is that of shocked outrage at the apparently universal collapse of civilization as he had hitherto known it and liked it. The third part of his book is given over largely to letters from correspondents of the 'Disgusted, Tunbridge Wells' variety, with Edwards claiming of the sectaries that 'I have discovered much more of their anarchical and antimagistratical spirit, many of these last errors plainly showing that they are enemies to all government, order, and distinction, and would bring all into a popular confusion . . . and that as often as the weak judgements and humours of the giddy inconstant multitude pleased'.

It was fear of 'the inconstant multitude' that was indeed the most frightening aspect of the upsurge in sectarianism as far as conservative opinion was concerned, and among the sectaries the General Baptists (such as Thomas Lambe and his church) naturally caught the eye as being amongst the more radical by virtue of their denial of pædobaptism, of a state church, and of Calvinist orthodoxy. The meetings at Lambe's church were, moreover, clearly something out of the ordinary; 'when one [preacher] hath done, there's sometimes difference in the church who shall exercise next, 'tis put to the vote, some for one, some for another . . .' (the spectre of popular rule again), and 'in this church 'tis usual and lawful, not only for the company to stand up and object against the doctrine delivered when the exerciser of his gifts hath made an end, but in the midst of it'.[1] Nor was it only a question of 'his' gifts; he made it clear a few pages later that there was a woman who preached at Lambe's church every week.

Thomas Lambe the soap-boiler had been released on bail from the Fleet Prison in London back in June 1640, on the strict condition that he refrain from preaching, baptizing and attending conventicles. He seems to have played a prominent rôle among the Baptists before his arrest in Colchester the previous year, a fact which, in turn, points to the existence of a Baptist church in or near Colchester at this date. Bruno Ryves, a royalist, claimed that there were such in 1642, and his testimony should not be dismissed as mere name-calling aimed at separatists or other radicals, for four years later he described in some objective detail the 'two sorts of Anabaptists' he found in nearby Chelmsford: 'the one they call the Old Men or Aspersi, because they were but sprinkled; the other they call the New Men, or the Immersi, because they were overwhelmed in their rebaptisation'.[2]

---

[1] T. Edwards, *Gangræna*, 2nd edn, i., pp. 92–95.

[2] M. Tolmie, 'Thomas Lambe, Soapboiler, and Thomas Lambe, Merchant, General Baptists', *Baptist Quarterly*, vol. xxvii, 1 (Jan., 1977), p. 5. It seems that the use of unnecessary elongations of, or unusual endings attached to, words in order to convey negative connotations ('rebaptisation') is not simply a modern phenomenon. ('Pentecostalist'; 'Marxoid'; 'fundamentalistic'.)

Ryves' testimony thus indicates the presence of Baptists in Essex prior to their general introduction of baptism by immersion in the early 1640s.

About seven months after his release on bail, Lambe had again been arrested for his part in a meeting at Whitechapel, but by the end of 1641 he had been released and was explaining his Baptist ideas to the separatists of Gloucestershire and baptizing them in the Severn in the middle of the night. Parliament passed an ordinance in 1645 forbidding lay preaching and, the Lord Mayor of London desiring to make a test case of Lambe, he was taken into custody yet again. But the parliamentary committee refused to prosecute him, and it became apparent that, under the prevailing chaotic political conditions, persecution was unenforceable. Later that year Lambe was touring Kent with Henry Denne, another leader of the General Baptists, and continued his evangelistic journey into the following year, preaching in Essex, Surrey, Hampshire and Wiltshire.

The manner of baptism had caused division, not only amongst the Chelmsford Baptists, but in the congregation at Lincoln also. Martin Mason, the Quaker, in his *The Boasting Baptist Dismounted* of 1656, distinguishes the 'sprinklers' of that city from the 'dippers', and it seems certain that both groups were Generals.[3] Nevertheless, if some General Baptists were slow to accept the practice of immersion, they were the exceptions; as early as 1642, Edward Barber felt free to write *A small treatise of baptisms or dipping* in which he assumed the synonymity of the two terms.[4]

Barber is generally believed to have been part of Lambe the soap-boiler's congregation, and his writing on behalf of the Baptists continued the following year with a petition – *The humble Request of certaine Christians* – inviting Parliament and the Westminster divines to debate doctrine with them, declaring that, if the Baptists could be worsted in such discussions, 'then we will thankfully be reduced to the truth and repent and revoke our errors and suffer for our presumption'.[5] The challenge went unmet but in 1645 Barber again took up his pen, this time

---

[3] *Ibid.*, p. 6.

[4] B.R. White, *The English Baptists of the Seventeenth Century*, p. 34.

[5] *Ibid.*, p. 35.

concerning *A true discovery of the ministery of the Gospell*. In this work he described the qualifications and work of an 'apostle or messenger', together with those of pastors, teachers and deacons. The first of these, an office distinct to the General Baptists, was to be not a master of the churches, but a servant, supporting himself by a trade, and effective in evangelism at large, rather than being permanently tied to a particular locality. In his last work, *An Answere to the Essex Watchmens Watchword* of 1649, he argued against tithes and in favour of religious toleration and a Spirit-taught ministry. Concerning toleration, he wrote that 'No man ought to be forced in matter of religion, the gospel being spiritual and requiring only spiritual worshippers who cannot be made so, but by the Word and Spirit of God, which breatheth where and when it listeth, and not where and when men's laws and statutes pleaseth.'[6] By this date, at least, the General Baptists were not entirely without sympathizers in arguing such a case.

Barber's ideas on learning and the ministry were the common stock, not only of General Baptists, but of a variety of other radicals. Samuel How, the separatist and former semi-separatist, had preached a famous sermon at the Nag's Head tavern near Coleman Street, London, published in 1640 as *The Sufficiencie of the Spirits Teaching, without Humane Learning*. He died that year and a conservative pamphleteer jeered that this mere cobbler, who had taken upon himself 'the mending of souls', was thus paid his 'wages' for having meddled with things 'above his reach'. There is more justice, perhaps, in the same pamphlet's observation that

> The ignorant will only be
> To human learning an enemy.[7]

Henry Haggar, who exercised an apostolic ministry for the General Baptists in the Shropshire and Staffordshire area in the 1650s, opined that

> It was always God's way (or for the most part) to choose his prophets
> out of unlearned men, and honest labouring men, that knew what it was
> to get their living by the sweat of their brows; and not such as were

---

6   J.F. McGregor, 'The Baptists: Fount of all Heresy' in J.F. McGregor and B. Reay eds., *Radical Religion in the English Revolution*, p. 49.
7   C. Burrage, *Early English Dissenters*, ii., pp. 328–330.

brought up idly, so that they cannot dig, and are ashamed to beg: and therefore prove unjust stewards. They are not fit to be ministers of Christ, because they must preach for hire . . . therefore they must please men . . . or else men will give them little or no wages. [8]

This last statement was a curious argument. Thomas Edwards had contended, with more reason, that the danger of preachers merely seeking to please was a weighty consideration against sectarianism. In his *Reasons against the Independant Government of Particular Congregations* of 1641, he had urged against toleration, for otherwise 'the most eminent ministers in this kingdom' would have little assurance that their congregations would not desert them 'upon any discontent taken, or any light occasion of demanding dues, or preaching against anything they like not'. [9] Edwards was again showing his squeamishness at what might happen if the inconstant multitude were allowed to think and act for themselves, and in this respect it was in the General Baptists (more than in the Independents or even the Particular Baptists) that his worst fears were realized. Daniel Featley, in his *The Dippers Dipt*, stigmatized all Baptists as 'Russet Rabbies, and mechanic enthusiasts, and profound watermen, and sublime coachmen, and illuminated tradesmen'; he could afford to be scathing about the possibility of God speaking through such social riff-raff, because of his certainty that God did not now speak – except in a metaphorical sense, through the learnedly constructed sermons of suitably educated and officially sanctioned preachers – at all. That the arguments of both How and Haggar, on the one hand, and Edwards and Featley, on the other, concerning who ought or ought not to be suffered to preach were transparently self-serving and self-vindicating is a point which hardly needs to be laboured.

The historian Murray Tolmie suggests that the General Baptists were 'looser in organization, more radical in outlook, and more fluid in membership' than the Particulars, whilst J.F. McGregor observes that, 'largely isolated by doctrinal differences from the radical Calvinist coalition, they appear to have found their support in a lower strata of the London population, less touched by Puritan influence'. Not only, he might have

---

[8] J.F. McGregor, 'Baptists: Fount of all Heresy', p. 50.
[9] M. Watts, *The Dissenters*, i., p. 88.

added, in the London population. John Onley, a leader among the Warwickshire General Baptists, 'painfully follows husbandry all the week days', and he was not an unusual specimen; the General Baptists were able to penetrate the countryside and win significant numbers of converts from the agricultural population, a characteristic they were to share only with the Quakers. Whereas separatists, semi-separatists and Particular Baptists were, in a certain sense, radicalized Puritans, and tended to win adherents from among those whose personal history was linked to one degree or another of Puritanism, the General Baptists had divested themselves of Calvinist theology, and thus could appeal to those segments of the population which had never been puritanised in the first place.

Not all the General Baptist leaders were from humble backgrounds; Henry Denne and Samuel Fisher were former clergymen within the established church. Even so, virtually all of the gentry and men of wealth or influence listed by J.F. McGregor in his article 'The Baptists: Fount of all Heresy' (the title is a reference to the Presbyterian Robert Baillie's tract of 1647) were Particular Baptists, not Generals.[10] What is more, when the 'other' Thomas Lambe, a wealthy linen draper of Cornhill, came to General Baptist conclusions in 1653 (he had previously belonged to the relatively well-to-do congregation of the radical Independent, John Goodwin), his wife remarked that they could not find 'any society in that engagement where they could have such means of edification as they had left'. Accordingly, they started their own congregation with seceders from Goodwin's rather than join the nearby fellowship of the lowly soap-boiler. The little social difficulty was to haunt this, the richer, Thomas Lambe; although his congregation grew to over a hundred, the influx tended to be those of a similar social standing to other General Baptists ('the poor people I now serve', he called them), and the prospect of being unable to marry his daughters to their social equals was to be a major factor leading him to renounce sectarianism completely in 1659.[11]

---

[10]   J.F. McGregor, 'Baptists: Fount of all Heresy' in McGregor and Reay eds., *Radical Religion*, pp. 37–9.
[11]   M. Tolmie, 'Thomas Lambe, Soapboiler, and Thomas Lambe, Merchant, General Baptists', p. 11.

The General Baptists were prominent in their support for the Leveller movement, sustaining their efforts on its behalf longer than did the Particulars, who had always been more half-hearted. The reasons are threefold. In the first place, as we have seen, their support came largely from the very lower middle-class which was also the bedrock of Leveller support. In the second place, the Generals had no links with Puritanism and had had a generation in which to forget their links even with Barrowist separatism. They thus had no pretensions to respectability, and no friend-ships to keep up with likeminded people to their right. The divide between themselves and competing religious factions was more absolute. That being so, they could afford to go out on a limb a little more sustainedly in this particular cause. Finally, since their thinking was not informed by Calvinist theology and by Puritan assumptions regarding the godly nation, they were more natu-rally attracted to the secular political vision of the Levellers, with its stress upon freedom from religious compulsion. As we noticed in the previous chapter, several General Baptist leaders got themselves into serious trouble for their Leveller involvements, and in the case of Henry Denne (present at the Burford mutiny in May 1649) that involvement almost cost him his life, which was only spared by an embarrassing and very public recantation, seen by his fellows as a betrayal.

This disastrous, and perhaps disgraceful, event did not finish Denne's career. But it seems to have marked the end of a period of uncertainty for him. John Drew suggested that year, in his *A Serious Addresse to Samuel Oates*, that Denne was drifting in the direction of the Seekers, a group which rejected all outward ordinances such as communion and baptism. Certainly Denne's *Antichrist Unmasked* of 1646 taught the doctrine of an inner light similar to the teaching that was to become a hallmark of the Quakers.

The tension between Spirit and letter was disturbing many religious people in the late 1640s and 1650s, and the exclusiveness of General Baptist ways did not easily retain the long-term loyalty of people brought up to think in terms of a Christian commonwealth. As William Grounds told his brothers and sis-ters of the Fenstanton congregation at the admonitory process preceding his excommunication, 'as for others they may find comfort in other ways, they being also the ways of God'. William Marriat, on his way out of the same church, told the leaders that, 'if you mean that I should so join with you as not to join with any other people, I will not do that . . . I do believe that other people which do not observe these ordinances, are the people of God as well as you'. Marriat's other statements show him to have been a confused man, but clearly Baptist exclusiveness troubled him. Widow Sanders told John Denne (Henry's son) and John Gilman that 'she did walk in the ways of God, and so did we; so did those people that did live under episcopal and presbyterial government, and those that walked under no ordinances; they all walk as God would have them'.[12]

Such generosity of spirit, however it may commend itself to a more ecumenical age, was hard to square with the task of per-suading people to leave their parish churches and cleave to gathered congregations of the converted. It was inevitable that such views, if persisted in, would lead to the excommunication of those who held them. Certainly the Cambridgeshire General Baptists suffered for this reason a haemorrhage of members during the 1650s that seems to have been almost as great as any gains made from evagelism.

And still the problem persisted. Isabel, the maid of Robert Kent and his wife (with whom John Denne and Christopher Marriat were staying while on an evangelistic expedition), claimed that 'she tried the Scriptures by the Spirit, and not the Spirit by the Scriptures' – a Quaker idea. Five days later the two men stayed with Fordam the tanner at Newport in Essex. Fordam had been a General Baptist until recently (this was November 1653) but, along with others in the town, had come to reject his former beliefs. What, he now asked, was 'the breath of life' which God had breathed into Adam at the beginning to make him a living soul? 'It was nothing but God himself, so that the soul and spirit of man is God.' His guests desired him to prove that 'all that proceeded from God is God', which he could not do to their satisfaction.[13] But the Quaker concept of the

---

[12]   E.B. Underhill ed., *Records of the Churches of Christ Gathered at Fenstanton, Warboys, and Hexham 1644–1720*, pp. 21, 27, 40.
[13]   *Ibid.*, pp. 74, 77–78.

indwelling light is clearly present, though perhaps here taken to the rationalist extreme of the Ranters, who tended to deny any traditional Christian doctrines of God.

Historians have pointed out that it was the Baptists' 'extreme literalism' which 'was the chief cause of Baptist losses to the Quakers', the Generals being particularly vulnerable because Quaker doctrine was, in some ways, 'a radical extension of general redemption'.[14] Anthony Yeule, making the familiar exit from the Fenstanton church, admitted that 'the anabaptists do walk the nearest to the rule in the scriptures of any that I know; but for my part I will not be tied unto it'. He claimed that God 'spake unto prophets formerly, and now he speaks unto me by his Spirit'. Widow Peppers likewise claimed to have received 'greater manifestations; for God dwelleth in me, and I in him. And now I see that to love, to clothe the naked, and to feed the hungry is enough'. The church officers answered her by reducing these good deeds to love according to 1 Corinthians 13:3, and reducing love to keeping Christ's commandments according to John 2:4. Legalism again. Widow Sanders also claimed that 'the manifestation of the Spirit is as sure a rule for me to walk by, as the scriptures are for you'.[15]

Along with such a belief went a denial of the necessity of ordinances. However, since a distinctive position on the ordinance of baptism was one of the central planks of the Baptist platform, the sojourn in Baptist company of the many people who had begun thinking along these lines was bound to be transitory.

The number of ordinances was, in any case, growing, and causing divisions even among those who remained loyal to the cause. The church in Norborough, Lincolnshire, had trouble in 1652–53 with their pastor, Robert Wright, who first resigned his office, and later separated from the church and set up a rival meeting. The points at issue, at least in his own estimation (for his behaviour appears to have been rather erratic), were those of footwashing, the holding of a congregational supper before

---

[14]   M. Watts, *The Dissenters*, i., p. 205; J.F. McGregor, 'The Baptists: Fount of all Heresy' in McGregor and Reay eds., *Radical Religion*, p. 61.
[15]   E.B. Underhill ed., *Fenstanton Records*, pp. 43, 46–49.

communion, and the laying of hands on all newly-baptized believers. Edmund Mayle and John Denne, the elders from Fenstanton, managed to patch up the quarrel on this occasion. Perhaps they had the advantage of experience in such matters, for the previous January one of their fellow-elders by the name of Gray had caused an argument over the issue of holding a supper before communion. In April 1655, the church at Easton, Welby and Westby reported that some of their number had separated over their insistence on the necessity of a pre-communion supper.

It was the issue of the laying on of hands, however, that was to occasion the greatest dispute. In 1654 the General Baptist leaders meeting in London decided to break communion with those who would not practise and receive the laying on of hands. Lambe the soap-boiler was on the other, losing side of this issue, and his career as a national leader among the General Baptists was submerged, until the end of the 1650s, as a result. John Lupton and Joseph Wright of the Coningsby and Tattershall church in Lincolnshire also favoured breaking communion with those not under the laying on of hands, while a majority of the church in Thorpe, Rutland felt equally strongly the other way, and excommunicated those who had received it. The Fenstanton church was uncharacteristic in displaying sufficient good sense to adopt one view (in favour of laying on of hands) while sharing communion, in its own meetings at least, with those of the opposing view.

This destructive dispute was, in some ways, analogous with that taking place among Particular Baptists over open, or closed, communion, only to far less purpose. Legalism and literalism continued to alienate many, and to create candidates for deser-tion to Quakerism, for the adoption of Seeker views, or even for a return to the Church of England.

Like the Particulars, the General Baptists did have a regional organization of sorts, but we simply do not possess the informa-tion to know how structured this was. Clearly, Fenstanton was at the hub of events in the East Midlands, and there were fairly frequent meetings of leaders from the area in Cambridge to discuss local problems. It is less clear, however, whether this was intended to be an association on the model of the Particular

Baptists. There were also general meetings at Cranbrook and Yalding, in Kent, in July 1652, and at Chatham and Biddenden, in the same county, five years later. There were also three general assemblies in London, meeting in 1654, 1656 and again in 1660, when *A brief confession or declaration of faith* was produced. But the records we possess, and possibly the meetings that took place, are too sporadic to indicate regional associations such as those of their Calvinistic brethren.

The Particulars and the Generals themselves, however, did not act as brethren. There were obviously differences on predestina-tion and the scope of the atonement, but there were also some social differences, with the Generals appealing to a slightly lower social stratum. As we have seen, General Baptist support for the Levellers tended to be firmer and of longer duration than that which obtained among the Particulars; the latter, however, were much more prone to Fifth Monarchist views. A document of 1660, *The humble apology*, appears to have been almost the full extent of inter-Baptist co-operation; faced with imminent perse-cution at the hands of a restored monarchy, leaders of both types of Baptist felt able to unite in stressing their obedience and loyalty to secular government. The previous December, with the republican government already in an advanced state of collapse, the two groups had similarly combined to declare, in *A Declara-tion of Several of the People called Anabaptists*, that they would ever be 'obedient to Magistracy in all things Civil, and willing to live peaceably, under whatever Government is, and shall be established in this Nation'.[16] Among the signators was Henry Denne, who was clearly putting his old Leveller days yet further behind him.

Denne died shortly afterwards, and the eighteenth-century Baptist historian Crosby relates that a 'clergyman' of Denne's acquaintance gave him the following epitaph:

> To tell his wisdom, learning, goodness unto men,
> I need to say no more, but here lies Henry Denne. [17]

---

[16] cited in J.F. McGregor, 'Baptists: Fount of all Heresy' in McGregor and Reay eds., *Radical Religion*, p. 55.
[17] cited in E.B. Underhill ed., *Fenstanton Records*, p. xxii.

Even his erstwhile Leveller comrades could have agreed with that.

The Particular Baptists

'Precious brethren', wrote Thomas Collier and Nathaniel Strange, on behalf of the 'assembled messengers' at Chard, Somerset on 18th April 1657:

> partakers of the heavenly calling [Heb. 3:1], the earnest breathing of our souls are for your growth in grace and establishment in the truth [2 Pet 1:12] in Jesus as it is in these shaking days. Oh, this is the time of Jacob's trouble [Jer. 30:7], Satan rageth, the world rejoiceth, and poor Zion's children, some are weeping and making bitter lamentation, others turn - ing aside from faith which once was delivered unto them [Jude 3; 1 Tim. 4:1], giving heed unto seducing spirits and doctrine of devils; others almost asleep in a worldly spirit, contenting themselves in the form without the power [2 Tim. 3:5] . . . [18]

The Association Records of the Particular Baptists (especially those relating to the West Country, which owed so much to the literary efforts of Thomas Collier) abound with this liberal use of the 'language of Zion'. The modern reader cannot but be consoled by such reassuring evidence that this speech impedi-ment characteristically affecting the pious is, after all, nothing new. Though the note of the verbose messengers gathered in Chard is often one of bewailing, the apostle Paul's comment about 'groanings too deep for words' (Rom. 8:26) seems to be one of the few scriptures not taken to heart.

The various writers of the *Association Records* were clearly men upon whose minds the language and ideas of Scripture had left an indelible stamp. They believed that the Scriptures were, as John Spilsbury said, 'the all sufficient Rule by the Spirit of God', and therein they expected to find one unalterable pattern for all necessary details of church life and personal behaviour. There is, in their questionings and discussions, a deadly earnestness about 'getting it right' that strikes a strange, even amusing, note to the modern ear.

---

[18]   B.R. White ed., *Association Records of the Particular Baptists of England, Wales and Ireland to 1660*, ii., p. 85.

Thus it was that the elders and messengers of the West Country Particular Baptists, at their fourth general meeting at Bridgewater on 17th–19th April 1655, set aside time to consider the burning question 'whether it be an ordinance of Christ for disciples to wash one another's feet, according to John 13:14?' We are relieved at the sanity of their answer: 'we understand that Christ in that scripture teacheth disciples humility and to serve each other in love and, if need call for it, to wash each other's feet.' Just to be on the safe side, they concluded their answer with two further Scripture references: Hebrews 13:1 and 1 Peter 5:5. [19]

In early June the following year, the messengers of the churches of the Midlands Association, met at Moreton-in-the-Marsh for their fifth general meeting, addressed themselves to the issue of 'whether it be the duty of church members always to call each other brother and sister'. Again, we are impressed by the balance of the reply. [20] And again, it is not the answers, but the questions, that betray a desperate earnestness to find the one true pattern and to follow it to the letter.

The third general meeting of the West Country messengers at Taunton in September 1654 had considered 'whether a servant of the Lord may purpose what to speak to the world or to the church beforehand and search the Scriptures concerning it?' There are overtones in this question of the kind of thinking engendered by Samuel How's famous sermon of 1640 at the Nag's Head Tavern off Coleman Street, London, on 'The Sufficiency of the Spirit's Teaching without Human Learning'. Once again, a sane answer was given, and yet again it is the question that reveals more to the modern reader of the state of mind of many of these early Baptists. [21]

For them, the whole conduct of Christian life and of church order was, in a sense, 'up for grabs', or at least open to question. Something like a complete break had been made with the traditional churches (the desire of the early leaders to establish their theological orthodoxy and to remain in some sense a part of the Puritan fraternity notwithstanding) and so, once the main

---

[19] *Ibid.*, ii., p. 60.
[20] *Ibid.*, i., pp. 25–6.
[21] *Ibid.*, ii., p. 57.

lines of development had been proclaimed in the early confessions of faith, there remained a felt need by the people on the
ground to settle questions of personal conduct and the details
of church polity. Sometimes these questions had wider theological implications – as for example in the debate about accepting
state maintenance of ministers. This was a question that was a
contentious issue for Particular Baptists during the 1650s, when
several of them accepted livings in the extremely unusual,
piecemeal state church under the various Cromwellian régimes,
which managed to encompass Presbyterians, Independents,
willing Particular Baptists (and even, in the quieter rural back-
waters, episcopalians using the now-illegal *Book of Common
Prayer*).

One meeting of the West Country messengers at Chard in
October 1655 was asked 'whether Christ Jesus our Lord died for
all and every man or for the elect only, and if for all, then how
far?'[22] But this was an exception. Most of the 'queries' raised by
individual congregations at the regional general meetings were
of a more immediately practical nature.

This is not to say, however, that the general meetings took
no interest in theological concerns. In 1655 the Midland Association, as one of its first acts, adopted a common Confession
of Faith. This is a brief, but firmly Calvinistic, document,
teaching that people 'have no power of themselves to believe
savingly. . . . Therefore consent not with those who hold that
God hath given power to all men to believe to salvation.'[23] The
Midlands was an area in which the General Baptists, with
strongholds in Lincolnshire and Leicestershire, greatly outnum-
bered the Particular Baptists during these years and this fact
together, perhaps, with the Baptist historian Whitley's conjecture that Daniel King (one of the prime authors of the Midlands
Confession) was a defector from the Generals to the Particulars,
may account for the robustness of expression on this question.

The *Somerset Confession* was produced in 1656, the historian
W.L. Lumpkin considering it 'evidently the work of [Thomas]
Collier', and 'an attempt to comprehend all Baptists of the district

---

[22] Ibid., ii., p. 61.
[23] W.L. Lumpkin, *Baptist Confessions of Faith*, p. 199.

irrespective of their Calvinism or Arminianism'.[24] (This is not the place to take issue with Lumpkin's designation of the General Baptists' brand of anti-Calvinism as 'Arminianism.') Although there seems to have been ample reason for Collier and his fellows to attempt to heal the divide – the Quakers were making serious inroads into Baptist congregations in the area at the time – the evidence that the *Somerset Confession* was so intended is far from obvious. Article IX states that 'God in his Son did freely . . . elect and choose some to himself before the foundation of the world', article XI claims that 'those that are chosen of God . . . shall never finally fall from him', and article XV says that Christ bore only 'the sins of his people' – which is presumably not the same as taking away 'the sin of the world' (Jn. 1:29)![25]

However, the humility that was so evident in the 1644 Confession ('if any shall do us that friendly part to shew us from the word of God that we see not, we shall have cause to be thankful to God and them') was continued in the provinces.[26] The messengers at Bridgewater in November 1656 answered a question on astrology by saying 'we cannot at present determine this question but desire to wait on the Lord for further light in it'. To another question they conclude their answer with 'This is our present light.' The previous year, they had answered a question about worship and added that 'This is that which at present we see and further we cannot speak but wait on the Lord for further light when he shall pour forth more of his Spirit.'[27]

There is an attractive combination of earnestness and self-effacing modesty in some of these discussions, especially in the dealings of the West Country association. Asked what should be done with members who refuse to abandon the wearing of 'gold, pearls and costly array', the meeting concluded that 'those who wilfully refuse to reform are to be dealt with as transgressors', yet 'we desire that persons in this case may be proceeded with in all sweetness, tenderness and longsuffering, it being not so clearly and generally understood among saints

---

24   *Ibid.*, pp. 200, 202.
25   *Ibid.*, pp. 205–6.
26   *Ibid.*, p. 149.
27   B.R. White ed., *Association Records*, ii., p. 58, 65–6.

to be a sin as other sins that are more contrary to the light of nature'.[28]

The Associations were formed partly in response to the needs of co-operation, not least in fending off the threat posed by Quakerism. More important, however, was the need to nurture young and struggling congregations. All of the earliest Particular Baptist churches had been situated in and around London. Even these had felt the need to justify their actions and beliefs by taking joint action in the form of a Confession of Faith, so that no one could suspect that such a statement was the work of one congregation 'more refined than the rest' whilst the others remained the devils which surrounding society seemed intent on taking them for.[29]

The Association was a form of organization that reflected the Independent belief in congregational autonomy whilst yet attempting to achieve unanimity on essentials and co-operation in practice between churches. As the Abingdon Association expressed the matter at its first general meeting in October 1652, 'there is the same relation betwixt the particular churches each towards other as there is betwixt particular members of one church. . . . Wherefore we conclude that every church ought to manifest its care over other churches as fellow members of the same body of Christ . . . to keep each other pure. . . .' In this way 'orderly walking churches' would be 'owned orderly and disorderly churches be orderly disowned'.[30]

In 1644, John Cotton, the famous Independent (erstwhile vicar of Boston, Lincolnshire and later, from 1633, pastor of Boston, Massachusetts), had published his work *The Keyes of the Kingdom of Heaven*, in which he had advocated a 'consociation' of churches 'to proceed with common consultation and consent'.[31] The purpose of such consociations, he envisaged, was 'to maintain brotherly love and soundness of doctrine in churches, and to prevent many offences which may grow up in this or that

---

28 *Ibid.*, ii., p. 64.
29 W.L. Lumpkin, *Baptist Confessions of Faith*, p. 155.
30 B.R. White, *Association Records*, iii. 126.
31 B.R. White, *English Baptists*, p. 66. See also *idem*, 'The Organisation of the Particular Baptists', *Journal of Ecclesiastical History*, xvii (1966), pp. 209–26.

particular church, when it transacteth all things within itself
without consent'. The Separatist stress on the immediate authority of Christ in a congregation of believers, and on each congregation's resultant autonomy from external human jurisdiction,
was a doctrine with potential for causing fragmentation. Indeed,
it had actually done so, and by the early 1640s there was already
a fair spectrum of separate churches in England: 'Ancient' Separatists and new, Jacobite semi-separatists and their breakaways,
General Baptists and Particulars. And the spectrum was widen-
ing. The device of the 'consociation' would enable mutually
acceptable churches, in the words of the Henley, Reading and
Abingdon Particular Baptists, 'to convince the world, for by this
shall men know . . . that we are the true churches of Christ'. By
owning – or disowning – one another, by collectively associating
in published confessions of faith, it was hoped 'to clear the
profession of the Gospel from scandal'.[32] At the very least, a
modest barrier was thus erected in the path of those who might
be the cause of further unwelcome diversity.

A fair proportion of time at association meetings was set aside
for prayer. It was only after the leaders of the Midlands Particular
Baptists (meeting in September 1657) had spent time together in
'solemn seeking of God by fasting and prayer' that the queries and
problems of the churches were given consideration. The meeting
of their West Country counterparts at Wells in April of the
previous year had clearly been a time of great spiritual refreshing.
Two days had been spent together in fasting and prayer before
'business' had been discussed, and then that business had been an
attempt to discern, through the words of Psalm 102, the strategy
and purpose of the Lord in respect of themselves. They were able
to report that 'we have seen the Lord exalted and his train filling
the temple. We have in some measure been embracing our dear
Jesus who hath even made us sick with love.' They had determined
to repeat the format at their October meeting, 'where we have
appointed to spend four days, two of them in waiting on the Lord
in fasting and prayer for the Spirit'.[33] The cohesion, not to mention
the encouragement, that such shared experiences would have given

---

[32]   B.R. White, *Association Records*, iii., pp. 26–7.
[33]   *Ibid.*, i., p. 32; ii., pp. 78–9.

to the group can well be imagined. The general meetings thus gave the leaders, and through them the churches, a sense of common purpose that might otherwise easily have evaporated in a small, scattered congregation, perhaps isolated from its fellows by some few dozen miles.

The congregations were admonished to have no truck with non-Baptist preachers. The West Country Association meeting in Chard in April 1657 was asked whether it was in order 'to hear a person that hath received a gift from the Lord, which gift hath been blessed by the Lord to the conversion of sinners and to the confirming of saints in the faith of Christ, being of a holy and grave conversation,' (it becomes almost impossible to believe that some particular messenger, with some particular case in mind, is not pleading for a 'yes' verdict) 'and denying wholly the world's ways' (except, of course, the baptism of Antichrist) 'and which, though not yet baptized, yet so far from opposing that ordinance that he is earnestly longing and diligently waiting for further information therein . . .?'

Normally such questions were answered in the flat negative. The same meeting had done so eighteen months earlier. It is somewhat surprising, therefore, that on this occasion, although inviting such a person to preach 'in the church assembled' was forbidden (with six reasons and a dozen scriptural proof texts supplied), the 'hearing of such a person when the church is not assembled' (i.e. in a state, or independent, church) was given an ultra-cautious 'maybe' for an answer.[34] Perhaps this is not so surprising after all, since at least one passionate advocate of an affirmative answer was clearly present!

The English Particular Baptist meetings consistently ruled out the lawfulness of preachers being maintained by the magistrate's authority. The Midlands Association did so in 1655, and the West Country Association in April 1656. In November, however, the latter meeting was informed that 'several churches . . . do still own the taking of a set maintenance from the magistrate and will not reform'. But the meeting did not take any action against these dissidents beyond 'bearing testimony against their practice'.[35]

---

[34] *Ibid.*, ii., pp. 67–8.
[35] *Ibid.*, i., pp. 22–3; ii., pp. 62–4.

Perhaps it was the churches of South Wales that the questioner had in mind. There John Miles, Thomas Proud and Thomas Joseph all accepted state support, while Walter Prosser (Particular Baptist leader at Hay) accepted the living of the parish of Tredunnock, Howell Thomas became the clergyman of Glyncorrwg, and Rhydderch Thomas accepted the benefice of Llanfihangel. Clearly, for the Welsh Baptists, the distinction between a state-sponsored church and a Baptist congregation was very blurred! These were a minority, however (the perpetual tragedy of the Welsh is that they have always been a minority *vis-à-vis* the English), and in the long run the Particular Baptists were able to establish themselves as a growing sectarian organization.

If the resolution of the issue was somewhat drawn-out, the reason is to be found in the somewhat ambiguous churchmanship of the Particular Baptists' origins. It was not only the London church pastored by Henry Jessey which contained both members who had been baptized as believers and those who had not; the Broadmead church in Bristol long continued the same latitude, though it later became commitedly Baptist. The independent church in Bedford, later famous as the 'Bunyan Meeting' after its most famous son (or, perhaps, father), continues that tradition of studied ambivalence to this day.[36] However, just as the issue of baptism marks the watershed – if the pun is at all excusable – between those churches unreservedly committed to religious voluntarism and the separation of church and state and those who are not, so ambiguity about the rite was inseparable from ambiguity about the place of religion in society. We are unsurprised, therefore, to find John Tombes acting as a cross between parish clergyman of Leominster – accepting state maintenance – and Particular Baptist pastor.

Even the eventual victory of the 'closed membership' principle among Particular Baptists, which limited belonging to those who had received believers' baptism, did not entirely end the discrepancies and confusions. Thus it was that John Miles could accept the parish living of Ilston, on Gower, in 1649 and yet exclude the majority of the populace from the ordinances whilst he organized

---

[36] This is one of the reasons, of course, that John Bunyan is claimed by both the Baptists and the Congregationalists.

the parochial structures as a closed-membership Baptist church. But such logic – or lack of it – carried less and less weight as the 1650s progressed. It was just as well. If even Presbyterians could find no place in the parish churches after the Restoration, the only place for Baptists in the structures of established religion would be the prisons.

* * *

By then, the Particular Baptists had grown to thirty thousand members, a figure equalled by the General Baptists. Between them, the two Baptist movements held the allegiance of one per cent of the population of England and Wales. If this does not seem an impressive figure today, it certainly impressed contemporaries. If opponents were inclined to vilify the radicals, the size of their following was the last thing they held in contempt. Rather, they were appalled at how quickly the contagion seemed to be spreading. It was not simply that seventeenth-century society was less accustomed to rapid social change than we are; the Baptists were far more influential than the figure of one per cent might imply. To that extent they 'outpunched their weight'. They converted the very people who counted in England, or who were starting to count: tradespeople and artisans; the newly literate; above all, soldiers in a standing army of unprecedented political influence. What is more, they were organized: regional meetings, associations, messengers, tracts, confessions of faith, petitions – all were products of a new age of improved communications and rising literacy, facilitated by social turmoil and cheap print. For the purpose of being heard, the Baptists had the *right* one per cent; they could not be ignored. And if they were sometimes legalistic and unwarrantably literalist, these were qualities on which they held no monopoly – either at this period or later. In any case, such characteristics seem to have been leavened by a warm piety which (if the records of the West Country Particular Baptists are at all typical) suffused their life as a whole. Their developing cohesion and self-consciousness as a group – or rather, as two groups – were to be needed in weathering the storms that lay ahead in the much harsher climate of Restoration England.

Chapter Fourteen

The Scriptures tried by the Spirit: the Coming of the Quakers

Origins of a Movement

It would be unjust to claim that George Fox, the most important of the early Quaker leaders, had no sense of sin. However, what he had was essentially a sense of other people's iniquity rather than of his own. As he says himself, 'When I came to eleven years of age, I knew pureness and righteousness; for while I was a child I was taught how to walk to be kept pure.' This conviction of his own righteousness – always, of course, with the Lord's help! – never seems to have left him; he admits to temptations, but the nearest he comes to an admission of sin is when he writes that 'all are concluded under sin, and shut up in unbelief as I had been. . . .'

Fox undoubtedly saw himself as specially anointed; his father is 'righteous Christer', his mother 'of the stock of the martyrs'. Of the shoemaker to whom he was apprenticed he writes 'While I was with him, he was blessed; but after I left him he broke, and came to nothing.' He also mentions 'one Brown, who had great prophecies and sights upon his death-bed of me. And he spoke openly of what I should be made instrumental by the Lord to bring forth. And of others he spake that they should come to nothing, which was fulfilled on some, that then were something in show.' It would, on the face of it, be hard to argue that Fox failed to take himself seriously. Speaking of himself as a boy, he claims that 'I never wronged man or woman in all that time [his apprenticeship], for the Lord's power was with me. . . . When boys and rude people would laugh at me, I let them alone and went my way. . . .'[1] One cannot help feeling that this was a forbearance which the young Fox would frequently have been called upon to exercise.

Belief in oneself is, perhaps, a prerequisite for success in a mission to change the world in which one lives. The Quakers were the most emphatically successful of the sects in the Civil War period. By 1660 they may have numbered as many as sixty thousand, equal to the Baptists' combined strength, and roughly one per cent of the population. In Bristol, with about a thousand Quakers, they were 5.6 per cent of the inhabitants; in Westmorland, again with one thousand, 3.3 per cent; in London, with eight to ten thousand, 1.5 per cent. Not a single county of England was without a Quaker meeting, a boast the Baptists were unable to make. And all of this had been achieved in less than a decade and a half. Some historians have argued with justice that fear of rapid Quaker expansion contributed significantly to the shift in public opinion in the late 1650s that led to the restoration of Charles II – 'so totally unexpected until a few months before it actually happened', as Christopher Hill observes.[2]

But where had the Quaker movement come from? Many people in England had, not surprisingly, been left confused by the religious turmoil of the 1640s. Familiar with the struggles between Protestant and Catholic, the substantial existence of the latter within England had been little more than a phantom for most ordinary people. Catholicism was a foreign threat; although papist fifth columns were greatly feared, these were merely 'reds under the beds', and few people knew Catholics at first hand.

The perpetual struggle between competing factions within the Church of England, generally between Puritans and ceremonialists, was more familiar to the person in the village street. Thoroughgoing pluralism and the possibility of real choice was, however, a novel experience to most people. In 1638 – in the world before the storm – William Chillingworth had been able to pronounce famously that 'The Bible, the Bible only I say, is

---

[1] G. Fox, *The Journal of George Fox*, ed. J.L. Nickalls, pp. 1–2, 20.
[2] C. Hill, *God's Englishman*, p. 241.

the religion of Protestants', though even then it had been obvious that 'what the Bible says' was not a question beyond all debate. But the experience of the 1640s had left many ordinary people with the impression that Scripture was a nose of wax, shaped in a bewildering variety of forms by an ever-proliferating assortment of competing expositors.

Almost inevitably, the negative aspect of the sectarians' message was found more persuasive than the positive. Martin Luther, as has often been remarked, had found it easier to convince sixteenth-century Germans that the Pope was Antichrist than he had done to persuade them that the just shall live by faith. So now; the idea that the Church of England was antichristian, and corrupt in both principles and ceremonies, found acceptance with many who yet could not bring themselves to believe that anyone had authority to set up a true church or a true baptism again – from scratch as it were – without a fresh revelation, or a new dispensation of the Holy Spirit. Praise-God Barbone, the London leather-seller who from 1640 led the eastern half of the gathered church in London previously cared for by Henry Jessey alone, took such a view of baptism, though not of churches. He reasoned that, if Anglican baptism were not true baptism, and that of Rome even less so, then there would have been a hiatus in true baptisms and no continuity of succession from the apostles; therefore, no one could presume to institute it anew. His argument (aimed against the Particular Baptists) was intended to call the premise into question by pointing out the unacceptable conclusion. Even so, it proved to be a catastrophic shot in the foot, and a shot in the arm for those who, nothing daunted by Barbone's warnings, were drifting towards a position that would be identified as Seekerism.

Broadly speaking, Seekers were those who accepted that 'all Christian ordinances had been lost by the apostasy of the churches and could be restored only by those who, like John the Baptist and the Apostles, had a special commission to do so. Until such qualified administrators appeared there could be no true Christian ordinances and therefore no true churches at all.'[3] Seekerism, then, consisted of an essentially orthodox faith

---

[3]   M. Tolmie, *The Triumph of the Saints*, p. 54.

combined with a definitely agnostic ecclesiology, a protest vote against the multiplicity of competing claims. Many were 'shattered Baptists', as Fox called them, who had had second thoughts about their baptism as believers whilst remaining unreconciled to the act perpetrated against them as infants. Many others had a history of differing varieties of radicalism. Yet others were simply bewildered, knowing enough to be disillusioned with parish religion but unconvinced by the legalistic obsessions of the various sects. Groups such as the Baptists had successfully propounded their radical critiques of established religion, but they had not so easily been able to replace the old certainties with their own new ones.

To be sure, the various groups of dissenters could present an unattractive enough aspect. Their mutual anathematising, their hard-edged exclusivism, their biblicist concern for extracting the one true pattern of belief and behaviour from Scripture: all of these things were repugnant to many who, however disillusioned with the Church of England, yet suspected that Christian faith might have something more to do with actually being kind to others and improving one's character than the sects seemed prepared to allow. It was possible to conclude that anything could be proven from Scripture; those who did so lost confidence in its authority and might be prone to slide into Ranterism.

Modern Marxist historians and others have found it useful to maximize the importance of the Ranters, and a lot of ink has been spilled since the 1970s in discussing them. In reality, they were so uncoordinated and variegated as hardly to qualify as a sect or movement at all. Effectively, they were a form of irreligion, enjoying the daring utterance of a variety of blasphemous denials. In that sense, they were as dependent and parasitic on piety and orthodoxy as is modern liberal theology; without orthodoxy, there would be nothing to deny, a condition which (in the absence of any constructive programme of one's own) is apt to prove embarrassing.

The Ranters existed ('operated' is too constructive a term) in large measure at the level of tavern atheism, though there were a number of more thoughtful souls among them. The Bible might or might not be historical. It might mean anything. Who made God? Who married Cain? According to the Puritan Richard

Baxter, they 'called men to hearken to Christ within them' and taught 'a cursed doctrine of libertinism, . . . that to the pure all things are pure (even things forbidden). And so, as allowed by God, they spake most hideous words of blasphemy; and many of them committed whoredom commonly. . . .'[4]

Baxter was less given to exaggeration and the repeating of scurrilous tittle-tattle than either Thomas Edwards or Daniel Featley. Accusations of immorality were not merely the fabrica- tions of the Ranters' enemies anyway; they were admitted to by themselves. Laurence Clarkson, one of their preachers, claimed that sin 'hath its conception only in the imagination. . . . What act so ever is done by thee in light and love, is light and lovely, though it be that act called adultery'. And he emphasized his sincerity by means of personal example on the point in question.[5]

The Ranters also employed a spiritualizing understanding of Scripture and of traditional Christian doctrines, which appealed to those disenchanted by biblicism and was to find an echo in Quakerism. Joseph Salmon, a Ranter, gave an interesting twist to 1 John 4:2 ('Every spirit that acknowledges that Jesus Christ has come in the flesh is from God') by arguing that both Christ and Antichrist were in every person. Indeed, it was the latter whose work was that of 'denying Jesus Christ to be come in thy flesh'. Christ was not come simply 'in *the* flesh', but 'in *thy* flesh'; Antichrist was not to be found in Rome, but was 'in all of us'; judgement day and the end of the world were not to be under- stood as future cosmic realities, but present spiritual experiences: 'Thou art therefore to expect Jesus to come to judgement in thee, and the end of the world to be in thee'.[6] The kingdom was not to be expected in the world; it had already arrived. Such unusual exposition could prove liberating, and was usually combined with a radically egalitarian social and political critique.

Even though the biblicist sects had tended to draw on lower social strata for their support than did, say, the Presbyterians, they did nevertheless tend to be dominated by an élite who had been educated, or were at least reasonably theologically literate,

---

4   R. Baxter, *The Autobiography of Richard Baxter*, ed. N.H. Keeble, p. 73.
5   Christopher Hill, *The World Turned Upside Down*, pp. 215–6.
6   cited in *ibid.*, p. 217.

because of the clear need to provide and understand a coherent view of biblical exposition. A spiritualizing approach, however, could undercut this. Then as now, the elevation of the Spirit above the letter shortcircuited intricate arguments about the true meaning of the text, and undermined the authority of those who depended upon their knowledge of (or, at any rate, their skill in) such arguments, and gave autonomy, and possible leadership even, to the unlearned.

Because the situation of religious pluralism was so novel and confusing to many people, and because of the instability of political and social conditions during the Civil War and its aftermath, membership of the sects could be very fluid. As often as not, sects recruited from one another. In part this was due to the fissiparous tendencies within sectarian groups themselves, a quality that had been amply demonstrated by the experience of the separatists in exile in the Netherlands earlier in the century. Furthermore, it was not unreasonable to assume that someone radical enough to join one previously illegal group was at least as likely as a non-sectarian to be possessed of sufficient intellectual and spiritual curiosity (or instability, as conservative critics might have said) to leave it and join another. Consequently, the biographies of individual radicals during the 1640s and 1650s often have a patchy quality, exhibiting a leftward – and sometimes even a rightward – drift from one group to another. Samuel Fisher was a Puritan clergyman who, having become a Presbyterian by 1643, later became a General Baptist, and in 1654 eventually turned Quaker. John Lilburne followed a similar path, from anti-episcopal (and so implicitly Presbyterian) agitation as a London apprentice in the late 1630s, through convinced separatism during his imprisonment by the Laudian authorities, into a period in which (as a Leveller leader) religious concerns became less important than his political causes, finally ending his days as a Quaker. Thomas Lambe the merchant had progressed from John Goodwin's brand of radical Independency to the General Baptists before returning to the bosom of the Church of England. A number of the Fenstanton General Baptists experienced serious troubles of mind over the degree of exclusivity and dogmatism which they were being required to accept; for some, their qualms were allayed by returning to their parish churches, whilst

others were prepared for the yet more radical position adopted
by the Quakers.

The Early Years

It is fair to say, then, that a number of people were disposed to
be receptive to the Quaker message when the movement began
to emerge at the end of the 1640s. The preaching of Fox and his
fellow-leaders appeared to present an escape from the narrow
biblicism of the sects, an affirmation of the religious and spiritual
potential within each individual, and a reinforced critique of all
those features of traditional religion and society – most notably
priestcraft and hierarchy – which religious and political radicals
of all hues had found so objectionable. In Fox's own case, his
early life was both a preparation and a foil for his later radicalism, and in that, at least, he was perhaps typical of many who
became Quakers.

He was born in July 1624 at Drayton-in-the-Clay (now Fenny
Drayton) in Leicestershire. His father was a weaver, and so
belonged to that section of the population which, since the time
of the Lollards, had been most predisposed to radical religious
influences. Although Fox received no formal education, his family is unlikely to have been very poor; though his earliest travels
appear to have entailed sojourns of sufficient length for him to
have maintained himself by taking employment, his wanderings
from 1647 (immediately prior to the establishment of networks
of supportive 'Friends') had no obvious means of finance. This
last fact lends itself to the conclusion that he was possessed of at
least some funds, an interpretation supported by his own testimony of this period that 'I had wherewithal both to keep myself
from being chargeable to others, and to administer something to
the necessities of others'.

He appears to have been unable to bear the sight or sound of
what he perceived to be the sins, or hollowness of religious
profession, in others:

> Now during all this time I was never joined in profession of religion with
> any, but gave up myself to the Lord, having forsaken all evil company
> . . . and travelled up and down as a stranger in the earth. . . . For I durst

not stay long in any place, being afraid both of professor and profane, lest, being a tender young man, I should be hurt by conversing much with either.[7]

As a result, he continued to be something of a loner – appropriately enough for one whose movement was to proclaim the spiritual autonomy of the individual. In 1647, he 'heard a voice which said, "There is one, even Christ Jesus, that can speak to thy condition", and when I heard it my heart did leap for joy.' The Quaker historian W.C. Braithwaite waxed eloquent about this speech, claiming that it 'takes us back to the primitive Christian experience of union with Christ' but, when he says of Fox that 'in communion with his deepest self he made his great spiritual discovery', the implied loss of transcendence comes as a sharp reminder of the Quaker emphasis on God's immanence; God was revealed, not so much *to* a person, as *in* them.[8]

Relying on this inner light, Fox began an itinerant preaching career. Starting in the north Midlands in the late 1640s, 'the real break-though', as one historian has called it, came in 1652, when he travelled north to the Pennines and Westmorland.[9] On Whit Sunday he preached to and converted to his views a congregation of Seekers at Sedbergh. The following Sunday a crowd of over a thousand gathered from the surrounding area, to whom Fox preached for over three hours on the fell-side at nearby Firbank. Hundreds were convinced on this occasion, and hundreds more over the days following. In the English Lake District – the 'Galilee of Quakerism', as it has been called – a following was built up over the succeeding months that was then used to launch evangelistic drives across the country, including the capital.

Seventy missionaries were sent into the south in the summer of 1654, including Francis Howgill, a leader of the original Seeker congregation at Sedbergh, and the nineteen-year-old Edward Burrough. The two rented a hall in Aldersgate, London and preached to congregations of up to a thousand. Another congregation of Seekers in Bristol felt that they had become finders

---

[7]   G. Fox, *Journal*, pp. 7, 10. In seventeenth-century English context, 'professor' means a devout person, who makes a profession of religious faith.

[8]   W.C. Braithwaite, *The Beginnings of Quakerism*, p. 35.

[9]   M. Watts, *The Dissenters*, p. 195.

when John Audland and John Camm came to preach to them, and they were soon joined by the defections of about a quarter of the Broadmead church. A flurry of missionary activity carried the message to Scotland, Wales and Ireland, the Netherlands, New England, the Palatinate, Danzig, Jerusalem, Alexandria, Rome, Malta and the West Indies. Impact was slight outside the Netherlands, North America and the countries of Britain, but the zeal was immense, and several paid for it with their lives.

A caveat is perhaps in order concerning the received wisdom that Fox was simply 'the founder' of the Quaker movement. The historian Barry Reay points out that a number of itinerant preachers of similar views were roaming the north of England during this period – he mentions Richard Farnworth, Thomas Aldam, Margaret Killam, William Dewsbury and James Nayler – and all of them were building up a following. Several wielded as much influence as George Fox in the 1650s. But whereas most of the other leaders died early, Fox lived on until 1691, and his longevity ensured his influence upon the movement over a greater timescale, while his massive *Journal* and other writings ensured that posterity would view the genesis of Quakerism through his eyes. 'So', Reay concludes, 'the birth of the Quaker movement was less a gathering of eager proselytes at the feet of a charismatic prophet, than a linking of advanced Protestant separatists into a loose kind of church fellowship with a coherent ideology and a developing code of ethics'. [10] Notwithstanding this caution, however, Fox was certainly central to events, even in the earliest years of Quakerism, and his views were typical of the movement as a whole.

Quaker Spiritualism

Fox's insistence that spiritual enlightenment came as 'openings' is a case in point. He told his hearers in Pickering, in 1651, that he 'directed them to the spirit and grace of God in themselves, and to the light of Jesus in their own hearts, that they might come to know Christ, their free teacher, to bring them salvation, and to open the

---

[10] B. Reay, *The Quakers and the English Revolution*, pp. 8–9.

Scriptures to them'. That was the order: the Spirit made alive, and only then could people have 'openings' in the Scriptures. If this order was not followed, one would be as the Jews of old who used to 'try their doctrines by the Scriptures, but erred in judgement, and did not try them aright, because they tried without the Holy Ghost'. When a minister in Nottingham taught his people, in 1649, that the Scriptures were the touchstone of faith, Fox (who had insinuated himself into the audience) felt constrained to cry out, 'Oh, no, it is not the Scriptures', and informed those present that it was 'the Holy Spirit, by which the holy men of God gave forth the Scriptures, whereby opinions, religions and judgements were to be tried'. In similar vein, he taught of the apostles and prophets that 'none can understand their writings aright without the same Spirit by which they were written'.

He denied the frequently levelled charge that he had 'slight esteem of the Holy Scriptures, but they were very precious to me, for I was in that Spirit by which they were given forth, and what the Lord opened in me I afterwards found was agreeable to them'. Concerning the things God had revealed to him, he did not at first know 'where to find it in the Scriptures; though afterwards, searching the Scriptures, I found it'. [11]

'That which may be known of God', Fox declared in *Gospel-Truth* in 1658, 'is manifest within people; thou needest no man to teach thee'. The elevation of the spirit above the letter, and the importance of personal revelation in the heart of the believer, were ideas that had been taught in England before the advent of the Quakers but never, perhaps, in such a compelling fashion or in such favourable circumstances. Roger Brerely, the curate of Grindleton in Yorkshire, had been accused of similar teachings during the reigns of James I and Charles I. The works of Jakob Boehme (1575–1624), the Lutheran mystic, had been translated and printed in London during the 1640s, though these had met an existing demand, rather than simply creating one. The Family of Love, who had continued to eke out a subterranean, albeit diminishing, existence in England from the end of the previous century, also set aside literalist understandings of Scripture in favour of spiritualizing interpretations.

---

[11]   G. Fox, *Journal*, pp. 34, 40.

The Familists were in decline, however, and had too much
vested in the reputation and esoteric writings of a now-dead
messiah, whilst the Grindletonians operated within the established church and were geographically limited in their appeal.
Boehme (like Niclaes) was dead, and his writings alone could
hardly have formed the basis for a new sectarian movement.
George Fox, for all his eccentricity and glaring absence of a sense
of humour (or even of proportion), seems to have been possessed
of a magnetic quality. If he took himself a little too seriously, he
was able to inspire those he met to do likewise, even if they were
unconvinced by his message.

That message insisted that Christian doctrines be understood
somewhat metaphorically, and concerned the inward spiritual
experiences of the believer as their primary point of reference. As
Niclaes had said in the previous century, 'True light . . . consists
not in knowing this or that, but in receiving and partaking of the
true being of the Eternal Life, by the renewing of the mind and
spirit and by an incorporation of the inward man into this true
Life and Light.'[12] Fox spoke approvingly of those who 'came,
with the light and spirit of Truth, to see into themselves, then they
came to say, "I, I, I, it is I myself that have been the Ishmael, and
the Esau" '. The Quaker who answered the question of Matthew
Caffyn, a Baptist leader, concerning the location of the heaven
into which Christ had ascended, clapped his hands upon his
breast and cried 'within me, within me'. What mattered was 'not
the history, but the mystery'. It was the same mode of thought
that prompted John Moone to tell another Baptist, John Tombes, that the True Cross was not a piece of wood outside Jerusalem but the power of God by which Paul was crucified to the
world.[13] Isaac Penington, a later Quaker leader, challenged his
readers to distinguish 'between that which is called Christ, and
the bodily garment which he wore. The one was flesh, the other
Spirit. The flesh profiteth nothing. . . . The body of flesh was but
the veil'.[14]

---

[12] cited in W.C. Braithwaite, *The Beginnings of Quakerism*, p. 23.
[13] H. Barbour, *The Quakers in Puritan England*, p. 146.
[14] I. Penington, *The Works of the Long Mournful and Sorely Distressed Isaac
Penington*, 2nd edn, i., p. 360.

Spiritualism and Docetism of this kind may have been useful lines of attack upon the more formal, rigid orthodoxies of the Presbyterians or even of the sects, but Fox himself had to reverse tactics when confronted by Ranters. In 1651 he came across a soldier in Nottingham, one Rice Jones, who had been a Baptist but had since fallen into Rantism. When Jones told him that 'Thy faith stands in a man that died at Jerusalem, and there never was any such thing', Fox responded by stressing that the historical Christ had indeed been 'persecuted and suffered there outwardly'. Two years previously, he had encountered a group of Jones' sort in Coventry prison who had justified their immoralities by reference to Peter's vision of the sheet declaring all things clean. On that occasion he had 'showed them that that Scripture made nothing for their purpose' – presumably by the orthodox method of comparing one scripture with another to obtain a sound exegesis.[15] Despite their disclaimers, what the Spirit revealed to Quakers had to remain a close approximation of what the Scriptures revealed to 'professors', albeit the latter, of course, did not 'possess what they professed'.

Though their less scurrilous critics did not accuse Quakers of Ranter immoralities, even the usually charitable Richard Baxter could see no essential difference in their principles: 'The Quakers were but the Ranters turned from horrid profaneness and blasphemy to a life of extreme austerity on the other side. Their doctrines were mostly the same with the Ranters.'[16] Justice Hotham of Lockington, in Yorkshire, disagreed, though he was a supporter of Fox and opined that 'if God had not raised up this principle of light and life, the nation had been overspread with Ranterism'.[17] W.C. Braithwaite unsurprisingly took the same view, claiming that the Quaker message became 'an antidote to Ranterism', reclaiming many Ranters for true godliness, as well as holding back many more from falling into the same errors. This, he maintained, was because of the Quaker insistence that

---

[15] G. Fox, *Journal*, pp. 47, 63.

[16] R. Baxter, *Autobiography*, pp. 73–4. Baxter also gave credence to the absurd conspiracy theories which insisted that the whole movement was just another Catholic plot, and that some Quaker preachers were really monks in disguise, intent upon creating trouble in Protestant England.

[17] G. Fox, *Journal*, p. 90.

'there could be no guidance of the Spirit apart from a walking in the light'.[18] Nevertheless, the distinction was not always so clear to other contemporaries as it was to Justice Hotham. When the Derby magistrates in 1650 asked Fox whether he had no sin, it was clearly Ranterism that they were smelling after. When Fox's answer seemed to confirm their fears, they asked if he were Christ and also 'if a man steal is it no sin?' Despite his more reassuring information concerning these last two points, they committed him for six months as a blasphemer and as a man who claimed to be without sin.[19]

Fox consistently mocked the more orthodox on the subject of perfection and accused them of 'pleading for sin'. For 'of all the sects in Christendom (so-called) . . . I found none that could bear to be told that any should come to Adam's perfection . . . to be so clear and pure without sin, as he was', he wrote. Lest any 'professors' should consider the issue not quite so clear-cut, biblically, as he maintained, Fox added, more embarrassingly, 'therefore how should they be able to bear being told that any should grow up to the measure of the stature of Christ . . .?' Again, he linked his teaching to the idea that the Spirit who inspired Scripture is necessary to understand Scripture aright. He made no bones about his own claim to have 'come up to the state of Adam which he was in before he fell'.[20]

This teaching, together with the generally internalizing tendency of Quaker ideas, was a protest against the habit of Puritans and the more orthodox sectarians whereby doctrinal and procedural correctness was emphasized more than pureness of heart. Hugh Barbour, the recent historian of Quakerism, points out that, for Quakers, God's grace was understood primarily as 'moral power', rather than in the traditional Protestant sense of 'forgiveness'. When Samuel Fisher, the General Baptist who turned Quaker in 1655, wrote that 'if we be not renewed by the Spirit, and saved from sin, then . . . grace is no more use . . . to us', his usage is perhaps patient of both definitions.[21] Pelagian

---

[18]   W.C. Braithwaite, *The Beginnings of Quakerism*, p. 22.

[19]   G. Fox, *Journal*, pp. 51–2.

[20]   *Ibid.*, pp. 18, 27, 32–3.

[21]   H. Barbour, *The Quakers in Puritan England*, pp. 145, 162.

though such soteriology must have seemed to those who had been reared upon Calvinist orthodoxy, to the Quakers themselves it seemed an actual release from legalism.

Quaker Egalitarianism

This release from the necessity of conforming to procedural niceties took the form of iconoclastic attitudes toward church buildings ('steeplehouses'), Sundays ('first days'), the wearing of hats in religious meetings, and university education as a qualifi‐ cation for ministry (though the rejection of this was already a sectarian commonplace). Meetings could be silent or ecstatic ('Quakers' was originally a mocking nickname for these people who trembled under the Spirit's power), but never formal or ceremonial. In their own eyes they were not 'Quakers' but 'Friends'; the possession of the Spirit by each was a sign, not of crankiness, but of fellowship based on equality.

This egalitarian propensity also spilled over into the social arena, with Quakers refusing to doff their hats to their social superiors, and addressing all as 'thou' and 'thee' without differ‐ entiation. This caused great anger and offence to non-Quakers, and could threaten to make regiments with Quaker soldiers (for they were not pacifists until after the Restoration) ungovernable by their officers. Fox quoted Christ's words: 'How can ye believe, who receive honour of one another, and seek not the honour that cometh from God only?', but added 'Oh, the blows, punchings, beatings and imprisonments that we underwent for not putting off our hats to men!' Thomas Ellwood, Quaker of a gentry family, was told by his father, 'Sirrah, if ever I hear you say Thou or Thee to me again, I'll strike your teeth down your throat.' And when Ellwood junior kept his hat on in his father's presence, Ellwood senior struck his son with 'both his fists'. [22]

Quaker egalitarianism also rejected Calvinist predestination. 'God would all men to be saved, mark, all men', Fox told his Irish listeners in 1669, and wrote of the period immediately after

---

[22]   B. Reay, *The Quakers and the English Revolution*, p. 58; G. Fox, *Journal*, pp. 206, 406.

his conversion: 'For I saw that Christ had died for all men . . . and had enlightened all men and women with his divine and saving light.' According to him, election stood in the second birth and reprobation in the first; God does not predestine which individuals come into either category. James Nayler, another Quaker leader, put the point more platonically when he insisted that reprobation referred to the seed of the flesh and election to the seed of the spirit. Fox blamed the 'priests' for having frightened people with their Calvinist doctrines and their insistence that 'the greatest part of men and women God had ordained . . . for hell, let them pray or preach or do what they could'.[23] Samuel Fisher expressed the Quaker position when he explained that 'we talk of an universal redemption by Christ's coming intentionally to save all men, though (through their own default) all are not, but few only actually saved', but then he had already practised such arguments during his time with the General Baptists.[24] The Quaker notion that the Spirit indwelt everyone was, indeed, a radical extension of General Baptist and other free-will theologies.

The Confrontation with Authority

Official attitudes toward the Quakers varied. There were a number of them in the army, an embarrassing point consistently over-looked by those who wish to read post-Restoration Quaker pacifism back into the period of Quaker origins during the English republic. The refusal of hat-honour by soldiers, and the addressing of officers as 'thee' and 'thou', was hardly conducive to military discipline. But a number of the officers were themselves infected with the new spiritual contagion. When General George Monck (the man eventually responsible for restoring Charles Stuart to his throne as Charles II) came to purge his army in Scotland of Quakers, he found that most regiments were affected, though their numbers ran into dozens rather than hundreds. Cromwell's instincts were torn between a personal desire for toleration on the

---

[23] G. Fox, *Journal*, pp. 316, 550.
[24] cited in B. Reay, *The Quakers and the English Revolution*, p. 33.

one hand, and the political need to pacify conservatives in Parliament and the counties on the other. The level of practical toleration
varied from area to area, depending upon the sympathies of the
local justices and magistrates. Colonel Adrian Scrope, who was in
charge of the army garrison in Bristol in the 1650s, said that 'if the
Magistrates did put them [the Quakers] in prison one day, he
would put them out the next'.[25] Even so, both popular and official
fear of Quakers and 'anabaptists' remained strong.

Many Quakers did not help themselves in this respect. Several
went naked 'for a sign', one music teacher of London doing so
with a pan of hot coals on his head; John Gilpin crawled up a
street in Kendal 'thinking that I bore a cross upon my neck'; John
Toldervy was moved by the spirit to put his hands in a pan of
boiling water, to burn his leg by the fire, and to put a needle in
his thumbs to the bone. But when James Nayler entered Bristol
in October 1656 (he had prophesied the millennium for that
year), riding a donkey, with women followers placing their garments before him on the ground and crying 'holy, holy, holy,
Lord God of Israel', Parliament's patience snapped. His life was
spared only by a 96 to 82 vote, and he was branded, bored
through the tongue, whipped, pilloried and imprisoned. At the
pillory his followers put up a placard informing bystanders that
'This is the King of the Jews', whilst Robert Rich stroked and
kissed him, and licked the brand on his forehead.

Nayler sent out papers from prison confessing his folly, and
renouncing 'all those false worships with which any have idolized
my person in the night of my temptation'.[26] But the damage had
been done. Conservative pamphlets, both in Bristol and nation-
ally, derided 'the Quakers' Jesus' and insisted that the aberration
was, in fact, typical. Parliament clamoured for stiffer legislation
against the sects.

Quaker denunciation of tithes – quite apart from their other
eccentricities – had already marked them out as subversives in

[25] B. Reay, 'Quakerism and Society', in J.F. McGregor and B. Reay eds., *Radical
Religion*, p. 156.
[26] P. Mack, *Visionary Women: Ecstatic Prophecy in Seventeenth-Century England*,
pp. 198–9; H.L. Ingle, *First Among Friends: George Fox and the Creation of Quakerism*,
pp. 147–9; B. Reay, *Quakers and the English Revolution*, pp. 54–5.

any case. Other sectaries, of course, also called for the abolition of tithes, but after the demise of the Levellers, the Quakers' voice was the shrillest on this subject, and a number of their imprisonments were due to refusal to pay.

The Marxist historian Christopher Hill has argued that the mid-seventeenth-century attack on tithes was not simply a religious protest, the refusal of those who had left the Church of England to support its ministry.[27] Tithes were a form of real estate, and the rights to revenue from particular parishes could be inherited or sold. In practice, the recipients were often gentry, who might collect the money and pay a pittance to a vicar (the long-term acceptance of 'vicar' as the popular generic term for a parish clergyman indicates the frequency of the practice). Since tithes formed part of real estate, so the argument goes, the attack on them was actually an attack on the property system. There is certainly something to be said for this way of thinking. The Quakers formed a spiritual home for many people of politically radical temperament after the failure of the Levellers; Lilburne and Winstanley both joined the movement, and Nayler was accused of having been at Burford.

The Quakers were radicals socially, politically and theologically. For this, they suffered even during the relatively tolerant years of the Interregnum. It was, in no small part, the fear of 'fanaticks' such as themselves that brought about the Restoration of the monarchy in 1660. And it was they who were to bear the brunt of persecution in the very different world that followed.

----

[27] C. Hill, *The Century of Revolution*, pp. 163–5.

Chapter Fifteen

A New Earth: America

A City upon a Hill

Of all the problems which faced the various radicals, one element ran through them like an endless thread: the denial of space and opportunity. The Reformed utopia which, in its different hypothesized variations, was yearned for by separatists and semi-separatists, and even by their non-separating brethren of Presbyterian and Independent persuasion, could not be enacted in England – at least not before the 1640s – because the authorities in church and state simply refused to countenance change. The Baptists and Quakers, like the continental Anabaptists, had no such ambition to build a godly commonwealth, but they also found it hard to live a normal life in line with their convictions, because government harassed them at every turn.

It takes no great effort of the imagination, therefore, to understand why some radicals, of all types, were attracted by the possibility of a New World – not on the other side of the Second Coming, but on the other side of the Atlantic Ocean. It was, to be sure, a wide Jordan that must be crossed, but once over yonder there would be space enough to be one's own magistrate, and thus to erect the city of God on that distant hill, or to gather the saints in the wilderness without disturbance.

It was not as if North America were devoid of Europeans before the religious malcontents of the Old World took it into their heads to go there. Well before the Pilgrim Fathers' famous crossing in 1620, the Spanish held Florida (by dint of their permanent settlement in 1565 of San Augustín), even as they strengthened their grip on Central and South America. The French had founded Quebec in 1608, while the Dutch had taken an interest in the area around the mouth of the Hudson River from 1609, founding New Amsterdam in the 1620s (known later, after the British captured it in 1664, as New York). English settlers too were scattered along the eastern seaboard of what would later become the United States, with the first permanent settlement in Virginia from May 1607.

Such religion as prevailed within these colonies, however, was of the official, state-backed varieties approved of by the governments of the respective mother countries. Although scattered patterns of settlement (along with the relative inability of Catholics and Anglicans to organize and adapt their structures to growing and moving populations) later made some of these areas amenable to religious radicalism, they were at first hostile or indifferent to it.[1] The first foray of English religious radicals into the New World proved to be a disaster, in any case. After Francis Johnson's death in exile in the Netherlands in 1618, most of his congregation sailed from Gravesend for Virginia. But only 50 of the 180 who set out survived the crossing.

A group from John Robinson's congregation – the famous Pilgrim Fathers – who made the attempt in 1620, were more fortunate. Making a living in the Netherlands had never been easy for the English immigrants, but their prolonged sojourn in exile was raising new problems for many of them, in particular the future of the second generation. Of all their sorrows, that which was

> most heavy to be borne, was that many of their children, by these occasions [the harsh poverty] and the great licentiousness of youth in that country, and the manifold temptations of the place, were drawn away by evil examples into extravagant and dangerous courses, getting the reins off their necks and departing from their parents. . . . So that

---

[1] In Virginia as late as 1662, there were only ten ministers to meet the needs of more than 45 Church of England parishes, many of which were huge by English standards. No bishop for the English colonies was ever appointed. The first Catholic bishop in North America was François-Xavier de Montmorency Laval, Bishop of Quebec from 1658. There was no Catholic bishop in the colonies that would later become the United Sates until the appointment of John Carroll as Bishop of Baltimore in 1790!

they saw that their posterity would be in danger to degenerate and be corrupted.[2]

The 'licentiousness of youth' and the 'manifold temptations' were the inevitable 'downside' of the toleration which permitted deviant English migrants to exist in the Netherlands without molestation. Since the government in England would not even tolerate the separatists, far less adopt their version of a godly commonwealth, and Dutch exile was merely serving to corrode their community, the only practical way to preserve their integrity seemed, to some of them at least, to be to ring-fence themselves in a distant wilderness. To describe the motivation of the Pilgrim Fathers in such terms is not to belittle them; it is necessary for an understanding of much of their subsequent history, as well as for understanding the attitudes of many of the non-separatist Puritans who joined them in New England during the 1630s.

Robinson himself never went to the New World. He continued to guide his flock by writing, however, from his base with the larger part of the church remaining in Leiden, down to his death in 1625. His sermon to the departing 'pilgrims' is memorable, among other things, for his stress on the notion of continuing revelation:

> I am verily persuaded the Lord has more truth yet to break forth out of His holy Word. . . . The Lutherans cannot be drawn to go beyond what Luther saw . . . and the Calvinists, you see, stick fast where they were left by that great man of God who yet saw not all things. This is a misery much to be lamented, . . . were they now living [they] would be as willing to embrace further light as that which they first received. I beseech you remember, it is an article of your Church covenant that you be ready to receive whatever truth shall be made known to you from the written Word of God.

The church and the world were to be made anew as God continued to reveal himself.

Armed with this confidence, the group of 102 separatists, and a crew of 25, set sail in the Mayflower for Virginia. Imperfect navigation brought them to Cape Cod instead, but they decided

---

[2] W. Bradford, *Of Plymouth Plantation* in C.L. van Steeg and R. Hofstadter eds., *Great Issues in American History*, i., p. 34.

to land anyway. The party had departed from Leiden in July, and then on from Plymouth in September, and the consequence was that they landed in the New World just in time to face the onset of winter. Cool reflection might have prompted them to make their journey in the spring, leaving at least some time for gathering what food they could before the weather closed in. As it was, they were fortunate to be given some provisions by the local Wampanoag tribe. Even so, half of the settlers died during the harsh New England winter that followed.

Undaunted, the company established farms and a permanent settlement, as well as an organized church life and a constitution. The leadership consisted of William Brewster (1567–1644), an elder of the church; Captain Miles Standish (1584–1656), the group's military commander; and William Bradford (1590–1657), governor of the new Plymouth colony from 1621. It is Bradford, a Yorkshireman who had joined the separatists as a teenager and gone with them to Leiden, where he worked in the cloth trade, who has left us the most vivid account of those early years in his book *Of Plymouth Plantation*. Once a base of homesteads was established, others could join them with somewhat less difficulty, and by 1630 the colony had grown to three hundred souls.

In that year, a huge addition was made to colonial strength in the area with the arrival of a thousand Puritans of congregational, or Independent, opinions who were fleeing the high-church régime of Charles I and William Laud. During the course of the next ten years they were joined by perhaps twenty thousand others, putting the colonist population of New England on a comparable level with that of the natives. By the mid-century, settlements in New England contained four colonies of similar churchmanship: Plymouth (planted by the Mayflower pilgrims from 1620), Massachusetts (settled by English Puritans from 1629), Connecticut (founded in 1636 by settlers who had moved on from several towns in Massachusetts) and New Haven (founded similarly in 1638).

Although the non-separatist newcomers might belong more properly to the history of Puritanism (and so arguably not to our narrative here), two factors go a long way to justify their inclusion in an account of restoration-ism, rather than of reformation-ism. In the first place, though the new arrivals from 1630 might claim to be non-separatists, they had in fact taken greater pains to remove themselves from the jurisdiction of the Church of England than Henry Barrow or John Greenwood had ever done. They had left England because they could not, in conscience, continue to live within its church. In the second place, once they were in the New World they took steps to organize their churches along lines which none of the territorial churches of the Old World would have countenanced: they made conversion a test for church membership. Again, this was a step further than the English separatists would have allowed.

Logically, linking conversion with church membership would have made the early settlers into Anabaptists (or perhaps Baptists), and have introduced toleration into the new colonies. However, since only (male) church members could vote or hold political office, the effect of the policy was almost the opposite of Anabaptism: it meant that a theocracy (of a kind) was in the process of being established.

The Puritans had argued their corner for a truly godly church polity for three generations but, because of the opposition of the ecclesiastical authorities, had never been able to do more than theorise. Here was the opportunity for action – for the setting up of a truly godly commonwealth in virgin country. As the first congregational churches were established in Massachusetts, ex-isting members 'screened' all subsequent applicants for member-ship, to satisfy themselves of the person's convertedness or otherwise. Those who gave a credible 'testimony' were admitted. In this way, about half of the men, and rather more of the women, became church members in Massachusetts during the 1630s and 1640s, although even those who did not were expected to attend upon the preaching of the word. One recent historian, though unable to hide his own distaste for the process, highlights some of its effects well:

> For ten years the human flood swept into Massachusetts, . . . some twenty thousand souls, and every soul was checked off as saved or damned. . . . As [the saints] gathered together in their pure churches, placing the mark of holiness on their own foreheads and of damnation on most of their neighbours, the experience could not fail to induce that intellectual arrogance which is the breeder of separatism. Though in

England they had denounced the evils of separation, the very act of
forming a congregational church necessitated an assumption of superior
purity and thereby encouraged a separatist frame of mind. [3]

The charge that is very frequently made against the separatists of
Plymouth Plantation and the Puritan congregationalists of Massachusetts Bay and elsewhere in New England is that of hypocrisy;
these were people who had fled persecution in their homeland and
gone to the New World for the cause of conscience, yet who now
denied freedom of conscience to dissenters within their own ranks
and to others who came after. Truly, the confusion is all ours. The
point bears repeating that the New Englanders had all aspired to
have a national church in England organized along lines of which
they themselves approved. None of them had advocated any
religious freedom in either the Old World or the New, save the
freedom to enforce their own preferred brand of ecclesiastical
polity upon others. John Winthrop (1588–1649), the governor of
Massachusetts, gave perhaps the most famous expression to the
Puritans' sense of American destiny:

> We shall be as a city upon a hill, the eyes of all people are upon us, so
> that if we shall deal falsely with our God in this work we have undertaken, and so cause him to withdraw his present help from us, we shall
> be made a story and a byword through the world . . . till we be consumed
> out of the good land whither we are going. [4]

The last phrase's evocation of the Israelites' journey to the
Promised Land was hardly accidental; the settlers believed themselves to be the recipients of a sacred trust to build a Zion in the
New World, untainted by the corruption and bondage of the Old.
As one recent historian has explained,

> Other peoples had their land by providence; *they* had it by promise.
> Others must seek their national origins in secular records and chronicles;
> the story of America was enclosed in the Scriptures, its past postdated
> and its future antedated in prophecy. [5]

Such an attitude should not be entirely beyond the sympathy of
moderns who take pluralism for granted. The settlers had left

---

[3] E.S. Morgan, *The Puritan Dilemma: the Story of John Winthrop*, pp. 79–80.
[4] cited in *ibid.*, p. 70.
[5] S. Bercovitch ed., *The American Puritan Imagination*, p. 9.

their homeland precisely because the enactment of their religious vision had been thwarted by authority. They had not travelled three thousand miles into the wilderness to have it subverted from below, as it were, by dissent. They sought room, not for religious liberty, but for their own holy experiment. 'All Familists, Anti-nomians, Anabaptists and other Enthusiasts', declared Nathaniel Ward in 1647, 'shall have free liberty to keep away from us, and such as will come to be gone as fast as they can, the sooner the better'.[6]

As one historian has pointed out, the very fact of such un-limited space made intolerance more of a practical proposition – at least in the short-to-medium term – than it was in Europe:

> A dissension which in England would have created a new sect . . ., simply produced another colony in New England. . . . In New England the critics, doubters, and dissenters were expelled from the community; in England, the Puritans had to find ways of living with them. It was in England, therefore, that a modern theory of toleration began to develop.[7]

Such a way of expressing the matter has, of course, the supreme merit of turning conventional wisdom about America as the home of religious toleration on its head. But it does also contain more than a grain of truth.

The Civil War in England precipitated such widespread religious pluralism in practice that at least some Puritans (mostly among the Independents) felt constrained to confront the problem with more than simply new suggestions for meth-ods of persecution. In the person of Cromwell, the English republic had a leader committed to the cause of religious toleration, at least within limits. And after 1689, even the restored royalist-Anglican régime called a moratorium, in its own interests, on imprisoning Protestant dissenters. There was nowhere to expel such people to, and there were too many of them for a general cull or incarceration to be practical politics. Slowly, grudgingly and grumpily, religious dissidents had to be granted the right to exist.

---

[6] N. Ward, *The Simple Cobler of Aggawam* (1647) in C.L. van Steeg and R. Hofstadter eds., *Great Issues in American History*, i., p. 206.
[7] D.J. Boorstin, *The Americans*, i., p. 20.

But religious toleration played no part in the Puritan vision, and in America there seemed to be no need for it either, at least in the early years. Freedom of conscience meant freedom only for those consciences in accordance with the truth. John Cotton (1584–1652), one of the greatest of New England's preachers, made this abundantly clear:

> The Word of God in such things is so clear, that he cannot but be convinced in conscience of the dangerous error of his way, after once or twice admonition, wisely and faithfully dispensed. And then if any one persist, it is not out of conscience, but against his conscience. . . . So that if such a man . . . shall still persist in the error of his way, and be therefore punished, he is not persecuted for cause of conscience, but for sinning against his own conscience. [8]

Such a situation demanded that the body of ministers be, quite literally, the conscience of the community, for it was they who decided what was, and was not, acceptable in doctrine. Their distaste for presbyterianism meant that the synods of ministers could not make binding decisions, but this did not prevent them from holding any synods at all, nor from making any decisions at all. As one historian has observed, 'most pious men and women' – and no *im*pious held any political authority – 'would hesitate to back their own views above the collective wisdom of the clergy'. [9]

Such collective wisdom was not always unanimous, however, and on those occasions when there was no unanimity, possibilities for conflict were engendered. In 1631, barely a year after the arrival of the Massachusetts congregationalists, the minister of Watertown, one of the new settlements, began to teach that, not only was the Church of England a true church, but that of Rome was also. It is possible that acquaintance with Baptists back in England had led George Philips, the pastor in question, to realize where any argument which consistently denied the churchhood of Rome would lead. If so, the large majority of his fellow settlers were less clear-sighted, and he was reproved. One of his elders, Richard Brown, refused to retract the opinion even in the face of opposition from the other ministers but, in keeping with the spirit

---

[8] cited in *ibid.*, p. 21.
[9] E.S. Morgan, *The Puritan Dilemma*, p. 82.

of congregational independency, he was not removed from his position for his deviation.

Where the judgement of the clergy and political authorities were defied, however, America afforded ample opportunity for other solutions. There was space to give full play to the geographical possibilities latent in the injunction to 'cast out the bondwoman and her son' (Gal. 4:30), and this is exactly what the Massachusetts authorities did in 1638 in the case of Anne Hutchinson and her children. In England, Hutchinson (1591–1643) had considered becoming a separatist – a temptation to many of those who ultimately arrived on the shores of New England – but in 1634 she went instead to Massachusetts. Her pastor, John Cotton, had been the Puritan minister of Boston, Lincolnshire, but in 1633 he had left episcopal harassment behind him to take up the position in his town's namesake in the New World. Seldom has any preacher created so much devotion (dependency, some might say) in his hearers as did Cotton; one later opponent sneered that his devotees 'could hardly believe that God would suffer Mr. Cotton to err'. Hutchinson felt she could not live without his sermons, and persuaded her husband to uproot the family and remove to Massachusetts, the better to hear the oracles of God from his mouth.

What most appealed to Hutchinson about Cotton's preaching was his development of Calvinist doctrines of 'free grace'. Calvinism had traditionally taught that a person can do nothing – not even believe – to save themselves. Even the believing was 'wrought' by God; it was evidence that one was among the elect, not the cause of being among them. Such thinking had led to embarrassing questions about whether, if all was predetermined, there was any point in doing anything, and so later Puritans had sought to meet such criticisms by laying stress on the need for 'preparation' to receive grace. Indeed, Cotton had at one time laid just such emphasis himself.[10] But if God did not 'suffer Mr. Cotton to err', then God himself must have changed his own mind, because from 1632 Cotton moved to the view that no

---

[10] R.T. Kendall, *Calvin and English Calvinism to 1649*, pp. 110–17. Kendall points out that, paradoxically, this defence of Calvinism takes one back close to a position of justification by works. Such argumentation has aroused the fury of some modern protagonists of the Puritans; see P. Helm, *Calvin and the Calvinists*.

works could prepare a person to receive Christ. His new position contained antinomian possibilities, and Anne Hutchinson did not hesitate to embrace them with fervour. Sanctification, she taught the group meeting in her house to discuss her mentor's sermons, was not evidence that a person was justified before God.

Such notions threatened to undermine good order in the new colony. Moral behaviour and group cohesion were at a premium if the settlers were to survive in the hostile environment. Neither did Hutchinson's new disclosure, that she was the frequent recipient of divine revelations, serve to reassure the religious and secular authorities. (Indeed, she claimed that it was the Holy Ghost who revealed to the elect who the other saints were, since their sanctification – or absence of it – was no guide to anything.) A sizable faction in the Boston church supported the prophetess and, for a while at least, Cotton and another teacher of the church, Hutchinson's brother-in-law John Wheelwright, gave their tacit approval. So did Henry Vane (1613–62), son of one of Charles I's Privy Councillors, and already governor of the colony in 1636, though he had arrived only the previous year. After much politicking, however, John Winthrop and his supporters succeeded in reducing Hutchinson's support to a rump, and brought her to trial in November 1637.

Here she did not flinch from defending herself by claiming the imprimatur of the Holy Ghost. When speaking of her struggles to understand difficult portions of Scripture she claimed, in language which would be echoed by Quakers in the years ahead, that the Lord 'must by his prophetical office open it unto me'. Furthermore, 'the Lord was pleased to bring this Scripture out of the Hebrews . . . and in this did open unto me and give me to see that those which did not teach the new covenant had the spirit of antichrist'.[11] When the officer of the court asked her how she

---

[11] E.S. Gaustad ed., *A Documentary History of Religion in America to the Civil War*, p. 133. The historian H.S. Stout ('Word and Order in Colonial New England' in N.O. Hatch and M.A. Noll eds., *The Bible in America*, p. 31) has added an interesting sidelight on the debate. 'The two sides of the controversy drew their inspiration and proofs from different translations of Scripture. The Hutchinsonian party spoke from the Geneva Bible [which had found favour among Puritans from the 1560s], while the leaders accused them from the Authorized [which, since 1611, had slowly been replacing it].'

knew that it was the Spirit of God speaking to her, she replied
with a question of her own:

> *Hutchinson:* How did Abraham know that it was god that bid him offer
> his son, being a breach of the sixth commandment?
> *Officer:* By an immediate voice.
> *Hutchinson:* So to me by an immediate revelation.
> *Officer:* How! an immediate revelation.
> *Hutchinson:* By the voice of his own spirit to my soul. [12]

In the opinion of most historians, the trial was a farce, partly
because the judges had already decided the verdict, and partly
because Hutchinson was the intellectual superior of most –
perhaps all – of her accusers, constantly worsting them in oral
debate. The fact that Hutchinson was a woman made matters
worse in the eyes of her accusers: indeed, it might be suspected
that it was this aspect of the question which constituted her
principal offence. As the minister Hugh Peter declared at her
trial, 'you have stepped out of your place, you have [acted]
rather like a husband than a wife and a preacher than a hearer;
and a magistrate than a subject'. [13] Once again, the socially
subversive aspects of religious radicalism – and the socially
conservative aspects of established religion – stood revealed.
Worse still, both Hutchinson and her friend and supporter,
Mary Dyer, had given birth, within a few months of each other,
to stillborn and badly deformed babies, a fact which was
uncharitably taken as evidence of the judgement of God upon
them. (The Puritans believed strongly in 'providential' judgements of this sort.)

None of the accusers' shortcomings could change the outcome
of the trial, however. Hutchinson and her followers were banished, removing themselves to Rhode Island, and later to New
York colony, where they were soon killed by the Indians. The
Puritan 'city on the hill' remained intact and, for the moment,
uncontaminated by the leaven of heterodoxy.

---

[12] *ibid.*, pp. 133–4.
[13] cited in A. Delbanco, *The Puritan Ordeal*, p. 151.

A Refuge in the Wilderness

But not all of the radicals who came to the New World were seeking a scenario for their particular brand of New Zion, or godly commonwealth. Not all wished to found a state espousing the kind of established religion which they had failed to persuade the government authorities of the Old World to enforce. There were a number who sought something more prosaic: a respite from persecution.

Roger Williams (1603?–83) was perhaps one of the most prominent of the settlers who represented this viewpoint, reject - ing John Cotton's insistence that 'separating from Babylon' was to be understood in a geographical sense. As Williams pointed out, if the analogy was to stand, there must be a localized Judæa also, and since Cotton had removed from England to New England on religious grounds, then he must consider the former to be Babel and the latter a new Israel. But 'the Lord Jesus', he concluded, '(John 4) clearly breaks down all difference of places, and Acts 10 all differences of persons'.[14] New England could not be seen as New Zion.

Williams was undoubtedly the most persistent and articulate advocate of the separation of church and state in early New England. He had not always been so enamoured of this ideal. His early career in England had been spent, in part, as a Puritan chaplain to a gentry family in Essex, before emigrating to Boston with his wife in 1631. By that time, however, he was already an explicit separatist. This was not compatible with the position of the Boston church, which represented a body of opinion anxious to remain on good terms with the government in London. Wil - liams therefore declined to serve as its minister and joined instead with the separatists at Plymouth plantation. Later, he left these also and served as a teacher in the church at Salem from 1633–35. However, he got into trouble several times during these years because of his increasing rejection of the Christendom model.

This rejection led him to question, among other things, the right of the settlers, under their royal charter, to take the natives'

---

[14]   Roger Williams, 'American Exceptionalism Rejected', cited in R. Reinitz ed., *Tensions in American Puritanism*, pp. 157–8.

lands from them simply because the latter were not Christians; religion conferred no special property rights. Similarly, he doubted the right of the courts to punish transgressions of the first table of the ten commandments; their duty lay in punishing civil wrongs, not religious ones. In January 1636, the Massachu-setts authorities expressed their disagreement with this last sen-timent by attempting to seize Williams personally for purposes of punishment, but he caught wind of the intention and fled, enduring, as he later said, 'a winter's miseries in a howling wilderness of frost and snow'.

Thus was he propelled into founding Providence Plantation, just outside Massachusetts jurisdiction, which was later to form the basis of the colony of Rhode Island. Williams and those who joined him in this new enterprise determined from the beginning upon abandoning the Christendom model. Their later charter, dating from 1663, stated that no resident was to be disturbed for 'differences in opinion in matters of religion' unless they 'actually disturb the civil peace of said colony'.[15] For a while, at least, Williams and his friends remained in the position of separatists, albeit of a very radical type, but in March 1639 Governor Winthrop confided scathingly to his journal that

> At Providence things grew still worse; for a sister of Mrs. Hutchinson, the wife of one Scott, being infected with Anabaptistry, and going last year to live at Providence, Mr. Williams was taken (or rather embold-ened) by her to make open profession thereof, and accordingly was rebaptised by one Holyman, a poor man late of Salem. Then Mr. Williams rebaptised him and some ten more. They also denied the baptising of infants, and would have no magistrates.[16]

The last point was a mere rhetorical flourish, the familiar charge against 'rebaptizers' that they would bring social anarchy in their wake; the civic government of Providence continued to function as before.

Williams' convictions could by now fairly be described as Baptist. Although this puts him at the fountainhead of a long and immensely influential religious tradition in America, his allegiance on this point was transitory at best. By the late summer

---

[15] cited in H.L. McBeth, *The Baptist Heritage*, p. 130.
[16] cited in *ibid.*, p. 131.

he had concluded that his second baptism had been a mistake – not because his infant baptism was valid after all, but because true apostolic succession for baptism of any kind had long since been broken. Thus did he arrive at the position, effectively, of a Seeker. Whereas before he had refused religious communion with almost everyone on the grounds of his hyper-separatism, now he 'would preach to and pray with all comers'. What he would not do was to join with any existing church; a true church could only be founded by 'a spiritual restoration' of the church of the apostles.[17] When this happened, he believed, God would 'pour forth those fiery streams again of tongues and prophecy in the restoration of Zion'.[18] This, in essence, was the position he held to his death in 1683.

Whatever one's opinions about the vagaries of Williams' personal spiritual pilgrimage, almost everyone today owes him good language for his achievements. In the first place, his stand on the issue of religious toleration forced the subject upon public attention. His (temporary) return to England in 1644 to obtain a charter for his new colony saw the publication of his famous book *The Bloudy Tenent of Persecution*. This urged that

> a permission of the most paganish, Jewish, Turkish, or Antichristian consciences and worships be granted to all men in all nations and countries . . . . The state of the land of Israel (the kings and people thereof, in peace and war) is proved figurative and ceremonial, and no pattern nor precedent for any kingdom or civil state in the world to follow. . . . Enforced uniformity, sooner or later, is the greatest occasion of civil war, ravishing of conscience, persecution of Christ Jesus in his servants, and of the hypocrisy and destruction of millions of souls. [19]

In contrast to the Puritans, Williams identified the fall of the church from its pristine purity, 'not from the failures of godly rulers, but from their very assumption of power over the church'.[20]

Unsurprisingly, the book was ordered to be burned by Parliament, and Puritan dignitaries rushed into print to denounce

---

[17] *ibid.*, p. 132.
[18] cited in C.L. Allen, 'Roger Williams and "the Restauration of Zion" ', in R.T. Hughes ed., *The American Quest for the Primitive Church*, p. 46.
[19] cited in A.S.P. Woodhouse ed., *Puritanism and Liberty*, p. 266.
[20] C.L. Allen, *op. cit.*, p. 40.

Williams for his effrontery and social heresy. Within five years, the rejoinders amounted to over a hundred. In answer to one of these, John Cotton's *The Bloudy Tenent Washed and Made White in the Bloud of the Lamb* of 1647, Williams brought out his predictably entitled *The Bloudy Tenent Yet More Bloudy* of 1652.[21]

In the second place, Williams made real attempts to place relations with the American natives on a footing more consistent with Christian principles than the simple expropriation which found favour, explicitly or implicitly, with the majority of his countrymen. His land at Providence was purchased from them, not simply taken. He took the trouble to learn several of the Indians' languages, traded with them (though not in weapons or liquor) and sought to win them to Christian faith by preaching to them on many occasions. Although Williams was not alone in this attitude – John Eliot (1604–90) and Thomas Mayhew, Jr. (1621–57) were instrumental in converting perhaps two and a half thousand Indians from the late 1640s onwards – he was certainly unusual.

Although Baptist beginnings in America were nothing like as promising as their later success might lead one to expect, the cause refused to wither simply because its first champion proved to be such a transitory adherent. By 1644 John Clarke (1609–76) had founded a second Baptist church at Newport, also situated in Rhode Island, the oasis of toleration established by Williams. The church had its origins in a congregation formed, by 1638 at the latest, a few miles away in Portsmouth. This had consisted of Anne Hutchinson and some followers, who stressed the 'inner light', and a party around Clarke, who were more strictly biblicist. This congregation split over the issue in 1641. Both halves later split again: the 'spiritualist' party divided into the Hutchinsonians, who moved northward and were killed by Indians in 1643, and a group which later became Quaker. The biblicists split for reasons unknown. Clarke's party, however, removed to Newport, where by 1644 it had become Baptist. This church grew so fast as to be able to afford the luxury of splitting several times

[21]   For a full discussion, see R.T. Hughes and C.L. Allen, *Illusions of Innocence: Protestant Primitivism in America 1630–1875*, ch. 3.

more during the 1660s without destroying its own viability in the process. On these occasions, disputes were between advocates of Particular (i.e. Calvinistic) Baptist views, and General (non-Calvinist) Baptists, but, for variety's sake, one Stephen Mumford generated a further schism from 1671 by his insistence upon observing Saturday – rather than the more usual Sunday – as a Sabbath.

Outside of Rhode Island, Baptist growth was more hazardous because of the threat of persecution. Nevertheless, John Miles, whom we last encountered attempting to turn a South Wales parish into a Particular Baptist church in the 1650s, fled the renewed persecution in England and Wales after the Restoration of the monarchy and arrived, with his congregation, in Massachusetts in 1663. His new settlement of Swansea was, nonetheless, situated judiciously close to the Rhode Island border. Like many early New England Baptist churches, the congregation contained both Particular and General persuasions, an inclusivity that was maintained for nearly two decades.

The first Baptist church to be formed in the Puritan stronghold of Boston, however, predictably faced quite fierce persecution. There John Gould, his wife and some followers separated from their Congregational meeting over the issue of infant baptism in 1665. Although a number of them were imprisoned, they were able to construct their own meeting house by 1679. Even then the authorities attempted to seal it off, but they eventually relented; persecution was becoming an increasingly impractical proposition, even in America. By the late seventeenth century, each species of Baptist was represented by several congregations, though the Generals were to remain the stronger in New England for some time to come.

If persecution of those who did not seek a city upon a hill, but a refuge in the wilderness, began to ease by the 1680s, then that fact was in no small part the achievement of the Quakers. Even more than was the case with the Baptists, Quakers coming to early New England had been given a welcome of the sort intended to persuade them to find their refuge elsewhere. This was a policy which led indirectly to the founding of Pennsylvania in 1681, but much was to happen before that date which changed the complexion of religious politics elsewhere in the colonies.

More than any other group of religious radicals since the early Anabaptists, the Quakers 'gloried in adversity and employed martyrdom as the early Christians had done – to gain sympathy, and then adherents, for their cause'.[22] By refusing to recant or stay away, the Quakers forced the civic leaders of Puritan New England to exact the retribution which they threatened, and incur the public odium which such violence inevitably brought with it.

Translation to the New World had robbed Quakerism of none of its predilection for provocative tactics. Adherents provoked scenes in parish churches or in the streets. When punished, they were prone to acts of heroism, publicly forgiving those who had just whipped them. When the victims were young women, as they frequently were, public revulsion against judicial severity was bound to grow.

The first appearance of the movement in America was in 1656, when Mary Fisher and Ann Austin arrived on a ship in Boston harbour. Both were immediately arrested and imprisoned, and their tracts burned. After five weeks, they were deported to Barbados. By that time, eight more Quakers had arrived and been similarly punished. Perhaps the strangest arrival was that of a boat called the *Woodhouse* which, its builder claimed, had been sailed across the Atlantic with its crew of eleven Quakers without the use of any navigational aids save that of the Inner Light. Most of these interlopers were whipped, branded, imprisoned and had their ears cropped but this was becoming *de rigueur*. If such measures failed to halt the influx of trouble-makers who, upon their arrival, immediately set about denouncing the established Congregational church by every possible method, what would stop them?

By 1659 there was ample evidence that the authorities' attempts had failed. Quaker missionaries – and their converts among the Massachusetts population – had been subjected to banishment and every kind of mistreatment. There had even been an attempt to sell the children of one Quaker family into indentured servitude.[23] There remained only the invocation of the death penalty. Cautiously, it was proposed to inflict it solely

---

22 P.U. Bonomi, *Under the Cope of Heaven*, p. 26.
23 H. Barbour and J.W. Frost, *The Quakers*, p. 51.

upon those Quakers who returned for a third time after having been twice expelled.

The Quakers proved equal to the challenge. Some years before, while still resident in his native Yorkshire, Marmaduke Stephenson had heard a voice of God calling him to be 'a prophet unto the nations', in response to which he had gone to Barbados. Upon hearing of the fearsome new law in Massachusetts, however, 'immediately came the Word of the Lord unto me, saying, "Thou knowest not but that thou mayest go thither" '. After heeding this second call, and being banished the requisite number of times, he was hanged in Boston in August 1659. He did not suffer alone. Another young Quaker, William Robinson, was hanged alongside him whilst a third, Mary Dyer, was spared at the last moment.

Dyer is a classic example of the dilemmas posed to magistrates when young women insisted upon courting the same penalties as men. On this occasion, extreme measures were taken to frighten her into obedience. She was offered her life – if she would give an undertaking not to return to Massachusetts. When she refused, she was marched to the gallows with her two male companions, drums playing loudly so that none of the condemned could start making speeches to the assembled throng. The men were hanged first and then Dyer's arms and legs were tied and her head covered as if for execution. Only then was a last minute reprieve read out, though it had been planned all along. Even a historian with as little patience for the Quakers as Boorstin feels compelled to describe this action by Governor Endicott as a 'barbarous proceeding'.[24] Although she refused to accept the reprieve unless the capital law against Quakers was repealed, and then refused to leave the territory, Dyer was unceremoniously bundled across the border into Rhode Island where, for a time, she rejoined her husband in Newport. But the Light within her was too strong; within the year she was back. And this time she was hanged.

That the death penalty ceased to be exacted from Quakers was brought about, surprisingly enough, by the Restoration government in England, which had even less affection for the Puritans

---

[24] D.J. Boorstin, *The Americans*, i., p. 53.

than it did for the Quakers. Fox's *Journal* gleefully records how, following news of the execution of a fourth Quaker, William Leddra, in Boston in March 1661, senior Friends in England approached Charles II. The king readily agreed to halt executions in New England, and the person chosen to deliver the royal decree on this point was, provocatively, himself a Quaker, Samuel Shattuck. Shattuck had qualified for execution under the law which he now came to have revoked; he had been twice expelled from Massachusetts, and this was his third appearance in Boston. On this occasion, however, he came bearing the royal *mandamus* and delivered it in person to Governor Endicott.[25]

If executions ended, repression did not. But the heaviest force of the persecution had been broken. No Quaker meeting house was officially permitted in the Puritan colonies until 1697, but Quaker activities had continued unofficially for years before that, especially in the outlying towns. In Rhode Island, the Friends had been unmolested from the beginning. Roger Williams disapproved of them, his own affinities with their doctrines notwithstanding, but his principles of toleration guaranteed them a safe haven within the colony. Indeed, it was there that they most prospered, particularly in the area of Aquidneck Island, and they may have constituted a majority in the Newport and Portsmouth area by the 1670s, when one of their number actually became governor.

In 1681, William Penn secured a charter for his new colony to the south. Pennsylvania was to become a Quaker stronghold in the years that lay ahead, though their principle of freedom for all comers (as had been the case with Roger Williams in Rhode Island) meant that they could not guarantee their own predominance by any means other than persuasion. It also raised the dilemma of how to balance private conscience with public responsibility.

Initially strong in the New Model Army back in the English republic of the 1650s, the Quakers had been pacifist since the Restoration of the monarchy. Holding sway over the government of Pennsylvania, Quakers found themselves divided, during the eighteenth century, over the question of how far to lend support

---

[25] Fox, *Journal*, pp. 411–3.

to the crown in its military conflicts with other colonial powers or even (which was more urgent) how far to use force in defending their own outlying settlements against Indian attacks.

By that time, however, the pluralism of the New World colonies and the position of radicals within that plurality were both assured. The difficulties faced by Baptists, Mennonites and Quakers in America were of a different order to those which had faced them in the Old World. These were problems of adaptation and self-redefinition: how could one be faithful to the original vision and apply its principles faithfully in the new environment?

By the eighteenth century the city on the hill was already dead, unless one agreed to redefine that city as a secular vision. To be sure, the Congregationalists remained the established church in much of New England, the Anglicans in Virginia, the Carolinas, Georgia and (after 1691) Maryland. But even in the South, pluralism could not for ever be held at bay. Instead, the New World had proved a refuge in the wilderness for countless groups of beleaguered, persecuted European sectarians, or for those Protestants and even Catholics who simply found themselves in a minority in their homelands. When they crossed the ocean, it was not to establish a new Zion, but to find space to breathe free air. America proved to be a sectarian triumph; when Lutherans, Anglicans, Reformed and Catholics came to America it was, in effect, on sectarian terms.

Conclusion

'The Great Restoration' is the title which we have given here to the enterprise upon which the radicals of the sixteenth and seventeenth centuries were embarked. 'Restoration' was indeed the term which many of them – perhaps most – applied to themselves and which illuminated their self-understanding. They posited a 'fall' of the church more drastic than that which the Protestant Reformers attributed to the Church of Rome and, as a result of this draconian analysis, insisted upon a restoration of the primitive church (as conceived by themselves) rather than a mere re-formation of Christendom.

Some, like the spiritualists, believed that such a restoration could only be inaugurated by God in a new dispensation. For most, it was the Christendom model itself, not just its particular shortcomings in the Roman Catholic Church, which had consti-tuted the 'fall'. The church that needed restoring was a church of true believers, or rather, of personally committed disciples; for most of them, doctrine was descriptive of the true church, not definitive, and adherence was to a body in relationship with Christ, not to a *corpus* of dogmas, however correct. If some of the radicals whose stories are recounted here were prone to legalism and wooden literalism, that is perhaps a tragedy born of their surroundings, and not necessarily inherent in their ideas. Like others in their age, they appealed 'to the New Testament *against* the prescriptive claims made by medieval tradition for nonbiblical forms in favour of congregational freedom. . . . They cited the gospel accounts . . . not to validate a [new] rule but to loosen [an old] one'.[1] It was in the heat of theological conflict that rigid positions were formulated.

Other understandings are possible. The demarcation between Reformers and radicals can be seen as one of psychological temperament – an instance of the divide that marks off moderates from radicals in every age and in every movement. In this scenario, the heroes of our story can be seen as nothing more than a collection of social misfits driven by intellectual outsiders who can never rest content unless some newly accepted principle (in this case biblicism, Christian primitivism or the assault upon priestcraft) is driven through to its logical conclusion, regardless of collateral consequences. This would be an uncharitable judgement, and a very partial one, since its strictures would apply much more clearly to some (the name of Karlstadt comes to mind) than to others.

Marxists have been prone, of course, to see all religious movements as political movements in fancy dress. Anabaptism was a continuation of the Peasants' War by other means; Quakers were sublimated Levellers; religious dissent was a form of artisan and lower middle-class protest against aristocratic or patrician domination. Again, there is some explanatory power in such analyses – the Münster débâcle could hardly have been played out in a circumstance of universal peace and plenty – but it hardly accounts for why so many radicals chose to act clean contrary to their material and economic interests in order to pursue their profoundest religious beliefs. Marxists may insist that, in the minds of such people, the religious 'projected reality' had taken on an autonomous existence to the point where it loomed larger than the material realities around them. But that can never be more than speculation and special pleading: psychologising brought in to make up for the deficiencies of a barren materialist reductionism.

On a different plane, the Great Restoration can be seen as one of the earliest chapters in the destruction (self-destruction, some might say) of western Christendom. The Protestant Reformers had opened a fissure which made growing pluralism all

---

[1]   J.H. Yoder, 'Primitivism in the Radical Reformation: Strengths and Weaknesses' in R.T. Hughes ed., *The Primitive Church in the Modern World*, p. 79.

but inevitable. By the mid-sixteenth century none of the competing orthodoxies could impose uniformity with any ease, even within the states supposedly adhering to them. The multiple nature of the magisterial Protestant secession – Lutheran, Reformed, Anglican – made a nonsense of any claim to universality. The struggles of the Anabaptists and of the English radicals were simply early episodes in the inevitable movement towards a secular society. Likewise, the attempts to suppress them represent the instinctive recognition of the difficulty of securing social order on any other moral base than that sanctioned by institutional religion.

In the long run, of course, it is the radicals who have won out and their persecutors who have lost. Western societies have had to be reconstituted on another basis than compulsory religion, though it is still far from clear quite what that basis is, or should be. But whatever Christianity is, it is not a fig leaf to cover the embarrassment of the kingdoms of this world at their inability to reflect the powers of the age to come.

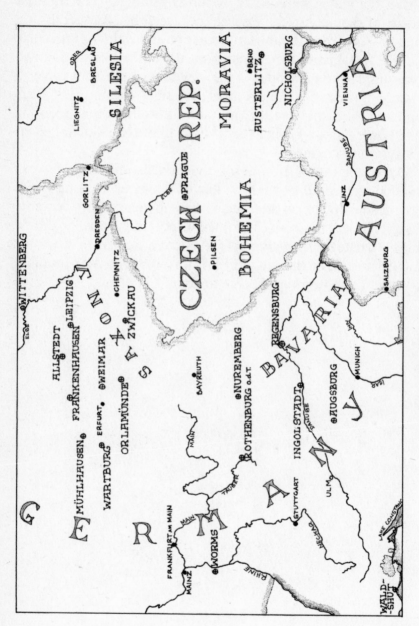

Map 1: Central Germany and Bohemia

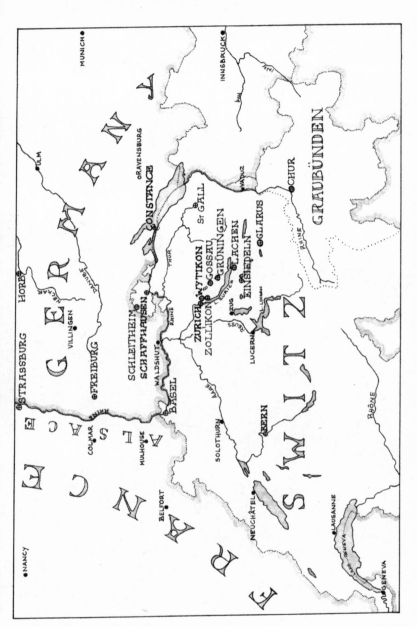

Map 2: Switzerland and southern Germany

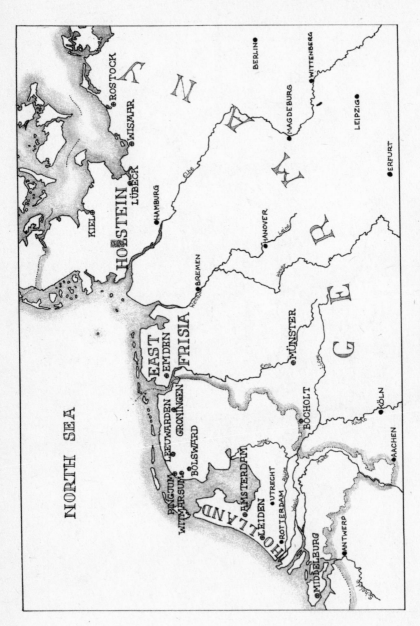

Map 3: Netherlands and northern Germany

Map 4: Southeastern England

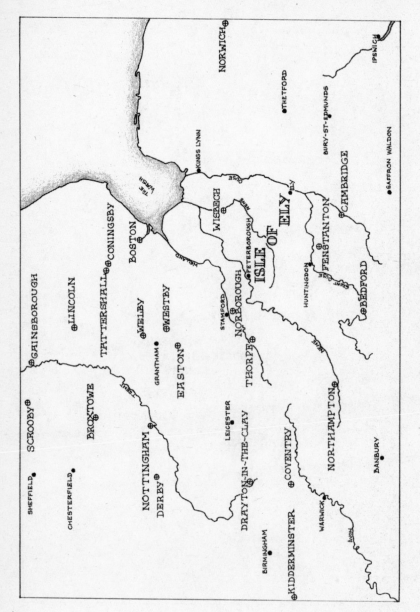

Map 5: East Anglia

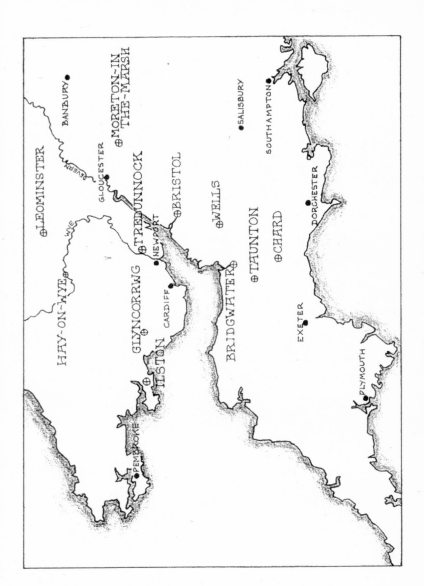

Map 6: Southwestern England and South Wales

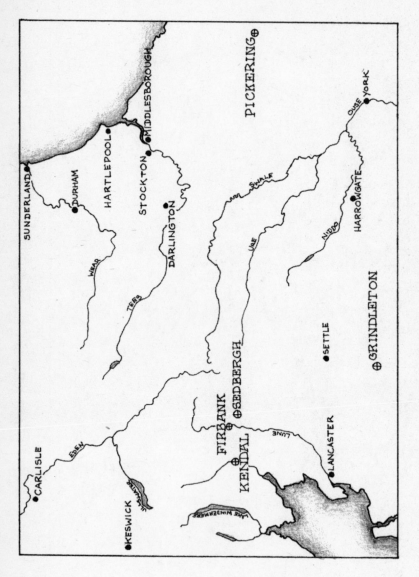

Map 7: Northwestern England

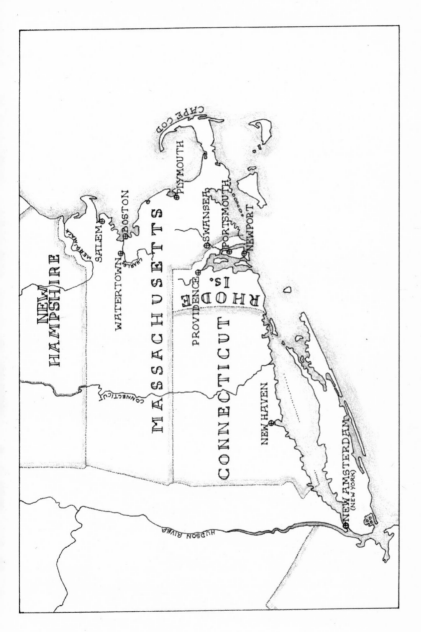

Map 8: New England

Bibliography

A: Primary Sources

Ainsworth, Henry, *An Epistle Sent Vnto Tvvo daughters of Vvarwick* (Amsterdam, 1608)

Bale, John, *A Mysterye of inyquyte* (Geneva, 1545)

Baxter, Richard, *The Autobiography of Richard Baxter* ed. N.H. Keeble (London, Everyman 1931)

Bray, G. ed., *Documents of the English Reformation* (Cambridge, James Clarke Ltd. 1994)

Bredwell, Stephen, *The Rasing of the Foundations of Brownisme* (London, 1588)

Brewer, J.S., Gairdner, J., Brodie, R.H. eds., *Letters and Papers, Foreign and Domestic, of the Reign of Henry VIII* (21 vols. in 36, Public Record Office, London, 1862–1932)

Bradford, John, *The Writings of John Bradford*, ed. A Townsend (2 vols., Cambridge, Parker Society 1848 and 1853, reprinted by Edinburgh, Banner of Truth Trust 1979)

van Braght, Thieleman J., *Martyrs Mirror*, (tr. J.F. Sohm, (Scottdale, PA, Herald Press, 1977)

Browne, Robert, *The Writings of Robert Harrison and Robert Browne*, eds. A. Peel and L.H. Carlson (London, George Allen and Unwin Ltd 1953)

Bucer, Martin, *Handlung inn dem offentlichen gesprech . . . gegen Melchior Hoffman* (Strassburg, 1533)

Burrage, C., *The Early English Dissenters in the Light of Recent*

Research (2 vols., Cambridge, Cambridge University Press 1912)

Cartlstadt – see Karlstadt

Champneys, John, *The Harvest is at Hand* (London, 1548)

Cole, Thomas, *A godly and frutefull sermon, made at Maydstone* (London, 1553)

Cranmer, Thomas, *Works*, ed. J.E. Cox (2 vols., Cambridge, Parker Society, 1844 and 1846)

Denck, Hans, *The Spiritual Legacy of Hans Denck*, ed. C. Bauman, (Leiden, E.J. Brill 1991)

Edwards, Thomas, *Gangræna*, 2nd edn, (London, 1646)

Fox, George, *The Journal of George Fox*, ed. J.L. Nickalls (London, 1952)

Foxe, John, *The Acts and Monuments of the English Martyrs*, ed. J. Pratt (London, 1870)

Gaustad, E.S. ed., *A Documentary History of Religion in America to the Civil War* (Grand Rapids, Eerdmans 1982)

Greenwood, John, *The Writings of John Greenwood 1587–1590*, ed. L.H. Carlson (London, George Allen and Unwin Ltd 1962)

Grindal, Edmund, *Remains of Edmund Grindal*, ed. W. Nicholson (Cambridge, Parker Society 1843)

Harder, L. ed., *The Sources of Swiss Anabaptism* (Scottdale, PA, Herald Press 1985)

Harrison – see Browne

Hubmaier, Balthasar, *Balthasar Hubmaier: Theologian of Anabaptism*, eds. H.W. Pipkin and J.H. Yoder (Scottdale, PA, Herald Press 1989)

The Chronicle of the Hutterite Brethren, tr. A.J.F. Zieglschmid (Rifton, NY, Plough 1987)

Joris, David, *The Anabaptist Writings of David Joris, 1535–1543*, ed. G.K. Waite (Waterloo, Ontario, Herald Press 1994)

Karlstadt, Andreas, *The Essential Carlstadt* ed. E.J. Furcha (Waterloo, Ontario, Herald Press 1995)

Karlstadt, Andreas, *Karlstadt's Battle with Luther*, ed. R.J. Sider, (Philadelphia PA, Fortress Press 1978)

Kenyon, J.P. ed., *The Stuart Constitution* (Cambridge, Cambridge University Press 1966)

Lumpkin, W.L. ed., *Baptist Confessions of Faith* (Valley Forge, Judson Press 1959)

McBeth, H.L. ed., *A Sourcebook for Baptist Heritage* (Nashville, Tennessee, Broadman Press 1990)

Marpeck, Pilgram, *The Writings of Pilgram Marpeck*, eds. W. Klassen and W. Klaassen (Scottdale, PA, Herald Press 1978)

Moore, R.I., *The Birth of Popular Heresy* (London, Edward Arnold Ltd. 1975)

Müntzer, Thomas, *Collected Works*, tr. and ed. P. Matheson (Edinburgh, T. & T. Clark Ltd. 1988)

Niclaes, Hendrik, *Evangelivm Regni* (1575?)

Pecock, Reginald, *The Repressor of Over Much Blaming of the Clergy*, ed. C. Babington (London, 1860)

Penington, Isaac, *The Works of the Long Mournful and Sorely Distressed Isaac Penington*, 2nd edn. (London, 1761)

Philips, Dirk, *The Writings of Dirk Philips*, eds. C.J. Dyck, W.E. Keeney and A.J. Beachy (Scottdale, PA, Herald Press 1992)

Reinitz, R. ed., *Tensions in American Puritanism* (New York, Wiley and Sons 1970)

Riedemann, Peter, *Confession of Faith* (Rifton, NY, Plough 1970)

Robinson, H. ed., *Original Letters relative to the English Reformation* (2 vols., Cambridge, Parker Society 1846 and 1847)

Robinson, H. ed., *The Zürich Letters* (2 vols., Cambridge, Parker Society 1842 and 1845)

Robinson, John, *The Works of John Robinson*, ed. R. Ashton (3 vols., London, 1851)

Rogers, John, *The Displaying of an horrible secte of grosse and wicked Heretiques* (London, 1578)

Rupp, E.G. and Drewery, B., *Martin Luther* (London, Edward Arnold Ltd. 1970)

Sattler, Michael, *The Legacy of Michael Sattler*, ed. J.H. Yoder (Scottdale, PA, Herald Press 1973)

Simons, Menno, *Complete Writings*, ed. J.C. Wenger (Scottdale, PA, Herald Press 1956)

Smyth, John, *Works*, ed. W.T. Whitley (2 vols., Cambridge, Cambridge University Press 1915) van Steeg, C.L. and Hofstadter, R. eds., *Great Issues in American History* (3 vols., New York, Vintage 1969)

Tobias, *Mirabilia opera Dei* (London, ca. 1650)

Trinterud, L.J. ed., *Elizabethan Puritanism* (Oxford, Oxford University Press 1971)

Turner, William, *A preseruatiue, or triacle* (London, 1552)

Underhill, E.B. ed., *Records of the Churches of Christ Gathered at Fenstanton, Warboys, and Hexham 1644–1720* (London, Hanserd Knollys Society 1854)

Veron, Jean, *An Apologye or defence of the doctryne of Predestination* (London, 1561)

White, B.R. ed., *Association Records of the Particular Baptists of England, Wales and Ireland to 1660* (3 vols., London, Baptist Historical Society 1971–4)

Whittingham, William, *A Brieff Discours of the Troubles Begonne at Franckford* (Zürich?, 1574)

Wilkinson, William, *A Confutation of Certaine Articles* (London, 1579)

Williams, G.H. and Mergal, A.M. eds., *Spiritual and Anabaptist Writers* (Philadelphia, PA, Westminster Press 1957)

Winstanley, Gerrard, *Winstanley: The Law of Freedom and Other Writings*, ed. C. Hill (Harmondsworth, Middlesex, Penguin 1973)

Woodhouse, A.S.P. ed., *Puritanism and Liberty* (London, Everyman 1986)

Zwingli, Huldrych, *Writings*, tr. E.J. Furcha and H.W. Pipkin (2 vols., Allison Park, PA, Pickwick Publications 1984)

Zwingli, Huldrych, *Commentary on True and False Religion*, ed. S.M. Jackson (Durham, NC, Labyrinth Press 1981)

B: Secondary Sources – Books

Barbour, H., *The Quakers in Puritan England* (New Haven, CT, Yale University Press 1964)

Barbour, H. and Frost, J.W., *The Quakers* (New York, Greenwood Press 1988)

Beachy, A., *The Concept of Grace in the Radical Reformation* (Nieuwkoop, Netherlands, B. de Graaf 1977)

Bercovitch, S. ed., *The American Puritan Imagination* (Cambridge, Cambridge University Press 1974)

Bonomi, P.U., *Under the Cope of Heaven* (Oxford, Oxford University Press 1986)

Boorstin, D.J., *The Americans* (Harmondsworth, Middlesex, Penguin 1965)

Braithwaite, W.C., *The Beginnings of Quakerism* (London, Macmillan 1912)

Cameron, E., *The Reformation of the Heretics* (Oxford, Oxford University Press 1984)

Clement, C.J., *Religious Radicalism in England 1535–1565* (Carlisle, Paternoster 1997)

Coggins, J.R., *John Smyth's Congregation: English Separatism, Mennonite Influence and the Elect Nation* (Waterloo, Ontario, Herald Press 1991)

Cohn, N., *The Pursuit of the Millennium* (London, Paladin 1970)

Collinson, P., *The Elizabethan Puritan Movement* (London, Cape 1967)

Delbanco, A., *The Puritan Ordeal* (Cambridge, Massachusetts and London, Harvard University Press, 1989)

Deppermann, K., *Melchior Hoffman* (Edinburgh, T. & T. Clark 1987)

Dickens, A.G., *The German Nation and Martin Luther* (London London, Edward Arnold Ltd. 1974)

George, C.H. and K., *The Protestant Mind of the English Reformation, 1570–1640* (Princeton, Princeton University Press 1961)

Goertz, H-J., *Thomas Müntzer: Apocalyptic Mystic and Revolutionary* (Edinburgh, T. & T. Clark 1993)

Hatch, N.O. and Noll, M.A. eds., *The Bible in America* (Oxford, Oxford University Press 1982)

Helm, P., *Calvin and the Calvinists* (Edinburgh, Banner of Truth 1982)

Hill, C., *Society and Puritanism in pre-revolutionary England* (Harmondsworth, Middlesex, Penguin 1991)

— *The World Turned Upside Down* (Harmondsworth, Middlesex, Penguin 1975)

— *God's Englishman* (Harmondsworth, Middlesex, Penguin, 1972)

— *The Century of Revolution* (London, T. Nelson and Sons Ltd. 1961)

Hughes, R.T. ed., *The American Quest for the Primitive Church* (Urbana, University of Illinois Press 1988)

Hughes, R.T. and Allen, C.L., *Illusions of Innocence: Protestant Primitivism in America 1630–1875* (Chicago, University of Chicago Press 1988)

Ingle, H.L., *First Among Friends: George Fox and the Creation of Quakerism* (Oxford, Oxford University Press 1996)

Kendall, R.T., *Calvin and English Calvinism to 1649* (Carlisle, Paternoster 1997)

Klaassen, W., *Living at the End of the Ages* (Lanham, Maryland, University Press of America 1992)

Krahn, C., *Dutch Anabaptism* (Scottdale, PA, Herald Press 1981)

Lambert, M., *Medieval Heresy* (2nd edn., Oxford, Blackwell 1992)

Lamont, W.L., *Godly Rule: Politics and Religion 1603–60* (London, Macmillan 1969)

McBeth, H.L., *The Baptist Heritage* (Nashville, Broadman 1987)

McGregor, J.F. and Reay, B. eds., *Radical Religion in the English Revolution* (Oxford, Oxford University Press 1984)

McFarlane, K.B., *The Origins of Religious Dissent in England* (New York, Collier 1966)

Mack, P., *Visionary Women: Ecstatic Prophecy in Seventeenth-Century England* (Oxford, University of California Press 1992)

Morgan, E.S., *Visible Saints: the History of a Puritan Idea* (Ithaca, NY, Cornell University Press 1963)

Morgan, E.S., *The Puritan Dilemma: the Story of John Winthrop* (Boston, Little, Brown and Co. 1958)

Morrill, J.S. *The Revolt of the Provinces: Conservatives and Radicals in the English Civil War, 1630–1650* (London, Allen and Unwin Ltd 1976)

Moss, J.D., *Godded with God: Hendrik Niclaes and his Family of Love* (Transactions of the American Historical Society, Vol. 71, part 8, 1981)

Neale, J., *Elizabeth I and her Parliaments* (2 Vols., London, Cape 1953 and 1957)

Oberman, H.A., *The Roots of Anti-Semitism* (Philadelphia, PA, Fortess 1984)

Packull, W.O., *Mysticism and the Early South German-Austrian Anabaptist Movement 1525–1531* (Scottdale PA, Herald Press 1977)

Pearse, M.T., *Between Known Men and Visible Saints* (Cranbury, NJ, Associated University Presses 1994)

Peel, A., *The First Congregational Churches* (Cambridge, Cambridge University Press 1920)

Preus, J.S., *Carlstadt's Ordinaciones and Luther's Liberty* (Boston, Harvard University Press 1974)

Reay, B., *The Quakers and the English Revolution* (New York, St. Martin's Press 1985)

Rothenberger, J.R., *Caspar Schwenckfeld von Ossig and the Ecumenical Ideal* (Pennsburg, PA, Board of Publication of the Schwenckfelder Church 1967)

Rupp, E.G., *Patterns of Reformation* (London, Epworth 1969)

Schultz, S.G., *Caspar Schwenckfeld von Ossig* (Pennsburg, PA, Board of Publication of the Schwenckfelder Church 1977)

Scott, T., *Thomas Müntzer: Theology and Revolution in the German Reformation* (Basingstoke, Macmillan 1989)

Shaw, H., *The Levellers* (London, Longmans 1968)

Snyder, C.A., *Anabaptist History and Theology* (Kitchener, Ontario, Pandora Press 1995)

Snyder, C.A. and Hecht, L.A. eds., *Profiles of Anabaptist Women* (Waterloo, Ontario, Wilfrid Laurier University Press 1996)

Sprunger, K.L., *Trumpets From the Tower: English Puritan Printing in the Netherlands 1600–1640* (Leiden, E.J. Brill 1994)

Thomas, K., *Religion and the Decline of Magic* (Harmondsworth, Middlesex, Penguin 1973)

Tolmie, M., *The Triumph of the Saints: the separate churches of London 1616–1649* (Cambridge, Cambridge University Press 1977)

Vedder, H.C., *Balthasar Hubmaier: the Leader of the Anabaptists* (New York, AMS Press Inc. 1971)

Wagner, M.L., *Petr Chelčický* (Scottdale, PA, Herald Press 1983)

Watts, M., *The Dissenters*, vol. 1 (Oxford, Oxford University Press 1978)

White, B.R., *The English Baptists of the Seventeenth Century* (London, Baptist Historical Society 1983)

White, B.R., *The English Separatist Tradition* (Oxford, Oxford University Press 1971)

Williams, G.H., *The Radical Reformation*, 3rd edn (Kirksville, Missouri, Sixteenth-Century Journal Publishers 1992)

Zeman, J.K., *The Anabaptists and the Czech Brethren in Moravia, 1526–1628* (The Hague, Mouton 1969)

C: Secondary Sources – Articles and Pamphlets

Abray, L.J., 'Confession, conscience and honour: the limits of magisterial tolerance in sixteenth-century Strassburg' in O.P. Grell and R. Scribner eds., *Tolerance and Intolerance in the European Reformation* (Cambridge, Cambridge University Press 1996), pp. 94–107

Cater, F.I., 'The excommunication of Robert Browne and his will', *Transactions of the Congregational Historical Society*, v.4 (Jan., 1912)

Finlayson, M.G., 'Puritanism and Puritans: Labels or Libels?', *Canadian Journal of History* 8 (1973), pp. 203–23

Greaves, R.L., 'The Puritan-Nonconformist Tradition in England, 1560–1700', *Albion* 17.4 (Winter, 1985), pp. 449–86

Jones, N.L., 'Elizabeth's First Year' in C. Haigh ed., *The Reign of Elizabeth* (London, Macmillan 1984), pp. 27–53

Jones, R.T., 'John Robinson's Congregationalism' (The Congregational Lecture 1987, London Congregational Memorial Hall Trust)

Kliever, L.D., 'General Baptist Origins', *Mennonite Quarterly Review*, xxxvi (1962), pp. 291–321

Stassen, G.H., 'Anabaptist Influence in the Origin of the Particular Baptists', *Mennonite Quarterly Review* (1962), pp. 322–48

Tolmie, M., 'Thomas Lambe, Soapboiler, and Thomas Lambe, Merchant, General Baptists', *Baptist Quarterly*, vol. xxvii, 1 (Jan., 1977)

White, B.R., 'The Organisation of the Particular Baptists', *Journal of Ecclesiastical History*, xvii (1966), pp. 209–26

Yoder, J.H., 'Primitivism in the Radical Reformation: Strengths and Weaknesses' in R.T. Hughes ed., *The Primitive Church in the Modern World* (Urbana, University of Illinois Press 1995)

Index

Richard Hooker and the Authority of Scripture, Tradition and Reason
Reformed Theologian of the Church of England?
Nigel Atkinson

There is no doubt that Richard Hooker (1554–1600) is one of the most important writers in the history of the Church of England. However since John Henry Newman presented him as a 'theologian of the *via media*' he had been consistently overlooked by evangelical Anglicans.

This well-documented and detailed analysis of the theological first principles of the 'father of Angelicalism' challenges the traditional consensus. The author examines three key elements of Hooker's theology – namely the authority of reason, tradition and Scripture and evaluates Hooker's approach in the light of his debates with contemporary Puritans including Walter Travers, Thomas Cartwright and William Tyndale. His views are then compared with ap -proaches of Erasmus and the Reformers, Luther and Calvin. Finally the interpretations of leading and influential Hooker scholars are examined to show how often his theological principles have been misrepresented.

This important study concludes that Hooker's debt to the Reformation is greater and more profound than generally acknowledged and that Hooker is consistently closer to the mainstream of Reformation thought than his Puritan opponents.

'a lucid, penetrating and immensely relevant study of Hooker's theological method which firmly repudiates the influential High Church stereotype of Hooker.'

From the foreword by Alister McGrath

An ordained priest in the Church of England, Nigel T. Atkinson is Warden of Latimer House, Oxford. He is married with four children.

0-85364-801-8

Protestant Scholasticism
Essays in Reassessment
Editors: Carl R. Trueman and R. Scott Clark

Traditionally Protestant theology, between Luther's early reforming career and the dawn of the Enlightenment, has been seen in terms of decline and fall into the wastelands of rationalism and scholastic speculation.

In this volume a number of scholars question such an interpretation. The editors argue that the development of Post-Reformation Protestantism can only be understood when a proper historical model of doctrinal change is adopted. This historical concern underlies the subsequent studies of theologi - ans such as Calvin, Beza, Olevian, Baxter, and the two Turretini.

The result is a significantly different reading of the development of Protestant Orthodoxy, one which challenges the older scholarly interpretations and clichés about the relationship of Protestantism to, among other things, scholasticism and rationalism, and which demonstrates the fruitfulness of the new, historical approach.

"This diverse (and sometimes polemical) collection of essays will provoke discussion and stimulate further research . . . It challenges the traditional denigration of Post-Reformation theology and makes a significant contribution to the more positive interpretation and evaluation of a range of Reformed and Lutheran theologians."

W.P. Stephens, Professor of Church History in the University of Aberdeen.

Contributors are: D.V.N. Bagchi; David C. Steinmetz; Richard A. Muller; Frank A. James III; John L. Farthing; Lyle D. Bierma; R. Scott Clark; Donald Sinnema; Paul R. Schaefer; W. Robert Godfrey; Carl R. Trueman; P.G. Ryken; John E. Platt; Joel R. Beeke; James T. Dennison; Martin I. Klauber; Lowell C. Green; and David P. Scaer.

R. Scott Clark is Academic Dean and Assistant Professor of Church History in Westminster Theological Seminary, California. He has written several articles exploring Calvin's theology and the relations between continental and British Reformed theology.
Carl Trueman is Lecturer in Historical Theology at the University of Nottingham. He is the author of *The Claims of Truth* (Paternoster Press).

0-85364-853-0

Claims of Truth
John Owen's Trinitarian Theology
Carl R. Trueman

The Claims of Truth presents an exposition and analysis of the theology of the great Puritan theologian, John Owen, which pays particular attention to his vigorous trinitarianism.

The author argues that he only way to understand Owen is to see him as a *seventeenth-century* representative of the ongoing Western trinitarian and anit-Pelagian tradition.

In chapters which deal with Owen's historical context, his understanding of the principles of theology, his understanding of God, his Christology, and his understanding of atonement, Dr Trueman demonstrates how Owen used the theological insights of patristic, medieval, and Reformation theologians in order to meet the challenges posed to Reformed Orthodoxy by his contempo - raries.

The picture that emerges is one of a theologian whose thought, in its context, represented a critical reappropriation of aspects of the Western tradition for the purpose of developing a systematic restatement of Reformed theology which was capable of withstanding the assaults of both the subtly heterodox and the openly heretical.

"Drawing on recent scholarship on the sixteenth and seventeenth centuries the author brings attention to the important continuity that exists between the theology of John Owen and Reformation thought on the one hand and the continuity between his theological method and that of the Church Fathers and Medieval doctors on the other hand . . . Sound historical methodology and . . . a successful attempt to debunk many of the myths surrounding Reformed scholas - ticism."

Willem J. van Asselt, University of Utrecht.

Carl Trueman is Lecturer in Historical Theology at the University of Nottingham. He has written numerous articles and is co-editor of *Protestant Scholasticism* (Paternoster Press).

0-85364-798-4